HEALTH INTERVENTION RESEARCH

SAGE was founded in 1965 by Sara Miller McCune to support the dissemination of usable knowledge by publishing innovative and high-quality research and teaching content. Today, we publish more than 750 journals, including those of more than 300 learned societies, more than 800 new books per year, and a growing range of library products including archives, data, case studies, reports, conference highlights, and video. SAGE remains majority-owned by our founder, and on her passing will become owned by a charitable trust that secures our continued independence.

Los Angeles | London | Washington DC | New Delhi | Singapore

HEALTH INTERVENTION RESEARCH

Understanding Research Design & Methods

SOURAYA SIDANI

Los Angeles | London | New Delhi
Singapore | Washington DC

Los Angeles | London | New Delhi
Singapore | Washington DC

SAGE Publications Ltd
1 Oliver's Yard
55 City Road
London EC1Y 1SP

SAGE Publications Inc.
2455 Teller Road
Thousand Oaks, California 91320

SAGE Publications India Pvt Ltd
B 1/I 1 Mohan Cooperative Industrial Area
Mathura Road
New Delhi 110 044

SAGE Publications Asia-Pacific Pte Ltd
3 Church Street
#10-04 Samsung Hub
Singapore 049483

Editors: Michael Carmichael and Jai Seaman
Editorial assistants: Keri Dickens and Lily Mehrbod
Production editor: Katie Forsythe
Copyeditor: Jane Fricker
Proofreader: Sarah Cooke
Indexer: Silvia Benvenuto
Marketing manager: Camille Richmond
Cover design: Wendy Scott
Typeset by: C&M Digitals (P) Ltd, Chennai, India
Printed and bound by CPI Group (UK) Ltd,
Croydon, CR0 4YY

Library of Congress Control Number: 2014936874

British Library Cataloguing in Publication data

A catalogue record for this book is available from the British Library

ISBN 978-1-4462-5616-9
ISBN 978-1-4462-5617-6 (pbk)

CONTENTS

ABOUT THE AUTHOR

Souraya Sidani is Professor and Canada Research Chair at the School of Nursing, Ryerson University. Her areas of expertise are in quantitative research methods, intervention design and evaluation, treatment preferences, and measurement. Her research areas of interest focus on evaluating interventions and advanced practice roles, on examining patient preferences for treatments, and on refining research methods and measures for determining the clinical effectiveness of interventions.

PREFACE

In an era characterized by an emphasis on evidence-informed practice, research plays a central role in helping us understand human conditions, behaviors, and emerging problems; and identifying interventions that effectively address the problems and promote well-being. Empirical evidence on the effects of treatments guides decision making regarding the selection, implementation, and evaluation of interventions to improve various domains of life at the local, national, and international levels. However, to be useful, research studies must be well planned and executed. Careful planning involves the selection of research designs and methods that 1) are appropriate to capture the problem under investigation, 2) are consistent with the study's purpose and aims, 3) ensure validity of the inferences and minimize potential biases, and 4) are feasible within the context in which they are applied. Careful execution consists of developing a detailed study protocol, adhering to it when carrying out research activities (i.e., recruitment, data collection, implementation of the intervention, and data analysis), and closely monitoring the study in order to ensure quality of performance, and to identify and remedy any challenges or deviations.

A range of research designs and methods is available to study the effects of interventions. Some have been commonly considered as the most useful in generating credible evidence, and others have been advanced as plausible alternatives in response to recent critique of commonly used designs and methods. The critique was prompted by the realization that most, if not all, designs and methods are based on assumptions and recommendations which have been taken for granted and not been systematically and critically evaluated. These are derived from logic that may no longer be tenable in light of accumulating experience and emerging empirical evidence. Specifically, the adoption of the experimental or randomized controlled trial as the 'gold standard' for determining the effects of interventions was based on theoretical reasons and intuitive attractiveness rather than a compelling evidence base of data. Empirical evidence derived from meta-analyses shows that results of randomized trials and well-designed non-randomized studies evaluating the same interventions are comparable in determining the success of the intervention. These findings raise questions about the necessity and utility of randomization in reducing selection bias and enhancing validity of causal inferences. Randomization increases the likelihood that study groups are similar at baseline, but it does not guarantee it. Further, it introduces biases related to who takes part in studies and the influence of their perception of the intervention on treatment adherence and outcomes. Practical, pragmatic trials and partially randomized clinical or preference trials have been proposed to enhance representativeness of the sample, account for participants' treatment preferences, and reduce attrition. Similarly, evidence is emerging that questions the utility of other methods such as the use of placebo.

This book represents a compendium of research designs and methods, encompassing commonly used ones and recent advances that can be used in the evaluation of interventions. The book content describes the theoretical, empirical, and practical knowledge required in choosing among designs and methods for intervention evaluation. Theoretical knowledge covers the logic underlying different designs and methods; it provides the rationale or the 'why' for methodological decisions. Empirical knowledge looks at the results of studies that investigate the effectiveness, utility, or efficiency of different methods; it informs the 'what', 'when', and 'where' of methodological decisions. Practical knowledge involves descriptions of the procedure for implementing different research methods; it points to the 'how' for carrying out selected methods. The aim is to inform researchers of the nature and effectiveness of various designs and methods. This information is essential to 1) make researchers aware of different designs and methods, each having its strengths and limitations at the theoretical and empirical levels, 2) assist researchers in making appropriate decisions related to the selection of most suitable methods that best fit the context of particular studies, 3) help researchers recognize that methodological decisions should be based on evidence rather than mere traditional recommendations which may not be well supported logically and empirically, and ultimately 4) move the research enterprise out of the 'inertia' of using commonly recommended designs and methods that produce empirical evidence of limited utility to decision making and policy development, and into the world of generating, testing, and using alternative relevant designs and methods.

ACKNOWLEDGEMENTS

The author gratefully acknowledges the encouragement, support, and informal feedback from colleagues and students, and the instrumental support of staff at the Health Intervention Research Center (Sarah I. and Laura C.).

1

AN OVERVIEW OF HEALTH INTERVENTION RESEARCH

Intervention forms a central element of healthcare in primary, acute, rehabilitation, and long-term care settings. Healthcare professionals assess clients' condition to identify the problems requiring remediation, select and implement interventions to effectively address the problems, monitor clients' responses to interventions, and evaluate their achievement of beneficial outcomes. Healthcare professionals include physicians, nurses, allied health therapists such as respiratory, physical, occupational and speech language therapists, psychologists, social workers, and health educators. They implement interventions, independently or collaboratively, that target problems manifested in different domains of health and experienced by individuals, families, groups (defined in terms of socio-cultural or clinical characteristics), or the entire community. The selection and implementation of interventions are informed by the best available evidence of their success in producing beneficial outcomes (Guyatt et al., 2002).

Research is widely recognized as a source of evidence because of its systematic process aimed at making valid inferences about the causal effect of the intervention on outcomes. Research is guided by a comprehensive understanding of the intervention, and of the notions of causality and validity. In this chapter, the logic of intervention research is described relative to the notion of causality. It rests on a lucid knowledge of the intervention and its contribution to the hypothesized outcomes, as delineated next. Validity is discussed in Chapter 2.

HEALTH INTERVENTION RESEARCH

Health intervention research involves the systematic evaluation of the merit, worth, or value of interventions. The value of interventions is indicated by the extent to which the interventions are appropriate, safe, and effective in managing clients' problems and in improving their health. The goal of health intervention research is to demonstrate the causal relationship between interventions and anticipated outcomes. The causal relationship implies that the interventions, and no other contextual factors, are responsible for inducing the beneficial changes in outcomes. Evaluation of the interventions' effects on outcomes requires an understanding of the problem that the intervention targets, the intervention, the outcomes, the mediators or mechanisms through which the intervention exerts its effects on the outcomes, and the moderators or factors that influence the intervention effects.

Problem

Problems are alterations in clients' health condition that put them at risk for illness or that interfere with their engagement in healthy behaviors and activities of daily living. The alterations include: bio-physiological malfunctions such as high blood sugar and hypertension; physical limitations such as difficulty walking; cognitive impairment such as delirium; emotional symptoms such as anxiety; engagement in risky behaviors such as smoking; and social issues such as isolation. An understanding of the problem clarifies its nature, manifestations, determinants, and level of severity. Nature of the problem refers to the domain of health in which it is experienced. Manifestations are the indicators (i.e., signs and symptoms) that point to the occurrence of the problem. Determinants are causative factors that contribute to the experience of the problem. Level of severity reflects the intensity with which the problem is experienced. This understanding of the problem is necessary for determining the appropriateness of the intervention and for guiding the design of the intervention evaluation study.

Interventions are considered appropriate when they are reasonable and logical in that they specifically address the problem requiring remediation (hereafter referred to as health problem). The nature of the intervention fits with the nature of the health problem. Awareness of the nature, determinants, and manifestations assists in identifying the aspects of the health problem that are amenable to change and hence, targeted by the intervention. Also, it is instrumental in delineating intervention strategies that are consistent with the modifiable aspects of the health problem and, hence, relevant in addressing or resolving it (Lippke and Ziegelman, 2008; Slater, 2006). Knowledge of the level of severity with which the health problem is experienced helps in specifying the dose at which the intervention is given to induce the desired changes in the problem experience (Sidani and Braden, 2011). Congruence between the health problem and the intervention enhances the specificity of the intervention. The intervention targets what exactly and significantly contributes to the health problem; it does not address its 'wrong' aspect and therefore, miss the target (Green, 2000; Nock, 2007). The specificity of an intervention increases its effectiveness.

A thorough understanding of the health problem informs the identification of the client population and the sample selection criteria for the intervention evaluation study.

The population is generally defined relative to the experience of the problem targeted by the intervention. The sample selection criteria are specified to ensure that persons report the particular aspects of the problem specifically addressed by the intervention. These persons are expected to benefit most from the intervention.

Intervention

Health interventions are treatments, therapies, procedures, or actions that are implemented by healthcare professionals to, with, or on behalf of clients, in response to the health problem with which clients present, to improve their condition and achieve beneficial outcomes. Interventions consist of a set of interrelated activities that healthcare professionals perform; the activities reflect the cognitive, verbal, and physical functions within the scope of the professionals' practice. Health interventions include bio-physical treatments such as medications or administration of intravenous fluids; physical procedures such as surgical removal of a cyst and therapeutic massage; psychological, cognitive, behavioral, motivational, and educational interventions to promote engagement in healthy lifestyle; and social actions such as facilitating social gathering of older adults residing in long-term care institutions.

Understanding of an intervention taps into its goals, specific and non-specific elements, mode of delivery, and dose. An intervention's *goal* refers to its overall direction, that is, what the intervention is set to achieve relative to the targeted health problem, such as prevention, management, or resolution of the problem, and to the clients' general condition such as improved functioning. The *specific elements* are the active ingredients that characterize an intervention and distinguish it from others. The active ingredients are theoretically expected to induce changes in the health problem and clients' general health condition. The *non-specific elements* are strategies or activities that facilitate the implementation of the active ingredients but are not anticipated to contribute to changes in the health problem and the clients' condition (Hart, 2009; Stein et al., 2007). For instance, stimulus control therapy is a behavioral intervention for the management of chronic insomnia. Its primary goal is to assist persons to re-associate the bed and the bedroom with sleep. Its active ingredients consist of instructions regarding activities to avoid (such as reading or thinking) and activities to do (such as getting out of bed if one can't fall asleep) around bedtime. Its non-specific elements include monitoring the application of the instructions for feedback and discussing barriers to the implementation of the instructions. *Mode of delivery* reflects the medium, format, and approach for offering the intervention. Medium is the means through which the intervention is given, which can be oral (e.g., facilitation of group discussion on barriers to healthy behavior performance), written (e.g., distribution of pamphlet), and hands-on (e.g., surgery, massage). Format is the specific technique used for providing the intervention. Different formats are available such as face-to-face meetings or videotaped presentations within the oral medium, and booklet and computer-based application within the written medium. Approach is the structure selected for providing the intervention, which can be standardized or tailored.

In a standardized approach, the same intervention is carried out in the same way, at the same dose, across all clients. In contrast, a tailored approach consists of customizing the intervention, its mode of delivery, and its dose, to be responsive to clients' characteristics, needs, and preferences. *Dose* is defined as the level at which the intervention is to be given in order to successfully achieve the preset goals. It is operationalized in terms of amount (i.e., number of sessions, length of each), frequency (i.e., number of times the sessions are given within a specified period of time), and duration (i.e., total time period for giving all sessions).

Knowledge of the intervention's goals, active ingredients, non-specific elements, mode of delivery, and dose gives direction for the operationalization of the intervention. This, in turn, facilitates its implementation with fidelity and monitoring its delivery. Implementation of the intervention with fidelity in an intervention evaluation study is critical for initiating the mechanisms responsible for producing the outcomes (Borrelli et al., 2005).

Operationalization of the intervention consists of translating the knowledge of the intervention's goals, active ingredients, and non-specific elements into components and activities that are performed within the selected mode of delivery and dose, by the healthcare professionals responsible for delivering the intervention (hereafter referred to as interventionists) and by clients receiving the intervention. A *component* is a set of interconnected activities that address one modifiable aspect of the health problem or that target a particular domain of clients' general condition. The number of components determines the level of intervention complexity. Simple interventions comprise a single component, for example, acupressure for the management of nausea and vomiting, or education for enhancing clients' knowledge of factors that trigger dyspnea. Complex interventions involve multiple components. The components may address different aspects of the health problem or domains of clients' general conditions. For example, a diabetes self-management program would include a component aimed at increasing clients' engagement in physical activity and a component aimed at promoting a low carbohydrate diet. The components may also represent different strategies to manage the same problem; the strategies may target individuals (e.g., cognitive and behavioral strategies to improve adoption of health behaviors), or several constituents in a community (e.g., behavioral strategies for individuals, organization of support groups, and involvement of the community in maintaining safe neighborhoods, to increase participation in physical activity). A list of specific activities is generated to operationalize each component and integrated into a meaningful sequence of activities to be carried out, in the specified mode, within and across all intervention contacts or sessions. A detailed description of these specific activities is compiled in the intervention protocol, which is detailed in a manual.

The nature of the intervention's specific activities point to the professional qualifications and personal characteristics required of the interventionists. The interventionists should have the professional qualifications (e.g., formal training, licensing) that enable them to carry out the intervention activities, as determined by respective regulatory bodies. Some personal characteristics (e.g., gender, ethnicity) may be important to facilitate delivery of some interventions such as those addressing sensitive topics to some client populations. For example, women are more comfortable discussing sexuality issues with female interventionists.

The intervention protocol is foundational for training interventionists in the competencies required for an appropriate implementation of the intervention (Borrelli et al., 2005). The competencies relate to the conceptual underpinning of the intervention and the practical skills for carrying out its activities. Through intensive training, interventionists should gain an understanding of the health problem targeted by the intervention; the intervention's goals, active ingredients, non-specific elements, mode of delivery, and dose; and the mechanisms responsible for producing its effects on the outcomes. The interventionists also should be familiar with the intervention protocol, the rationale for each specific activity, the standards for carrying out the activities, potential challenges in carrying out the activities and ways to manage them (Sidani and Braden, 2011).

The intervention protocol serves as the reference for implementing the intervention and for developing instruments to monitor fidelity of intervention implementation. Interventionists are requested to follow the protocol when delivering the intervention. The activities to be performed are incorporated in an instrument for assessing the fidelity of implementation (Stein et al., 2007). Fidelity refers to the consistency between the actual delivery and the original design of the intervention; that is, the specific activities constituting the intervention are carried out as specified in the protocol. Deviations in the implementation of the intervention from its original design and across clients result in inconsistency in the intervention activities to which clients are exposed. This inconsistency contributes to variation in the level of outcome improvement reported by clients following implementation of the intervention, which reduces the power to detect significant intervention effects (Carroll et al., 2007; Leventhal and Friedman, 2004).

Furthermore, knowledge of the intervention's active ingredients, non-specific elements, and dose is necessary for:

1. Selecting the comparison treatment that serves as a control condition for determining the effects of the intervention on outcomes. The comparison treatment should not contain components or activities that may reflect the intervention's active ingredients in order to maintain a clear distinction between the two treatments and maximize the difference in the outcomes.
2. Identifying the most appropriate time, within the trajectory of the health problem, to provide the intervention such as before, during, or following its experience.
3. Determining the most accurate methods for collecting data on the intervention dose to which clients are exposed and for conducting dose-response analyses, which is important in specifying the optimal dose associated with beneficial outcomes.

Outcomes

Outcomes represent the consequences of the intervention. They capture the changes in a clients' condition expected to take place following receipt of the intervention and reflect the criteria for determining its benefits. Outcomes are derived from the goals of the intervention and classified into immediate and ultimate outcomes. Immediate outcomes entail the expected changes in the aspects of the health problem that are directly targeted by the intervention, and occur within a short time interval after the implementation of the intervention. Immediate outcomes are operationalized as modifications in the health problem's determinants, manifestations, or level of severity. Ultimate outcomes include resolution of the problem and improvement in other aspects of clients' general condition such as prevention of illness and promotion of healthy functioning. Achievement of ultimate outcomes follows changes in the immediate outcomes. Therefore, the immediate outcomes mediate the effects of the intervention on the ultimate outcomes. For example, stimulus control therapy is designed to assist persons with insomnia to re-associate the bed and the bedroom with sleep. Application of its instructions is expected to reduce the time it takes to fall asleep and the time awake after sleep onset, which yields an increase in sleep efficiency (immediate outcomes). Increased sleep efficiency is associated with the perception of low levels of insomnia severity (resolution of the problem), which decreases daytime fatigue and improves physical, psychological, and social functioning (ultimate outcomes).

Understanding the nature, classification, and interrelationships among outcomes has implications for outcome assessment and analysis in the intervention evaluation study. Awareness of the outcomes' nature directs their operationalization. Each outcome should be clearly defined at the conceptual level; its domains and dimensions that are expected to demonstrate changes post-intervention delivery (i.e., post-test) are identified, as they will guide the selection of the instrument to measure the outcome. A correspondence between the outcome domains and dimensions as defined conceptually and as captured in the content of the instrument is required to accurately assess the outcome and quantify the changes in the outcome. For example, the cognitive, more so than the physical, domain and the intensity, more so than frequency, dimension of daytime fatigue are expected to improve after delivery of the stimulus control therapy.

Classification of outcomes into immediate and ultimate informs the specification of the anticipated pattern of change in the outcomes. Usually, significant changes in immediate outcomes are hypothesized to take place within a short time (e.g., 1 week) post intervention and maintained over time (e.g., 9 months). No or small changes in ultimate outcomes are expected immediately following intervention delivery; however, the amount of change is anticipated to increase gradually over time. The anticipated pattern of change helps in specifying the points in time following implementation of the intervention to assess the outcomes; carefully planning the post-hoc comparisons to determine when the changes in outcomes actually occur; and interpreting statistically significant or non-significant findings related to the intervention effects on the immediate and ultimate outcomes at different time points post-intervention.

Knowledge of the interrelationships among the outcomes is necessary for elucidating the mechanism underlying the intervention effects and for planning outcome analysis accordingly.

The analysis focuses on examining the direct impact of the intervention on the immediate outcomes and the indirect effects of the intervention on the ultimate outcomes.

Mediators

The mechanism underlying the intervention effects reflects the pathway of changes that are responsible for producing the anticipated improvement in the outcomes. It refers to the series of events or alterations in status that occur during and after receipt of the intervention and that mediate the effects of the intervention on the ultimate outcomes (Nock, 2007; Vallance et al., 2008). The mechanism is operationalized in a causal path that links the delivery of the intervention with the mediators and subsequently the ultimate outcomes. There are three general categories of mediators: clients' reactions to the intervention, enactment and adherence to the intervention, and immediate outcomes.

Clients' reactions to the intervention include their understanding of the treatment recommendations they are expected to carry out in their day-to-day life (Borrelli et al., 2005) and their satisfaction with the intervention (i.e., perceived usefulness of treatment in managing the presenting problem). Client reactions contribute to the enactment (i.e., initiation) of and adherence (i.e., consistent and appropriate application) to the treatment recommendations. Clients who develop a good grasp of what the treatment is about and view it as helpful in addressing the health problem are likely to engage in the intervention and perform the treatment recommendations in the correct way and at the prescribed dose in their daily life (Carroll et al., 2007). Adherence to treatment yields improvement in the immediate outcomes, which in turn is associated with changes in the ultimate outcomes. To illustrate, the following generic mechanism underlies the effects of an educational intervention on quality of life: 1) clients attending all sessions of the intervention gain an understanding of the information relayed and find it meaningful, that is, suitable to address the problem, applicable within the context of their lifestyle, and useful in producing the outcomes of interest to them; 2) clients showing these favorable reactions to the intervention retain the information taught and apply it; 3) clients who apply properly what they learned experience improvement in the immediate outcomes; and 4) improvement in the immediate outcomes motivates clients to continue application of the treatment recommendations and produces the ultimate outcomes.

Understanding the mechanism mediating the intervention effects on the ultimate outcomes guides the following aspects of the intervention evaluation study:

1. Generation of conceptual definitions of the mediators, which directs their operationalization and selection of instruments to measure them directly;
2. Delineation of the points in time during and following the implementation of the intervention at which the mediators are to be assessed; and
3. Specification of the path model for testing the hypothesized interrelationships among receipt and dose of the intervention, mediators, and ultimate outcomes.

Moderators

Moderators are factors that influence the implementation of the intervention, the mechanism underlying its effects, and/or the achievement of ultimate outcomes. The moderators include characteristics of the clients who receive the intervention, the interventionists who deliver the intervention, and the setting within which the intervention is implemented. Client characteristics influence the experience of the health problem; for instance clients with a particular characteristic may experience a severe level of the problem, which may not be successfully managed by the intervention. Client characteristics affect the understanding, enactment, or adherence to treatment recommendations; for example, clients with low levels of education or high levels of cognitive impairment may not fully grasp the treatment, precluding them from applying the recommendations appropriately; thus, they do not show the expected improvement in outcomes. Client characteristics influence responses to the intervention; clients with a particular characteristic or certain level of the characteristic respond more favorably than others to the intervention. The favorable responses are exhibited in higher improvement in immediate and ultimate outcomes. For example, clients who lead an active lifestyle prior to cancer therapy report larger reduction in fatigue after receiving a behavioral intervention to promote physical activity, than those who had a sedentary lifestyle.

Interventionists' characteristics relate to their personal qualities (e.g., communication skills) and professional qualifications (e.g., experience working with the target population). These characteristics may interfere with the implementation of the intervention. For example, interventionists with poor communication skills may not relay information about treatment recommendations clearly and in simple terms. Interventionists' characteristics may affect the development and maintenance of a working alliance with the clients. This alliance impacts clients' satisfaction with and adherence to treatment, and improvement in outcomes (Dinger et al., 2008; Fuertes et al., 2007).

Setting characteristics relate to physical (e.g., high ambient temperature during performance of relaxation, and non-availability of walking trails in the neighborhood) and social (e.g., gender composition of clients attending a group session to discuss intimate sexual behaviors for the prevention of HIV, and neighborhood safety) features of the environment in which the intervention is delivered or the treatment recommendations are applied. Some features facilitate and others hinder performance of a subset or all intervention activities by the interventionist, and of the treatment recommendations by the clients.

Understanding of the moderators has implications for the design of the intervention evaluation study. Client characteristics that interfere with the implementation of the intervention, the trigger of the intervention mechanism, and the achievement of outcomes are considered potential confounds, and are controlled experimentally or statistically. Experimental control is exerted by screening clients and excluding those who have the characteristics. Statistical control is done by including clients with these characteristics, collecting pertinent data, and residualizing their influence when examining the intervention effects. Interventionist characteristics that affect the intervention delivery are specified and used for selecting interventionists, and are addressed during training. Clients' perception of the interventionists' working alliance is assessed and accounted for when evaluating the intervention effects. Setting characteristics guide site selection and assessment of the site features, particularly if more than one site is included in the study. Differences across sites are accounted for at the stage of data analysis.

AIMS OF INTERVENTION RESEARCH

The overall goal of intervention research is to generate evidence that supports the appropriateness, safety, and effectiveness of interventions in producing the beneficial outcomes. The evidence is used to develop guidelines that inform healthcare professionals' practice. To help in directing healthcare professionals' decision making about client care, empirical evidence synthesized across studies evaluating the same intervention has to provide answers to the following clinically relevant questions: What clients, presenting with which personal, health, and clinical characteristics, benefit most from which treatment, given at what dose, in what mode, and in what context?

Underlying these questions and relevant empirical evidence is the notion of causality. In other words, the evidence should demonstrate that the intervention causes the outcomes and that this causal relationship is robust, meaning that it is observed when the intervention is implemented by different healthcare professionals, to different clients, in different contexts, and in different modalities and doses.

CAUSALITY

A causal relationship is a structural relation that underlies the dependence among phenomena (*Stanford Encyclopedia of Philosophy*, 2008). In intervention research, the focus is on demonstrating the causal relationship between the intervention and the outcomes. This is accomplished by determining the causal dependence of the outcomes on the intervention. Causal dependence means that changes in the outcomes are contingent on the receipt of the intervention in that improvement in the outcomes occurs in the presence of the intervention and conversely, no changes in the outcomes take place in the absence of the intervention. This view of causal dependence is rather simplistic and deterministic, emphasizing the direct connection between an intervention and an outcome, and ignoring the context in which the intervention is implemented and the mechanisms through which the intervention produces its effects (Pawson and Tilley, 1997).

There is increasing acknowledgement of multi-causality in the health field. Multiple factors, experienced in different domains of health (e.g., physical, psychological) and at different levels (e.g., individual, community), are recognized as determinants of the health problems of clients requiring remediation. For instance, engagement in a healthy behavior is conceptualized as a function of the interpersonal, intrapersonal or individual, institutional or organizational, community, and public policy factors (National Institutes of Health, National Cancer Institute, 2005). The complexity of these problems demands multi-component interventions to comprehensively address them. Multi-component interventions contribute to changes in several interrelated outcomes. Accordingly, the simplistic view of causal dependence is no longer tenable, yielding a reformulation of causality as a chain representing the set of conditions that promote the connection between the intervention and the outcomes, and the interdependence among the intervention and the outcomes (Cook, 1993; Tilley, 2000). This notion of multi-causality highlights the importance of examining the mechanisms that mediate the effects of an intervention on the outcomes; and the factors that could moderate the ability of the intervention to trigger the mechanism and to produce the intended effects on the outcomes.

The criteria for inferring simple and multi-causality are temporality, covariation, contiguity, congruity, and ruling out plausible alternative causes of the intervention effects (Larzelere et al., 2004; Shadish et al., 2002). Although the same criteria are used, the evidence required to support the criteria differs slightly when inferring simple or multi-causality.

Temporality

Temporality has to do with the temporal order of the cause and the effect, where the cause should occur prior to its effects. Thus, the intervention has to precede changes in the outcomes in order to logically attribute the improvement in outcomes to the intervention. If the changes in the outcomes are observed before the implementation of the intervention, then they cannot be linked to the intervention because the changes in outcomes occurred irrespective of the intervention. To determine temporality, the outcomes should be assessed before and after delivery of the intervention. Changes in the level of the outcomes that are observed post-intervention represent the evidence to support temporality in simple and multi-causality.

Covariation

Covariation is the criterion that operationalizes causal dependence. It implies that the changes in the outcomes occur when the intervention is delivered, and do not occur when the intervention is not given. Covariation is often demonstrated by creating two groups of persons who experience the health problem targeted by the intervention. The groups are comparable in all respect except receipt of the intervention; that is, the intervention is given to one group and withheld from the other group. Evidence required for inferring covariation should show comparability of clients in both groups before implementation of the intervention, changes in the outcomes in the hypothesized direction among clients who receive the intervention, no changes in the outcomes among clients who do not receive the intervention, and significant differences in the outcomes between the two groups assessed post-intervention (Shadish et al., 2002).

The utility of having the two groups to demonstrate covariation is being questioned on two grounds. First, historically the effectiveness of several interventions, such as insulin for decreasing high blood glucose, blood transfusion for hemorrhagic shock, and closed reduction for fracture, was established in a series of case studies rather than comparison of outcomes for clients who did and did not get treatment (Cook et al., 2010; Glasziou et al., 2007). Second, withholding the intervention may be unethical, which is the case when equipoise (i.e., not knowing whether treatment is better than no treatment) cannot be maintained (e.g., antibiotics to control septicemia) when the target population is in critical, immediate need for treatment (e.g., severely dehydrated infants), and when depriving clients from the intervention is associated with unfavorable reactions that negatively contribute to the outcomes (i.e., clients who do not receive the intervention exhibit worsening of the outcomes). In these instances, covariation can be inferred from repeated observations of the same clients under two conditions: 1) when they are not offered the intervention (which precedes the second condition) and 2) when they receive the intervention. Outcomes are assessed before and after each condition. Evidence indicating no changes in the outcomes following the first condition (i.e., no treatment) and significant changes in the outcomes after the second condition (i.e., treatment), supports the criterion of covariation (Rossi et al., 2004) in simple and multi-causality.

Contiguity and Congruity

Contiguity has to do with the time lag between implementation of the intervention and the occurrence of changes in the outcomes. In simple causality, the changes in outcomes are expected within a short time interval following the intervention delivery. In multi-causality, changes in the immediate outcomes take place within a relatively short time interval after the implementation of the intervention, whereas changes in the ultimate outcomes occur within a long time interval and once the immediate outcomes are achieved.

Congruity reflects the magnitude of the changes in the outcomes, which should be congruent with the nature and dose of the intervention. In simple causality, interventions that are highly specific to the health problem, intense, and of high dose, are expected to yield large changes in the outcomes. In multi-causality, congruity is considered in association with contiguity, based on outcome data gathered repeatedly following implementation of the intervention. The evidence supporting these criteria includes: 1) large changes in the immediate outcomes are observed within a short time frame post-intervention; this level of change is maintained or a small increment is reported in the immediate outcomes over time; 2) small, if any, changes in the ultimate outcomes are found within a short time frame post-intervention; however, the amount of change in these outcomes increases gradually or sharply over time; and 3) the magnitude of the relationship between the intervention and the immediate outcomes is larger than the magnitude of the direct relationship between the intervention and the ultimate outcomes; this expectation is consistent with the mediating role of the immediate outcomes (Green, 2000; MacKinnon and Fairchild, 2009).

Ruling out Other Plausible Causes of the Intervention Effects

This criterion is considered the most defensible warrant for simple and multi-causality (Cook et al., 2010). It implies that the changes in the outcomes found after the implementation of the intervention are solely and uniquely attributable to the intervention. In other words, the outcomes are consequences of the intervention itself, and not other factors inherent in the context in which the intervention is delivered and evaluated. The factors are substantive or methodological. The substantive factors are associated with the characteristics of the clients who are included in the intervention evaluation study and who receive the intervention; the interventionists who deliver the treatments under evaluation; and the context of the study or the implementation of the intervention. Methodological factors relate to issues in the conduct of the evaluation study such as measurement of outcomes and statistical tests used in data analysis. Substantive and methodological factors present sources of bias or threats to the validity of inferences regarding the effects of the intervention on the outcomes, as discussed in Chapter 2.

Threats to validity, or biases, reflect alternative explanations for the intervention effects. Ruling out plausible causes involves: 1) exerting experimental control by eliminating possible sources of bias, as is done in the experimental or randomized controlled trial (RCT) design and 2) identifying, *a priori* and based on the theory underlying the intervention (i.e., understanding of the health problem, intervention, outcomes, mediators, and moderators), factors that could potentially confound the intervention effects, collecting data on these factors and examining statistically the extent to which the factors influenced the implementation of the intervention and the achievement of its outcomes, as is recommended when investigating the intervention under less well controlled conditions of day-to-day practice (Nock, 2007; Schafer and Kang, 2008).

Summary

- Design of an intervention evaluation study starts with a good understanding of the intervention and the notion of causality
- Understanding of intervention guides the plan and conduct of the evaluation study as follows:

- o Target health problem → sample selection
- o Intervention specific and non-specific elements, mode of delivery, dose → operationalization of intervention, development of protocol, implementation of intervention and monitoring fidelity of its delivery, selection and training of interventionists, selection of comparison treatment
- o Mediators, immediate and ultimate outcomes → specification of times for data collection, analysis of outcome data, interpretation of findings
- o Moderators → experimental or statistical control of potential confounds

- Understanding of causality also guides design of trial:

- o Temporality → plan sequence of outcome data collection and intervention delivery
- o Covariation → generation of comparison condition
- o Contiguity and congruity → interpretation of intervention effects observed at different time points post-treatment
- o Ruling out of plausible causes of intervention effects → selection of designs and methods to minimize bias

2

VALIDITY IN INTERVENTION RESEARCH

The primary concern in intervention research is to generate empirical evidence for making valid inferences about the effects of the intervention on the hypothesized outcomes. The evidence should indicate that the improvement in the outcomes is attributable to the intervention, and not to any substantive or methodological factors inherent in the context of the evaluation study. In this chapter, an overview of validity is presented. Threats to validity and approaches to minimize their influence are discussed. The foundations for choosing research designs and methods for evaluating interventions are laid out.

OVERVIEW OF VALIDITY

Validity refers to the approximate truth of inferences about the intervention effects (Shadish et al., 2002); that is, the claim that the intervention causes the outcomes is correct in that it accurately reflects reality or corresponds to the world. Accordingly, the empirical evidence obtained in an evaluation study has to support this claim and be consistent with the criteria for causality (see Chapter 1). The study findings should indicate that: 1) clients who receive the intervention exhibit improvement, of a magnitude which is congruent with the nature and dose of the intervention, in the outcomes after implementation of the intervention; 2) clients who do not receive the intervention experience no change in the outcomes post-treatment; 3) outcomes, assessed following treatment delivery, differ significantly between the two groups of clients (i.e., do and do not receive the intervention); and 4) the between-group differences observed in post-treatment outcomes are related to the receipt of the intervention and not associated with other conceptual and methodological factors. These factors could lead to partly or completely wrong claims regarding the causal effects of the intervention on the outcomes (Jepsen et al., 2004). They represent threats to validity or sources of bias.

Incorrect inferences are of two types. The first is called type I error and has to do with a false positive claim that the intervention is effective, when in fact it is not. This erroneous claim may inspire additional research to further evaluate the effectiveness of the intervention under the same or different context. Often, the favorable findings observed in a particular study do not replicate or are refuted in subsequent studies (Ioannidis, 2005; Yong, 2012). For instance, recent evidence indicates that commonly prescribed antidepressant drugs are as effective as placebo pills; and mammograms, colonoscopies, and PSA tests are not as useful in detecting cancer as initially thought (Freedman, 2010). As a result, human and financial resources are wasted (Simmons et al., 2011), and researchers, healthcare professionals, and clients are disappointed. The second type of incorrect inference is called type II error. It has to do with a negative claim that the intervention is not effective, when in fact it is. This erroneous claim results in the abandonment of a potentially beneficial intervention. In this case, the actual intervention effects may have been masked by factors other than the intervention (Green, 2000).

Several factors related to the characteristics of the clients, interventionists, context in which the intervention is delivered, the design and implementation of the intervention, and the methods used to evaluate the effects of the intervention on the outcomes may distort the empirical evidence for making inferences. They influence the validity of the inferences that can be made from the operationalization of the intervention and the outcomes to the concepts they are intended to represent (issue of construct validity). The factors weaken the validity of inferences about the causal relationship between the intervention and the outcomes. They may contribute or be directly responsible for the changes in outcomes observed post-intervention and offer plausible alternative explanations of the effects (issue of internal validity). The factors affect the validity of inferences about the covariation between the intervention and the outcomes as they yield incorrect (over or under) estimation of the intervention effects (issue of statistical conclusion validity). Lastly, the factors may limit the validity of inferences related to the extent to which the causal relationship holds under different contexts (issue of external validity) (Shadish, 2010).

Shadish et al. (2002) provide comprehensive lists of specific threats to each type of validity. The following sections review the mechanisms through which the main threats weaken the validity of inferences and propose general approaches to minimize their influence. Specific strategies for addressing the threats are presented in the remaining chapters.

CONSTRUCT VALIDITY

Construct validity relates to the operationalization of the intervention and the outcomes, which should be consistent with their theoretical definitions. Discrepancies between the theoretical and operational definitions preclude meaningful interpretation of the results obtained in an intervention study due to the lack of clarity on the nature of the intervention implemented and the outcomes assessed. In other words, the operationalization of the intervention and the outcomes has the potential to introduce confounds in that the treatment delivered and the outcomes assessed are deficient in reflecting what is intended or contaminated with elements of other concepts. The threats to construct validity include inadequate explication of concepts, method bias, inadequate implementation of the study treatments, and reactivity of clients.

Inadequate Explication of Concept

Inadequate explication of concepts refers to the lack of a clear conceptualization of the intervention and the outcomes. The theoretical foundation of the intervention is not well articulated, resulting in poor delineation of its specific and non-specific elements and hence, the translation of these elements into components and activities that comprise the intervention. Therefore, the intervention delivered to clients is not what was intended and does not produce the hypothesized outcomes. Similarly, an inadequate conceptualization of the outcomes results in unclear identification of the domains and attributes that characterize the respective outcome. This, in turn, leads to the selection of instruments whose content either does not correspond with the identified domains and attributes, or reflects domains and attributes of related concepts. Accordingly, the selected instruments do not capture the hypothesized outcomes, leading to the erroneous claim that the intervention is not effective. The prevalence of this threat in health intervention research has not been examined. However, Keller et al. (2009) found that only 15 of 470 studies evaluating interventions aimed to promote engagement in physical activities reported clear conceptualization and operationalization of the intervention and outcomes. Conversely, Painter et al. (2008) reviewed studies investigating the effects of interventions targeting health behaviors; their findings indicated that theoretically informed interventions showed higher levels of effectiveness in changing health behaviors than interventions that were not explicitly informed by a theory.

This threat to construct validity can be prevented by developing clear conceptualization of the intervention and the outcomes. A clear conceptualization of the *intervention* is achieved with a detailed explanation of its active ingredients, generation of a matrix that specifies the components, activities, and mode of delivery that correspond to each active ingredient, and translation of the activities into the intervention protocol. The protocol describes the logical sequence of actions to be performed when implementing the intervention. This strategy has been recommended to maintain theoretical fidelity when designing interventions (Borrelli et al., 2005; Sidani and Braden, 2011). A clear conceptualization of an *outcome* involves a theoretical analysis of the concept that depicts the domains and attributes that define it and distinguish it from other concepts. This definition guides the selection of outcome measures, ensuring congruence between the conceptualization and operationalization of the outcome.

The content of the measure should also be relevant to the target population, reflecting the way in which the outcome is experienced by members of that population (Rothwell, 2005). In addition, it is important to choose outcome measures that demonstrate acceptable content and construct validity (see Chapter 12).

Method Bias

This bias refers to systematic error of measurement inherent in the method and measures for assessing outcomes. The error stems from various sources, listed in Table 2.1. For a detailed description of measurement bias, refer to Bowling (2005) and Podsakoff et al. (2003).

TABLE 2.1   Sources of measurement error

Source of error	Example
Characteristics of clients completing the measure	Transient mood state, social desirability, tendency for acquiescence, literacy level
Items contained in measure	Complexity, ambiguity, negative wordings leading to misinterpretation of content Number of items inducing response burden and fatigue Broad categorization of behaviors resulting in misinterpretation of what exactly is observed Intermixing of items reflecting different concepts making it difficult for clients to distinguish among concepts Restricted range of response options leading to forced choice
Method for obtaining data	Self-report: is prone to social desirability but increases disclosure of sensitive information Observation: introduces evaluation apprehension Interview: introduces bias in responses
Context of administration	Timing (e.g., exact time for taking blood sample) Handling of specimens Uncomfortable or noisy environment

Error of measurement is reflected in clients' responses to the outcome measure that may be inconsistent or tainted by other factors. The responses introduce artificially inflated or deflated scores on the outcome measure and consequently an over- or underestimation of the intervention effects. Although the extent of measurement error has not been systematically examined in intervention research, the results of a meta-analysis (Podsakoff et al., 2003) indicated it is present in organizational research. Specifically, about 26 per cent of the variance in a measure is associated with sources of measurement error; the amount of measurement error variance differed by type of concept (e.g., 22 per cent for job performance and 41 per cent for attitude).

General approaches for reducing method bias rely on using multiple instruments to measure the same outcome, using different methods for obtaining data if relevant (i.e., outcome is operationalized in various domains such as psychological and physiological), or from different sources if applicable (e.g., measuring clients' adherence to treatment through clients' self-report and significant others' report). The content of the measures should be clear, easy to understand, and relevant to the range of client subgroups constituting the target population. Clients are informed there is no right or wrong answer as a means to reduce evaluation apprehension. The context under which outcome measures are administered is standardized, to the extent possible.

Inadequate Implementation of Study Treatments

This threat has to do with fidelity of intervention implementation, and manifests as deviations in the actual delivery of the intervention from the original design and/or as variability in the intervention delivery across clients. Deviations in the actual delivery of the intervention are likely to take place when its active ingredients are not clearly specified, particularly in complex interventions; the activities operationalizing the active ingredients are not well specified in a protocol or manual; and several interventionists assume the responsibility of implementing the intervention but do not strictly follow the intervention protocol in doing so. These deviations may lead to the omission of some active ingredients or the inclusion of some active ingredients that characterize other interventions than the intended one when providing the intervention, which precludes the achievement of the outcomes. Deviations also occur in the actual delivery of the comparison treatment and significantly influence the validity of inferences if the comparison treatment incorporates some of the intervention's active ingredients.

Variability in the implementation of the intervention across clients is often associated with the interventionists' flexibility, which consists of adapting the intervention's components, activities, mode of delivery, or dose to be responsive to clients' needs and preferences. Therefore different clients receive different components of the intervention at different dose levels and consequently, respond differently to the intervention. This variability in responses is manifested in increased variability in the post-test outcomes, which reduces the statistical power to detect significant intervention effects. The same applies to variability in the delivery of the comparison treatment, which is highly likely when it consists of usual care.

Inadequate implementation has been discussed in the methodological literature under the notions of treatment diffusion, dissemination, or contamination, and low reliability of treatment implementation. These have been frequently considered as significant threats to validity (Bamberger and White, 2007; Buckwalter et al., 2009; Cook et al., 2010); however, the extent to which they are present in intervention research has not been investigated because of the prevailing assumption that interventionists strictly adhere to the intervention protocol. The concern with the fidelity of treatment implementation was recently brought to the forefront in studies evaluating interventions targeting health behaviors (Bellg et al., 2004; Carroll et al., 2007), and has been associated with type III error of inference (Basch and Gold, 1986). This type of error involves the incorrect conclusion that an intervention is ineffective when it has not been implemented as originally designed.

The general approaches for addressing this threat to construct validity include the development of a protocol that details the activities reflecting the active ingredients and are to be performed when implementing the intervention; intensive training of the interventionists; and monitoring the fidelity of treatment implementation (see Chapter 11). Monitoring implementation is expected to improve adequacy of treatment delivery and consequently achievement of outcomes. In a review of 542 intervention studies, Durlack and DuPre (2008) reported larger effect sizes in studies that did, as compared to those that did not, monitor the implementation of the intervention.

Reactivity of Clients

Reactivity of clients entails their reactions to the treatment to which they are assigned and to the assessment of outcomes. Clients' reactions to treatment include:

1. Expectancy: the expectation that the treatment received will produce beneficial outcomes induces positive responses to treatment often labeled as placebo response (Autret et al., 2012; Finnis et al., 2010), or increases clients' motivation to comply with treatment and therefore show large improvements in the outcomes.
2. Hypothesis guessing: guessing the hypothesis being tested prompts clients to respond accordingly and demonstrate the expected changes in outcomes.
3. Novelty: novelty of the intervention generates two types of responses. Some clients are enthusiastic and respond favorably, whereas others find it disruptive of their routine practices and respond negatively (Shadish et al., 2002).
4. Desirability of allocated treatment: through the recruitment and informed consent processes, clients become aware of the treatments under evaluation. If allocated to the less desirable treatment, some clients attempt to compensate by seeking care elsewhere or by reporting improvement in the outcomes (compensatory rivalry). Other clients react with anger or by 'giving up', leading to their withdrawal from treatment or the evaluation study; alternatively, they respond in a way that reflects worsening of the outcomes (resentful demoralization).
5. Positive responses to non-specific elements of treatment: examples of non-specific elements are the interactional style or working alliance that develops between clients and interventionist and instrumental support provided by other clients attending the treatment group sessions. Clients respond favorably to these elements and report improvement in the outcomes.

The influence of clients' reactivity to the allocated treatment has been explored to various extents. Traditionally, expectancy and positive responses to non-specific elements of treatment have been considered as mechanisms underlying the placebo effects. Several studies and meta-analyses have investigated the placebo effects in trials evaluating pharmacological (i.e., medication) and psycho-behavioral treatments. For instance, meta-analysis of studies comparing the effects of antidepressant drugs to those of placebo found that 65–80 per cent of the response to the drug is duplicated in the placebo treatment condition (Van Die et al., 2009). Similarly, in a review of studies evaluating medical treatments for headache, Autret et al. (2012) reported that placebo effects reflected about one-fifth of the active drug effect. This evidence indicates that clients' reactions to treatment contribute to outcome achievement, potentially confounding or masking its effects. The contribution of guessing has not been examined directly because of the widespread application of blinding as a strategy to prevent this bias. However, a few studies evaluated the success of blinding by asking clients and their physicians to guess the treatment clients actually received. Findings suggested that a large percentage (> 50 per cent) of participants made a correct guess (Boutron et al., 2005; Sackett, 2007). Specifically, participants who experienced improvement in the outcomes and adverse reactions knew they received the active drug, whereas those who did not experience changes in their condition realized they got the placebo treatment. The influence of clients' reactions to treatment novelty and desirability has not been investigated; however, recent interest in exploring the contribution of treatment acceptability and preferences to outcomes sheds some light on the extent to which these two threats affect the validity of inferences about intervention effectiveness (see Chapters 7 and 10 for information on treatment preferences).

The way and extent to which clients' reactions to allocated treatment threaten the validity of inferences depend on the distribution of clients expressing different reactions across the treatment conditions. When clients with favorable reactions are primarily assigned to 1) the intervention, then these clients show high levels of improvement in the outcomes, potentially leading to an overestimation of the intervention effects, or 2) the comparison condition, then these clients demonstrate changes in the outcomes that, when compared to those of the intervention group, yield small differences in the two groups' outcomes, potentially leading to an underestimation of the intervention effects. Alternatively, when clients with unfavorable reactions are primarily assigned to 1) the intervention, then these clients show no changes in the outcomes, resulting in the incorrect conclusion that the intervention is ineffective, or 2) the comparison condition, then these clients show no change or worsening of the outcomes, resulting in overestimated intervention effects. Lastly, a balanced distribution of clients with favorable and unfavorable reactions in the two groups dilutes the intervention's effects on the outcomes, suggesting that the intervention is ineffective.

The general approaches suggested to reduce the potential for these reactions rest on masking the hypothesis being tested; blinding clients to the nature of the treatment conditions by not divulging, if ethical, which condition is the intervention and which is the comparison condition; and using a research design, such as cross-over or delayed treatment, in which all clients receive the intervention at different points in time. Other approaches rely on assessing clients' reactions to the allocated treatment, such as their perception of the working alliance and exploring their contribution to outcome achievement.

Reactivity to outcome measurement involves evaluation apprehension and testing effects (Becker et al., 2003). Evaluation apprehension refers to volitional changes in clients' responses to outcome measures, whether verbal or behavioral, which are related to their awareness that they are being evaluated and monitored (McCarney et al., 2007). Clients who are aware of being evaluated alter their behaviors or verbal answers in a way that is consistent with their desire to be viewed as competent (Hawthorne effect), or that is socially acceptable (social desirability). Testing effects occur when the same outcome measures are administered at two points in time and the responses at the second time point capture changes induced by familiarity or practice; that is, clients alter their responses because of learning the appropriate answer that takes place following the first administration. Testing effects are highly likely with short time intervals between administrations of outcome measures. Changes in outcomes that are associated with reactivity of measurement may mimic the hypothesized improvement in outcomes. If this improvement is observed in clients assigned to the intervention, then it masks or is mistaken for the intervention effects. If the improvement is reported by clients allocated to the intervention and comparison group, then the magnitude of the between-group differences in the post-test outcomes is reduced, potentially leading to the incorrect inference that the intervention is ineffective. Whereas no study that has examined testing effects was located, two recent studies that investigated evaluation apprehension, specifically the Hawthorne effect, were found. Campbell et al. (1995) compared the documentation of paramedics following notification of 1) the importance of documentation, 2) an upcoming research project, or 3) an upcoming quality improvement audit. The results showed enhanced documentation with the notification of the quality improvement audit, which consisted of monitoring participants' performance. Similarly, McCarney et al. (2007) reported better outcomes in the intervention group with intensive follow-up than in the intervention group with minimal follow-up.

Evaluation apprehension can be addressed by 1) making the conditions for outcome assessment less threatening, such as emphasizing that there are 'no right or wrong' answers (Podsakoff et al., 2003), and ensuring privacy and confidentiality of responses (Shadish et al., 2002); 2) providing adequate training for research staff to collect data (through observation or interview) in a non-judgemental manner; and 3) assessing social desirability and controlling statistically its influence when analyzing the effects of the intervention on the outcomes. The effects of testing can be minimized by using alternate forms of the same outcome measure at different points in time, and estimated with the implementation of the Solomon four group design in which one intervention and one comparison group complete the outcome measures before and after treatment, and one intervention and one comparison group do not complete the outcome measures at pre-test but do so at post-test.

INTERNAL VALIDITY

Internal validity relates to the relationship between the intervention and the outcomes. The relationship should be causal in that the implementation of the intervention precedes improvement in the outcomes, and no other explanations for the relationship are plausible. Thus, internal validity addresses the issue of confounding, that is, the extent to which the changes in outcomes are attributable to the intervention and not to other factors. The factors are associated with clients' characteristics, context, and co-intervention.

Clients' Characteristics

In an intervention evaluation study, clients' characteristics are assessed before the implementation of the intervention. The characteristics encompass personal qualities (e.g., socio-demographic, cultural), health-related factors (e.g., lifestyle, beliefs), clinical condition (e.g., presence of comorbid conditions), and status on the outcomes (e.g., severity of clinical problem targeted by the intervention). Clients' characteristics may introduce bias in different ways.

Selection bias

Selection bias refers to differences in the characteristics, measured prior to intervention implementation, of clients assigned to the intervention and the comparison groups. These baseline differences may be observed for characteristics that are directly associated with post-test outcomes. The distribution of these characteristics within and between the two groups influences the levels of the outcomes reported at post-test. If clients in the intervention group possess characteristics known to be associated with favorable post-intervention outcomes, then the characteristics' influence can take two forms. First, the characteristics confound the intervention effects resulting in the incorrect inference that the intervention caused the outcomes when in fact the baseline characteristics are responsible for the post-test outcomes. For example, McEwen and West (2009) found an association between clients' characteristics and an outcome of nicotine replacement therapy: older clients and men had high chances of achieving abstinence within 3–4 weeks of initiating therapy, whereas those with high levels of nicotine dependence had low odds of abstinence. Second, the characteristics result in restricted range in the outcomes, which occurs when clients report high levels on the outcomes measured before intervention delivery leaving no room for demonstrating additional improvement (Becker et al., 2003). Although clients in the intervention group show no significant changes in the outcomes over time, their post-intervention outcomes are more favorable than those reported for clients in the comparison group, potentially leading to the incorrect conclusion that the intervention is effective. Alternatively, if clients in the comparison treatment group have characteristics associated with favorable outcomes, then the differences between the intervention and comparison groups on the post-test outcomes are minimal, leading to the erroneous inference that the intervention is ineffective. Similarly, when the number of clients with these characteristics is balanced within the intervention and comparison groups, then the post-test outcomes are comparable between the two groups, yielding the incorrect conclusion that the intervention is ineffective.

In contrast, if clients in the intervention group have characteristics known to be associated with unfavorable post-test outcomes, then low levels on these outcomes observed in this group imply worsening in the outcomes, resulting in the erroneous conclusion that the intervention is ineffective, even detrimental. If clients in the comparison group present with these characteristics, then they report low levels on the post-test outcomes resulting in a large difference between the two groups that potentially overestimate the intervention effects. When clients with these characteristics are equally distributed in the intervention and comparison groups, there is increased within-group variability in the levels of post-test outcomes, which reduces the power to detect significant intervention effects.

Two general approaches are recommended for minimizing selection bias. The first consists of randomly assigning clients to the intervention and the comparison group. Randomization is believed to increase the likelihood of maintaining the comparability of clients in the two groups on all measured and unmeasured variables (Chatterji, 2007; Weinberger et al., 2001). The second rests on residualizing the influence of the characteristics in the statistical analysis of post-test outcomes.

Baseline differences may also be associated with receipt of the treatments under evaluation. Clients with some characteristics may be exposed to different components and dose of the treatment to which they are assigned. Some receive the full scope, and others are exposed to selected components and variable dose levels of the allocated treatment. The mechanisms through which clients' characteristics influence exposure to treatment and achievement of outcomes, as well as the prevalence of selection bias in intervention research, are discussed in Chapter 9.

Attrition bias

Attrition, also referred to as mortality, occurs when clients withdraw from the intervention evaluation study, at any time after providing consent. Attrition influences the validity of inferences about the intervention's effects through three mechanisms. First, when a large number of clients drop out of the study, the remaining sample size is decreased; this reduces the power to detect significant intervention effects (i.e., statistical conclusion validity). Second, clients who withdraw differ from those who complete the study on some characteristics including poor health, competing demands, and preferences for treatment (Coday et al., 2005; Thoolen et al., 2007). Therefore, the clients who complete the study do not represent all segments or subgroups constituting the target population (i.e., external validity). Third, and of most relevance to internal validity, is differential attrition. Differential attrition is a situation in which the characteristics of clients who withdraw from the intervention group differ from the characteristics of clients who withdraw from the comparison group. Consequently, the pre-intervention (i.e., pre-test or baseline) profile of clients who complete the study is no longer comparable between the two groups, resulting in selection bias that can potentially confound the intervention effects (Ahern and Le Brocque, 2005; Valentine and McHugh, 2007).

Different approaches are applied to address this serious threat to validity. The one most recommended is to prevent attrition by incorporating various retention strategies in the intervention evaluation study (see Chapter 8). Another approach is to conduct intention-to-treat analysis. This approach, along with the prevalence of attrition in intervention research, is described in Chapter 9.

Spontaneous changes in outcomes

Clients may experience changes in the health problem and their general health condition over time. The changes are spontaneous in that they are not related to any treatment; however, they may be associated with some client characteristics or the context of outcome assessment. Specifically, clients with a particular profile exhibit changes in their physical function, cognitive reasoning ability, and psychosocial experience (i.e., maturation) during the study period (Becker et al., 2003). The changes may affect clients' responses to treatment favorably or unfavorably. Favorable responses reflect the hypothesized positive outcomes, which are incorrectly attributed to the intervention. Unfavorable responses yield no changes or worsening of the outcomes, which mask the intervention effects. In some instances, clients present with extreme levels on the outcomes. Clients with such high or low pre-test outcome levels tend to show a change (decrease or increase, respectively) in their post-test outcome levels; the latter values are closer to the average outcome level reported for the group to which the clients are allocated or for the total sample, following implementation of the intervention (i.e., regression to the mean). If the changes in the outcome levels take place in the intervention group and in the same pattern as hypothesized, then the changes confound the intervention effects. If the changes are experienced by clients in the intervention and the comparison groups and in the same or different pattern than hypothesized, then the within-group variability in the post-test outcomes is increased, which reduces the power to detect significant intervention effects.

Sometimes, the context of outcome assessment before and after the implementation of the intervention affects clients' reported values, which mimic the pattern of change in the outcomes expected of the intervention. This tends to happen for outcomes for which the levels are known to vary within specified time intervals such as diurnal changes in the level of certain hormones, seasonal changes in some conditions (e.g., seasonal affective disorders), symptoms (e.g., rhinitis due to hay fever), and severity of a symptom experienced over time (e.g., severe pain felt in the immediately post-operative period dissipates within 1 week after surgery; or breathlessness reported with ambulation is no longer experienced within 5 minutes of rest). If the intervention is given within this time interval, the changes in the outcomes levels can be inaccurately attributed to the intervention. No systematic examination of this threat has been reported.

Approaches to address this potential threat include: incorporation of a comparison group of clients to assist in identifying the effects of the intervention above and beyond the spontaneous changes in the outcomes (as experienced by the comparison group); assessing the outcomes repeatedly before the intervention allowing the regression to the mean to take place prior to implementation of the intervention and measuring the post-test outcomes repeatedly following the intervention delivery to accurately capture the pattern of change in the outcomes; adjusting statistically for extreme values reported prior to the intervention or conducting sensitivity analysis to determine the effects of the intervention for clients having high or low pre-test outcome levels; and carefully planning the time for outcome assessment before and after the intervention.

Context

Context refers to external factors that occur during the study period, the implementation of the intervention, or in the time period between the intervention implementation and the outcome assessment, and that influence clients' responses to treatment (Buckwalter et al., 2009; West and Thoemmes, 2010). The external factors include features in the environment in which the intervention is provided or in which clients carry out the treatment recommendations, and events occurring in these time periods. Examples of environmental features are: uncomfortable seating while listening to music for relaxation purposes, unsafe neighborhood for walking to promote health, and unavailability of fresh fruit and vegetables (for healthy eating) in some locations and seasons. Examples of events include unexpected life events and changes in healthcare services or policy. These contextual factors interfere with the implementation of the intervention. They may facilitate its delivery resulting in the achievement of the outcomes or may hinder its application with fidelity and consequently, clients' experience of the outcomes. The factors influence clients' responses to the intervention either favorably, potentially leading to an overestimate of the intervention effects, or unfavorably, potentially weakening its effects.

Contextual factors may not be controllable by the researcher or the clients. Accordingly, collecting data on environmental features and on events that take place during the implementation of the intervention by the interventionists and the clients is a useful approach to identify and account for these factors in the analysis of outcome data and in the interpretation of the findings.

Co-intervention

Co-intervention or co-treatment refers to clients' exposure and receipt of additional therapies, above and beyond the intervention under evaluation. The additional therapies could be part of usual care to which all clients participating in intervention research are entitled, and which cannot be withheld for ethical reasons. In some situations, the healthcare professionals offering usual care decide to compensate clients by enhancing the quality of usual care or by providing some components of the intervention that are widely disseminated through best practice guidelines (i.e., compensatory equalization of treatments; Shadish et al., 2002). In other instances, clients enrolled in an intervention evaluation study may seek additional therapies for various reasons such as dissatisfaction with the allocated treatment.

The mechanism through which this threat influences the validity of inferences depends on the group of clients who implement the additional therapies and the effectiveness of these therapies. When clients in the comparison group carry out additional therapies, and if the latter therapies are effective, then these clients report improvements in the outcomes; this in turn, reduces the magnitude of the between-group differences in the post-test outcomes, resulting in the erroneous conclusion that the intervention is ineffective. Conversely, when clients allocated to the intervention group implement additional therapies, then the following situations may arise. First, the additional therapies might exert independent effects on the outcomes: if not partialed out, then improvements in the outcomes are incorrectly attributed to the intervention rather than the combination of treatments that actually produced the outcomes. Second, the additional therapies might interact with the intervention positively in that they strengthen its impact on outcomes, yielding an overestimate of the intervention effects. Third, the additional therapies may interact with the intervention negatively in that they weaken its impact on outcomes, leading to an underestimate of the intervention effects. The extent to which this threat to validity permeates intervention research has not been systematically examined.

Three general approaches are recommended to address this threat to construct validity. The first approach rests on excluding clients who report use of additional therapies from the study. The second approach involves requesting clients taking any treatment for the management of the problem targeted by the intervention or other health problems to continue with the same treatment at the same dose during the study period. The third approach consists of collecting data on additional therapies applied by clients assigned to the intervention and comparison group, and accounting for their influence in data analysis.

STATISTICAL CONCLUSION VALIDITY

Statistical conclusion validity is primarily concerned with the covariation between the intervention and the outcomes. It focuses on the accuracy in the results of the statistical analysis done to determine the effects of the intervention, that is, whether or not the intervention is associated with the outcomes, and the strength of the association (Shadish, 2010). The covariation between the intervention and the outcomes is evidenced in significant differences in the outcomes measured at post-test between the groups of clients who do and do not receive the intervention. The between-group differences should exceed the inter-individual differences (i.e., those observed between individuals and captured in the within-group variance) to make valid inferences about the presence and strength of the association. Three sources of bias can affect the detection of significant group differences: inadequate sample size, inappropriate use of statistical tests, and random error.

Inadequate Sample Size

Empirical evidence indicates an inverse relationship between sample size (i.e., number of clients participating in an intervention evaluation study and assigned to the intervention and comparison groups) and the magnitude of the intervention effects. Large sample sizes increase the potential of finding small intervention effects whereas small sample sizes increase the potential to detect large intervention effects (Lipsey, 1990; Lowenstein and Castro, 2009). Furthermore, Schmidt (2010) states that the p-value, conventionally set at .01 or .05 and used to determine whether or not the observed between-group differences in the outcomes are statistically significant (i.e., not due to chance), is a function of sample size. Taken together, sample size, effect size (i.e., magnitude of the intervention effect), and p-value influence the power to detect the intervention effects. For instance, with a small number of clients and a low preset p-value (e.g., $\leq$ .01), there is low probability that the observed effect size, even if large, is claimed to be statistically significant; this leads to the incorrect inference that the intervention is not effective.

Generally, the approaches to address this potential threat to validity include conducting a power analysis and focusing on point estimates and confidence intervals for quantifying the intervention effects. Power analysis assists in determining the number of clients needed to detect the hypothesized effect size at the preset p-value. Confidence intervals provide information on the precision of the intervention effects estimated in a particular intervention evaluation study and across studies. Schmidt (2010) reports that confidence intervals overlap across studies. This observation, in contrast to findings based on statistical significance, implies that the studies' results are not conflicting in estimating an intervention's effects.

Inappropriate Use of Statistical Tests

The statistical tests used to examine differences in outcomes between the intervention and comparison groups are based on a set of assumptions such as independence of the observations, normal distribution of the outcome scores, and equal variance of the outcome scores within the two groups. Violations of these assumptions reduce the chance of detecting the intervention effects. Addressing this potential threat involves: careful examination of the outcome data to determine the extent to which the data meet the assumptions prior to selecting a statistical test, and application of the appropriate formula of the statistical tests, if available, in case of minor violations. For example, the t-test and the F-test were found to be robust (i.e., produce the same results in face of challenges; Lowenstein and Castro, 2009) in the presence of non-normally distributed data obtained in large samples (Shadish et al., 2002); alternative formulae (available in most statistical packages) for the t-test and F-test can be used when the assumption of equal variance is not met. Consideration of other statistical tests is recommended when serious violations of the assumptions are found. For example, multi-level modeling is used to account for non-independence, which is likely when participants are recruited from different naturally occurring clusters (see Chapter 6). In addition, repeated testing done on the same data set increases the likelihood of detecting significant differences between groups or across time points; however, the differences may be due to chance. Two general approaches have been recommended to avoid this error. The first rests on adjusting the type I error rate for the number of tests to be performed (e.g., Bonferroni correction). The second involves the application of multivariate statistical techniques followed by planned comparisons, guided by clearly stated hypotheses regarding where or when the differences lie.

Random Error

Random error represents fluctuations in the clients' scores in the post-test outcomes. The fluctuations are related to unreliability of the measures, inconsistency in treatment implementation, variability in context, and natural heterogeneity of clients. Instruments with low reliability lead to variability in the clients' responses that does not capture their true levels on the outcome being measured. Inconsistent implementation results in clients' exposure to different components and dose levels of the intervention, which yields differences in the outcomes' levels achieved by the clients within the intervention and comparison groups. Similarly, variability in contextual factors operating during the implementation of the intervention and the time interval between treatment delivery and outcome assessment influences the clients' responses to the intervention. Natural heterogeneity of clients refers to inter-individual differences in the characteristics of clients that may be correlated with the outcomes and may yield differences in how clients respond to the allocated treatment. All these factors increase the variability in the post-test outcome levels reported by clients assigned to the intervention and the comparison groups. The high within-group variance (often considered error variance in the t-test and F-test) reduces the power to detect significant between-group differences, leading to the inaccurate inference that the intervention is ineffective. The general approach to minimize error relies on managing its sources, such as using a reliable measure, monitoring the fidelity of treatment implementation, and experimentally or statistically controlling contextual factors and sample heterogeneity. Experimental control is exerted by carefully selecting the context and holding its features constant for all clients, and clients based on preset eligibility criteria to enhance sample homogeneity relative to personal and health characteristics, and to responses to treatment. Statistical control consists of measuring the contextual factors and the clients' characteristics, and using them as covariate in outcome data analysis to account for their influence on post-test outcomes.

EXTERNAL VALIDITY

External validity relates to the generalizability of the causal relationship between the intervention and the outcomes across client populations and contexts. It is concerned with the extent to which the intervention is reproducible, and its effects on the outcomes hold over conditions representing variations in clients, contexts, and outcome measurement (Shadish, 2010). The local circumstances of the intervention evaluation study related to clients, context, intervention delivery, and outcome measures limit the reproducibility of the observed intervention effects to other conditions.

Client Characteristics

Clients' personal, health, and clinical characteristics influence their participation in the study and the achievement of outcomes expected of the intervention. There is ample evidence showing that clients who enroll in a study differ from those who decline enrollment, resulting in what has been called non-consent bias (Kaptchuk, 2001). Frequently reported reasons for refusal to participate are lack of interest in the study topic; practical inconvenience related to lack of time, lack of transportation, and concerns about costs of participation; perception of the treatments under evaluation (e.g., preferences for a particular treatment option, uncertainty about treatments' effectiveness, demands associated with carrying out the treatment recommendations); and poor understanding of study design (e.g., consent process, random assignment) (Baker et al., 2005). Further, the profile of participants and non-participants is not always comparable. For example, Thoolen et al. (2007) found that clients with type 2 diabetes who refused to enroll in a trial of a brief self-management intervention were less educated and reported higher self-management and self-efficacy levels than those who participated in the trial. In addition, low enrollment rates are increasingly observed in intervention research. For example, Bottomley (1997) stated that $\leq$ 30 per cent enrollment rates are frequently found in cancer trials and Rothwell (2005) indicated $\leq$ 10 per cent enrollment rates are common for clients with the target disorders. As well, the specification of stringent eligibility criteria, often done to enhance the homogeneity of the sample and to control for potentially confounding client characteristics, constrains participants to a subgroup of the client population (Rothwell, 2005; Stirman et al., 2005). The non-consent bias, combined with low enrollment rates and stringent eligibility criteria, yields a selective sample that is unrepresentative of all subgroups forming the target population, and that responds to the intervention in a particular way (see Chapter 5). Accordingly, the reported intervention effects may not be reproduced when the intervention is given to other subgroups of the client population encountered in different practice settings.

The approaches for addressing this limitation vary with the phase of the intervention evaluation (see Chapter 3) and the purpose of the evaluation study. In general, they involve examination of the same intervention's effects in different subgroups of the population, which is done within a program of research, or of the moderating influence of theoretically or clinically important client characteristics on the same intervention's effects, which is done in a large-scale study.

Context Characteristics

The physical and psychosocial features of the environment affect the implementation of the intervention and the clients' reactions and responses to the intervention. When the setting is carefully selected to have the features that facilitate intervention delivery and promote positive responses, then the improvement in outcomes may not be observed in other settings with less favorable features. For example, in a meta-analysis of studies that evaluated the effectiveness of educational interventions in enhancing diabetes self-management, Brown (2002) found larger effect sizes for interventions offered in in-hospital units than those given in out-patient clinics. Variability in the implementation of best practice guidelines or interventions and in the level of outcomes achieved has been reported across healthcare settings (e.g., hospitals) located within the same or in different geographic areas (Eccles et al., 2005; Lugtenberg et al., 2009). The same approaches for addressing client characteristics are applicable for the contextual limitation to external validity.

Intervention Delivery

Careful selection and training of interventionists, the close monitoring of their implementation of the intervention, and the availability of expert support throughout the study contribute to the fidelity with which the intervention is delivered. As mentioned previously, high fidelity is associated with large intervention effects (Durlack and DuPre, 2008). The latter effects may not be reproduced when healthcare professionals with different training and experience provide the intervention in the absence of expert support and under the time constraints of day-to-day practice. Variations in the intervention components, mode of delivery, and dose ensue and interfere with the achievement of the outcomes. A systematic, sequential evaluation of the effects on outcomes associated with alterations in the intervention components and dose, implemented by different healthcare professionals, is required to determine the reproducibility of the intervention and its effects.

Outcome Measures

The instruments used to measure the outcomes in an intervention evaluation study are valid, reliable, and sensitive to change, and hence able to detect the beneficial intervention effects. The extent to which the expected intervention effects are reproduced with the use of alternate measures of the same outcomes may be limited. Specifically, the former measures may not be clinically relevant (Rothwell, 2005). Their administration is demanding and time consuming, increasing the burden on healthcare professionals and clients; the scoring procedure is elaborate; and the interpretation of the scores is limited in clearly and easily identifying graded levels of improvement. Therefore different outcome measures, considered more clinically meaningful, may be used to evaluate the effects of an intervention under the conditions of day-to-day practice. The utility of such measures should be explored.

FOUNDATION FOR SELECTION OF RESEARCH DESIGNS AND METHODS

Health intervention research involves the systematic evaluation of the extent to which interventions are effective in producing the hypothesized outcomes. Systematic evaluation is applied within the context of a particular study and a multi-phase, multi-study process, with the goal of generating valid, cumulative, and meaningful evidence that will inform treatment-related decisions in day-to-day practice.

Studies aimed to evaluate the effects of an intervention should be designed and conducted following a rigorous process. Traditionally, the design is focused on demonstrating the single and direct causal relationship between the intervention and the outcomes while controlling, experimentally, for sources of bias. The experimental or randomized controlled trial (RCT) design was adopted as the 'gold standard' (Hyde, 2004) for examining the effects of health interventions including medication, education, self-help groups, and behavioral therapies. The adoption of this design was based on theoretical reasons and intuitive attractiveness (Kaptchuk, 2001). The features of the RCT were believed to operationalize the criteria for inferring causality and to reduce bias (see Chapter 4).

The adoption of the RCT as the gold standard resulted in what Kaptchuk (2001: 547) described as a 'mechanical ritual'. The experimental or RCT design is considered of high quality and therefore, the most appropriate in generating valid inferences about the effects of health interventions. Accordingly, it is the most highly recommended, if not mandated, and the most frequently selected design irrespective of the study aims, nature of the intervention under evaluation, and context. Recent reviews and analysis of the field of health intervention research characterize the widespread application of the RCT design as uncritical, inconsistent with the notion of multi-causality, and unresponsive to the expressed need for clinically relevant evidence that can meaningfully guide practice.

The uncritical adoption was based on an uncontested recognition of the strengths of the RCT design; its features are advantageous in controlling factors that may confound the causal connection between the intervention and the outcomes. However, the weaknesses of the RCT design were ignored, and in some cases dismissed, on the basis of its intuitive logic or reasonableness (Proctor and Capaldi, 2001), rather than compelling empirical evidence of its utility in generating valid inferences about the intervention effects (Kaptchuk, 2001; Westen et al., 2004). Emerging empirical evidence (e.g. Concato and Horwitz, 2004; Heinsman and Shadish, 1996) dispels the gold standard myth and suggests that there is no universally best research design and method (Cartwright, 2007). Each design and method has inherent strengths and limitations in providing valid inferences about the intervention effects. Thus, the application of different designs and methods will complement their strengths and counterbalance their limitations, which enhances the accuracy of the inferences within and across studies investigating the same intervention (Noar and Mehrotra, 2011). Accordingly, the selection of a design and methods for a particular intervention evaluation study should be informed by a critical analysis of their strengths and weaknesses, and relevance in addressing the study aims, in combination with empirical evidence supporting their utility, as presented in subsequent chapters.

Recent critique points to the limited relevance of RCT-generated evidence in guiding practice. The evidence is often grounded in the single and directional notion of causality, and in a controlled context that eliminates the potential influence of various factors (Donaldson and Christie, 2004). This evidence lacks ecological validity in that it does not mirror the conditions of day-to-day practice, under which the interventions will be ultimately implemented (Chatterji, 2007). In practice, multiple factors operate to affect treatment and outcomes (Noar and Mehrotra, 2011). The practice conditions are characterized by variability in clients receiving the intervention, the interventionists delivering the intervention, the components and dose of the intervention provided, and the environment in which the intervention is implemented. Clients present with different experiences (i.e., determinants, manifestations, level of severity) of the health problem targeted by the intervention, different illness representations, different values and preferences for treatment, in combination with a range of comorbid conditions. Clients are not denied treatment, and their characteristics, some of which may have rendered them ineligible for participation in research, influence initiation, adherence, and satisfaction with treatment, as well as outcome achievement. Thus, they confound or moderate the intervention effects, raising the clinical question: What clients, with which personal, health, or clinical profile benefit most from the intervention? Similarly, interventionists vary in their professional preparation, theoretical orientation, and perceived acceptability of the intervention, as well as interactional style. They may not have received intensive training to enhance their competencies in implementing the intervention. Most may have been socialized to attend to the individual clients' needs and individualize care to be responsive to these needs. These interventionists' qualities affect the implementation of the intervention as well as clients' reactions and responses to treatment, requiring answers to the clinical questions: What healthcare professional groups are most suited to deliver the intervention? To what extent and in what way does the interventionists' interactional style contribute to clients' adherence to treatment and outcome achievement?

Modifications in the implementation of the intervention is the norm in day-to-day practice (Goldfried and Eubanks-Carter, 2004); these may involve provision of some, but not all, components of the intervention, at various dose levels, using a different mode of delivery than specified for the intervention. The modifications are done to fit individual clients' needs and preferences or to accommodate for contextual constraints. In addition, any treatment addressing the same problem or the comorbid conditions is not withheld. Accordingly, clinicians wonder: What modifications can be safely made to the intervention without reducing its potency in improving the outcomes? How does the effectiveness of the intervention compare to the effectiveness of other treatments currently in use for the same problem? To what extent and in what way does the intervention interact with other treatments?

The context of practice is unstable due to changes in staff, policies, and availability of material and financial resources, which constrain the interventionists' ability to implement the intervention with fidelity. Similarly, clients may live in an environment that is not supportive of the treatment recommendations or not conducive to improvement in outcomes. The clinical question is: What environmental features are needed to implement the intervention by healthcare professionals and clients? Lastly, healthcare professionals want to understand not only that the intervention works in producing the intended effects but also how it works (i.e., the mechanisms responsible for the effects) and what unintended favorable or unfavorable (i.e., adverse) effects it has (Brown, 2002; Green, 2000).

The investigation of the contribution of multiple factors to intervention implementation and outcome achievement, and the generation of empirical evidence that addresses the clinical questions, demand changes in the conceptualization and conduct of health intervention research. Changes in conceptualization consist of acknowledging the potential influence of these factors and considering them of substantive relevance, rather than a mere source of bias which should be eliminated (Berwick, 2008). Hence, a wider range of aims, that go beyond just determining the effects of an intervention compared to no-treatment, is set for individual studies and for sequential studies within a program of research focusing on the same intervention (see Chapter 3). Changes in the conduct of intervention research involves the realization that different designs and methods have advantages and disadvantages in addressing different aims, and that the integration of different methodologies is beneficial in maintaining validity of inferences about intervention effects and in producing evidence of relevance to practice.

Summary

- Intervention evaluation studies should be carefully designed to enhance the validity of inferences regarding the effectiveness of the intervention in producing the outcomes
- Validity is maintained by recognizing potential threats to validity, incorporating strategies to prevent or minimize the influence of these threats and critically appraising the strengths and limitations of different designs and methods prior to selecting the most appropriate ones
- Selection of designs and methods is also guided by the research question and the need to produce clinically relevant evidence

3

PHASES OF INTERVENTION EVALUATION RESEARCH

The systematic evaluation of health interventions is done through a multi-phase process to generate the empirical evidence needed to inform practice. The phases are logically sequenced to design optimal interventions, explore their reasonable benefits and safety, and determine their impact, prior to translating them into practice. The sequential, multi-phase process meets scientific requirements and satisfies ethical obligations (Robey, 2004) for providing safe, appropriate, and effective treatments. It is relevant and followed in the evaluation of newly developed, single and multiple component interventions and of an intervention with demonstrated beneficial outcomes in a new context (i.e., new target population or setting).

Different scientific organizations (Medical Research Council in England, National Institutes of Health in the United States, and Canadian Institutes of Health Research in Canada) and scientists (e.g., Craig et al., 2008; Robey, 2004) have described the multi-phase process using slightly different terminology to label the phases. There is, however, a general sense of agreement on the goals to be attained within and across phases. Each phase is conceptualized to address a particular set of aims related to the value of health interventions. This conceptualization directs the selection of research designs and methods, and highlights the type of validity of most concern in studies planned for the different phases. For comprehensiveness, a five phase process is discussed next and summarized in Table 3.1 at the end of the chapter.

PHASE 1: MODELING OF THE INTERVENTION

The first phase, referred to as modeling of the intervention (Campbell et al., 2007; Eldridge et al., 2005; Hardeman et al., 2005), is foundational to the multi-phase evaluation process.

The emphasis is on the development of an optimal intervention and of a comprehensive understanding of the health problem targeted by the intervention, the active ingredients and non-specific elements of the intervention, the immediate and ultimate outcomes expected of the intervention, and the mediators and moderators of the intervention effects. This understanding is summarized in the intervention theory described in Chapter 1. The intervention theory guides the operationalization of the intervention, mediators, outcomes, and moderators; the statement of hypotheses to be tested; and the design and conduct of studies aimed to evaluate the effects of the intervention in subsequent studies. Maintaining consistency between the conceptualization and the operationalization of the intervention and related variables, which is an issue of construct validity, is of primary concern in this first phase. The goals to be attained in Phase 1 and the respective methodology are discussed next.

Conceptualization of the Problem

Phase 1 aims to gain an understanding of the health problem requiring remediation and targeted by the intervention. This involves conceptual and empirical work to define the problem at the theoretical (i.e., essential attributes) and the operational (i.e., its manifestations) levels, identify its determinants, and describe the level of severity at which it is experienced by the target client population. The conceptual work consists of a critical review of theories that can assist in explicating the health problem, and of quantitative and qualitative research findings that specify its prevalence and most significant determinants (Campbell et al., 2007). Drawing on pertinent theory and findings, the pathway through which the health problem is caused and sustained, is mapped. It is highly advisable to validate the conceptualization of the health problem in the target client population. This is important to ensure that clients experience it as defined and that the identified determinants are relevant to the population. Quantitative or qualitative methodology can be used in the evaluation. A quantitative methodology entails non-experimental designs carried out to examine the prevalence of the health problem and its relationships with the determinants in a large sample representative of the target population. A qualitative methodology applies a grounded theory or concept mapping approach, in an individual or group format, to capture the target population's input relative to their understanding of the problem. For a detailed presentation of the different approaches for understanding the problem refer to Sidani and Braden (2011). A critical analysis of the conceptualization assists in identifying aspects of the health problem that can be modified in order to prevent, manage, or resolve it. The identified aspects are targeted by the intervention.

Conceptualization of the Intervention

Phase 1 also aims to develop the intervention that will address the health problem. Different approaches can be followed. The first is theoretical. The theory that conceptualizes the health problem proposes strategies to manage its modifiable aspects (Hardeman et al., 2005). The second approach is empirical. It rests on a review of pertinent literature to identify strategies that have been used and found effective in addressing each modifiable aspect of the problem (Craig et al., 2008). The third approach is participatory. The clients' perspective on what constitutes reasonable strategies for managing the modifiable aspects of the health problem is explored. For an explanation of the procedure for applying these strategies, refer to Sidani and Braden (2011). Subsequent analytical work includes the selection of strategies that are most appropriate for each aspect of the health problem using intervention mapping (Kok et al., 2004). The selected strategies form the active ingredients that characterize the intervention and the targeted aspects of the health problem represent the immediate outcomes expected of the intervention. The strategies for each aspect of the problem are integrated into a component. The mode for providing each component is carefully selected. The nature of the strategies and the number of components guides the specification of the intervention dose. The analytic work culminates in the specification of the intervention in terms of its components, mode of delivery, and dose.

In addition, conceptualization of the intervention involves modeling the mechanisms through which it achieves its effects on the ultimate outcomes (Campbell et al., 2007; Craig et al., 2008). As explained in Chapter 1, the mechanism specifies the pathway of changes that take place following implementation of the intervention and mediate its impact on the ultimate outcomes. The changes relate to clients' reactions to treatment and improvement in the immediate outcomes, derived from relevant theory underlying the intervention or logical reasoning. Each mediating variable is defined at the conceptual level. The pattern (i.e., direction and magnitude) of change in the mediator over time is also described. The conceptualization of the intervention and its underlying mechanism gives directions for their operationalization.

Operationalization of the Intervention and its Mechanism

Operationalization of the intervention entails the development of the intervention protocol (Robey, 2004). The protocol specifies the nature and the sequence of activities to be performed when delivering the intervention. It is described in a manual that details the resources needed, the actions to be carried out and the information to be relayed by the interventionists, and the activities in which clients are to engage in each treatment session or contact, as well as the treatment recommendations that clients are expected to apply, in their day-to-day life in the time interval between treatment sessions or contacts. The protocol forms the basis for delivering the intervention and for monitoring the fidelity of its implementation. Similarly, the conceptualization of mediating and outcome variables gives directions for selecting instruments to measure them.

Most of the work done in Phase 1 is conceptual, requiring critical analytic skills and logical reasoning. It generates knowledge that informs decision making related to the plan and conduct of an intervention evaluation study, as discussed in Chapter 1.

PHASE 2: PILOT TESTING OF THE INTERVENTION AND RESEARCH METHODS

The second phase represents the first step in the empirical evaluation of the intervention. The goals are to examine the acceptability, feasibility, and effects of the intervention, and to explore the feasibility of research methods that are planned for the next phase of the intervention evaluation. These goals have different implications for the primary focus and the design of the pilot study.

Examining Acceptability of the Intervention

Acceptability refers to the clients' perception of the intervention as appropriate and reasonable in addressing the health problem as they experience it; convenient, suitable, and easy to apply in the context of daily life; effective in managing the problem in the short and long term; and associated with minimal risks or adverse effects (Tarrier et al., 2006). An acceptable intervention meets the clients' expectations for treatment of the problem (Kazdin, 1980). Clients' acceptability of the intervention affects initiation and adherence to treatment, and outcome achievement (Craig et al., 2008). Clients who judge an intervention as unacceptable may not adopt it or may be selective in applying treatment recommendations (i.e., those considered suitable), and therefore may not exhibit the hypothesized level of improvement in the outcomes (Eckert and Hintze, 2000).

Clients' acceptability of the intervention can be evaluated in stand-alone small-scale projects executed prior to pilot testing. Three approaches can be used. The first is consultative, aimed at eliciting clients' input regarding the appropriateness, convenience, effectiveness, and risks of a newly designed or refined intervention, or an intervention to be implemented in a newly selected client population, particularly clients of diverse cultural backgrounds. Clients are invited to an individual or a group interview. The interview is semi-structured and proceeds by: reviewing the health problem addressed by the intervention; giving an overview of the intervention to clarify its goals, components, mode of delivery, and dose; describing the activities in which the interventionists and clients engage during each intervention session, as well as the treatment recommendations that clients are asked to follow; requesting clients to comment on the acceptability of the activities planned for each session and the treatment recommendations to the target population, and to suggest modifications to enhance acceptability of the intervention. Transcripts of the interview are content analyzed to identify aspects of the intervention considered acceptable and hence are retained, and aspects requiring refinement and the nature of the changes to be made.

The second approach for examining acceptability relies on a quantitative methodology. A non-experimental, survey-type design is used to administer a questionnaire assessing acceptability of the intervention. The questionnaire 1) introduces the health problem targeted by the intervention; 2) describes the intervention in terms of its goals, components, activities, mode of delivery, and dose; and 3) presents items for rating the appropriateness, convenience, effectiveness, and risks of the intervention, as suggested by Tarrier et al. (2006). In addition, a list of activities, content to be covered in each intervention session, and treatment recommendations is presented. For each activity and recommendation, clients are requested to rate its overall acceptability. Further, open-ended questions can be used, asking respondents to comment on any aspect of the intervention and to suggest ways to modify it to enhance its acceptability (Sidani and Braden, 2011). Descriptive analysis of the quantitative ratings and content analysis of qualitative responses identify the clients' perceived acceptability of the intervention and its specific activities.

The third approach involves a small-scale implementation of the intervention (e.g., case studies) and simultaneous assessment of acceptability using a mix of quantitative and qualitative data collection methods. A small group of clients representing the target population are invited to attend what can be called a 'mock' implementation of the intervention, offered in an individual or group format. Prior to providing the intervention, participants are informed of the need and importance of their feedback regarding acceptability, and the procedure for obtaining it. The procedure consists of delivering one intervention component at a time, followed by requesting clients to rate its acceptability and engaging them in a discussion of its relevance to the target population, of aspects that require refinement, and of content or activity that is important to the target population but are missing. The procedure is repeated for all intervention components. Converging quantitative and qualitative findings indicate what aspects of the intervention are acceptable and how to refine the intervention. This approach has been used to examine the acceptability of educational interventions offered in different modes: face-to-face (e.g., Chung et al., 2009), written (e.g., Gwadry-Sridher et al., 2003), and computer-assisted (e.g., Vandelanotte et al., 2004), and behavioral interventions (e.g., Ames et al., 2008).

Acceptability can also be examined in any study (pilot or otherwise) evaluating the intervention. A questionnaire similar to the one described previously for assessing acceptability of the intervention, can be administered prior to or following implementation of the intervention. Additional indicators of acceptability are inferred from reasons given by clients for declining enrollment or for withdrawing from treatment, in particular those reflecting perception of the intervention as demanding, not relevant, not helpful, or time consuming. Some researchers have considered adherence to treatment as an indicator of acceptability, which is not consistent with the conceptualization of treatment acceptability adopted in this book. Rather, the stance here is that acceptability represents a perceived value that drives adherence to the intervention, as proposed by health behavior theories such as the theory of planned behavior (Ajzen, 1991).

Examining Feasibility of the Intervention

Feasibility refers to the practicality of the intervention implementation. It has to do with the adequacy of the logistics encompassing the resources and procedures for delivering the intervention as designed (Becker, 2008). The goals are to determine the extent to which the intervention activities are carried out in the specified mode of delivery and at the recommended dose, and to identify any challenge in applying any of the intervention components and activities (Hertzog, 2008). The challenges relate to the skills of interventionists, availability of material resources, suitability of context, and the intervention protocol. The challenges interfere with the proper implementation of the intervention and may reduce the interventionists' and clients' enthusiasm for the intervention. Interventionists facing difficulties may experience frustration that adversely affects their interactions with clients; alternatively, they may be forced to modify the intervention delivery to fit with what is possible or feasible. Clients may react unfavorably to the intervention, leading to their withdrawal from treatment or non-adherence to treatment recommendations. Interventionists' and clients' responses to challenges in intervention implementation influence clients' achievement of outcomes.

Feasibility of intervention implementation can be evaluated in a stand-alone small-scale pilot study. A case study or single group design is appropriate to address this purpose. The design involves providing the intervention to a group of clients representative of the target population and using primarily qualitative methods for collecting data related to the indicators of intervention feasibility presented next.

The *adequacy of the interventionists' training* in enhancing their cognitive and behavioral skills required for implementing the intervention is assessed upon completion of the intensive training and throughout the pilot study. Interventionists are requested to rate the extent to which the training was helpful in understanding the conceptual underpinning of the intervention, learning about the intervention protocol, providing ample opportunities to apply the skills, and discussing potential challenges encountered in the treatment delivery and solutions for these challenges. Also, interventionists are invited to comment on the usefulness of different aspects of the training. Their knowledge of the intervention conceptualization and operationalization (Kovach, 2009) is tested with a self-administered questionnaire and through observation of their performance when providing the intervention to clients participating in the pilot study.

Availability of material resources needed for the implementation of the intervention is discussed with interventionists and research staff. The resources include equipment (e.g., laptop for computer-assisted delivery of the intervention), printed materials (e.g., booklet summarizing treatment recommendations), general supplies (e.g., items for demonstration of health-related skills such as menu to illustrate food selection), and medical supplies (e.g., blood specimen containers). The resources should be available in an adequate number and in proper functioning order. Interventionists and research staff are asked to report any difficulty in obtaining the resources informally, during regular research staff meetings.

Suitability of context is examined formally when selecting the sites for intervention delivery and informally during the conduct of the pilot study. The formal evaluation is done with a checklist that contains the features needed to facilitate the intervention implementation, and determining whether or not the selected sites have the key features. The informal evaluation consists of reviewing complaints about contextual factors that influence intervention implementation, made by clients (e.g., limited parking space which may frustrate clients and prevent them from attending the treatment sessions), interventionists (e.g., external noise that may distract clients), and research staff (e.g., difficulty booking rooms or enlisting the support of the IT staff in delivering the equipment promptly).

The *intervention protocol* is critical for implementing the intervention with fidelity. Evaluating its adequacy in specifying the sequence of activities to be performed and in describing the steps to be followed in carrying out the activities is of primary concern when testing the feasibility of the intervention. This is accomplished by closely monitoring the implementation of the intervention and by eliciting interventionists' feedback. Fidelity is monitored by observing the interventionists and documenting the intervention activities carried out (Kovach, 2009); by requesting interventionists to report on a checklist the activities performed and the reasons for non-performance; and having clients complete a short questionnaire to indicate the intervention components or activities to which they are exposed (see Chapter 11). Interventionists' feedback is obtained relative to 1) the comprehensiveness and clarity of the content covered in the intervention manual, 2) the ease with which the intervention activities are performed, in the specified mode, 3) the time it takes to deliver each intervention component, and 4) challenges encountered in providing the intervention.

The information gathered in a stand-alone feasibility study is useful in determining what aspects of the intervention delivery are easy to carry out and what aspects need refinement. Suggested modifications are incorporated into the design of the intervention. The revised intervention is subjected to further feasibility testing prior to evaluating its effects.

Examining Intervention Effects

In Phase 2 of the systematic evaluation process, the focus is on exploring the extent to which the intervention triggers the mechanism underlying its desired effects and on identifying possible adverse effects (Campbell et al., 2007; Kovach, 2009). Demonstrating that implementation of the intervention induces favorable client reactions and improvement in the immediate outcomes is an important initial step toward determining its impact on the ultimate outcomes. If changes in these variables do not take place following delivery of the intervention, then the hypothesized improvement in the ultimate outcomes may not appear. The Phase 2 pilot study provides an excellent opportunity for investigating factors that may have contributed to such unexpected results. The factors relate to the characteristics of clients, interventionists, context, and intervention (see Chapter 1), or to the conceptual and operational definitions of the variables constituting the pathway linking the intervention with the ultimate outcomes. Identifying adverse effects is essential for safety purposes.

Different exploratory research designs have been suggested for pilot studies aimed to examine the effects, desired or adverse, of the intervention; these include case studies or single-subject design, retrospective design, pre-experimental or single group pre-test–post-test (Robey, 2004) or repeated measures (Hertzog, 2008) design. A mixed, quantitative and qualitative, methods design is most appropriate to generate a comprehensive understanding of the range of intervention effects, particularly those unexpected, and of how the intervention works. In a mixed methods design, the intervention is provided to a small group of clients. Quantitative data related to the immediate (and ultimate, if possible) outcomes are collected before and after implementation of the intervention at the time intervals specified in the intervention theory. Quantitative and qualitative data pertaining to clients' reactions to the intervention are obtained during and following intervention delivery. Understanding of treatment recommendations and satisfaction with treatment, measured with validated instruments, can be assessed upon completion of each intervention component and of the whole intervention. Semi-structured interviews, using open-ended questions, can be held at post-test to explore clients' perception of the intervention (e.g., what did they like most/least, what was most/least helpful), the intervention implementation process (e.g., appropriateness of the mode of delivery and the dose, interactional style of interventionists, setting features; factors that may have facilitated/hindered application of treatment recommendations), the intervention hypothesized effects (e.g., did the intervention help in managing the health problem and how the intervention contributed to its management), and the intervention's unintended, whether beneficial or adverse, effects (e.g., how else did the intervention affect clients, what were positive or negative effects). The interviews can incorporate additional questions related to suggestions for improving the delivery and effectiveness of the intervention. Data analysis is primarily exploratory, aimed at 1) describing clients' reactions to the intervention, 2) estimating the extent of improvement or delineating the pattern of change in the immediate outcomes for all clients and those expressing different reactions to the intervention, and 3) identifying the range of responses (i.e., beneficial/adverse) to the intervention. The results inform decisions to refine, as necessary, the operationalization of the intervention (e.g., modification of aspects clients reported as least helpful), the context for its implementation (e.g., selecting new sites or additional training of interventionists), the conceptualization of the mechanism responsible for producing the hypothesized effects, the timing for measuring the outcomes, and the specification of its adverse effects.

Exploring Feasibility of Research Methods

Traditionally, pilot studies have been advocated to explore the feasibility of the research methods planned for the next phase of the intervention evaluation process in addition to examining the intervention effects (Forbes, 2009; Robey, 2004; Thomas Becker, 2008). In these studies, feasibility refers to the adequacy, effectiveness, and efficiency of the study protocol. The study protocol encompasses the procedures for recruiting clients, screening clients for eligibility, assigning clients to intervention and comparison groups, retaining clients in the study, and collecting pertinent data (Lancaster et al., 2004). The aims of feasibility pilot studies are to 1) identify the research procedures that are appropriate and acceptable to the target population and conveniently performed, and yield quality information within a reasonable timeframe, and 2) recognize difficulties in carrying out the research procedures. The results give advance warning about possible deficiencies in the research design, methods, and logistics planned for the large-scale evaluation of the intervention's efficacy. Awareness of these deficiencies and understanding their determinants guide the search for appropriate solutions or refinement of the procedures, which are incorporated in the design of Phase 3 trials. Examination of the intervention effects has dual purpose: to determine that the intervention, implemented as designed, does indeed produce the hypothesized changes in the mediators and outcomes, and to estimate the effect size for the primary outcome. The effect size, defined as the standardized difference in the post-test outcomes between the intervention and comparison groups, is used in the sample size estimation for the large-scale efficacy trial (Lancaster et al., 2004). Some scholars have raised concerns with this highly recommended practice, arguing that effect sizes estimated with values obtained from a small sample are biased (Hertzog, 2008) and should be interpreted with caution when calculating the sample size required for Phase 3 efficacy trials (Craig et al., 2008).

The design of pilot studies focusing on the feasibility of methods should mirror the one planned for Phase 3 trials. It is often an experimental or RCT design, in which eligible clients are randomly assigned to the experimental group that receive the intervention under evaluation or to the comparison group that do not receive the intervention. Clients in the latter group may be requested to stop any treatment they are taking to address the health problem (if ethical to do so) or given usual care.

Adequacy of the recruitment procedures is examined in terms of the sampling pool, the effectiveness of procedures used, and the recruitment time. The sampling pool refers to the number of clients representing the target population and available at the sites selected for the study. In a pilot study, it is important to estimate the number of clients who meet the eligibility criteria and agree to enroll in the study. A small sampling pool poses potential difficulty in accruing the sample size required for the Phase 3 trial and has implications for 1) increasing the number of sites from which to recruit clients, 2) expanding recruitment efforts within and across sites to reach a large number of potentially eligible clients, and 3) revising the study eligibility criteria to be more encompassing while also minimizing the potential for confounds. Effectiveness of recruitment procedures is assessed with their yield, that is, the number of clients recruited with the application of each strategy and the representativeness of the total sample. Data on the number of clients recruited are gathered with a log that documents the number of inquiries received following the implementation of a particular strategy or by requesting clients to indicate the source of information about the study (see Chapter 8). Results of descriptive analysis of the socio-demographic, health and clinical characteristics of clients who participate in the pilot study delineate their profile. Qualitative comparison of the sample profile to the characteristics of the target population (known from previous research or vital statistics) is a means for determining the sample representativeness. In addition, the time it takes to recruit the total number of participants required for the pilot study is determined. Data are obtained from the pilot study's administrative records documenting the date recruitment started and completed. Information on the recruitment yield and time gives directions for selecting the most effective and efficient, single or multiple strategies, to recruit a large number of clients, and for delineating the timeframe for the Phase 3 trial. This information has implications for the Phase 3 trial budget.

Adequacy of screening procedures relates to their practicality and accuracy in determining client eligibility. Practicality has to do with the ease with which the screening is done, at the specified time, and in accordance with the ethical principles of research. Information on the practicality of the screening procedures is collected informally. This can be done through observing or video/audio recording the conduct of screening, which provides data on the length of time it takes to complete the screening, difficulties encountered in the process such as clients' refusal to answer questions they perceive as intrusive, and the appropriateness of the screening process (i.e., the screening activities are properly sequenced in a way that reduces burden on the research staff and clients). Second, there should be discussion with the staff responsible for the research activity, who may experience challenges in the application of the screening process or report on complaints about the content, the length, and the timing of screening voiced by clients. The timing for conducting the screening should be carefully scheduled so that it takes place as soon as possible after recruitment to identify eligible clients and prevent them from participating in unnecessary research activities. However, the administration of some screening tests (e.g., Brief Symptom Inventory for detecting psychological impairment, or lung function tests to identify extent of lung malfunction) requires written consent. Clients are requested to consent twice, for the screening and for the study if found eligible. Alternatively, screening may be done after obtaining consent for the study, which clearly explains that participation in the study is contingent on the results of screening. The Phase 2 pilot study provides excellent opportunities to test the instruments used to assess for eligibility, for the relevance of their content, comprehension, ease of understanding and administration, and most importantly their sensitivity and specificity in identifying eligible clients. Modifications in the procedures are made and alternate instruments are selected to improve the practicality and accuracy of screening in the Phase 3 trial, as needed.

Assignment of clients to the intervention and the comparison groups in an RCT design is done randomly. The logistics of carrying out the randomization procedure (see Chapter 10) are evaluated informally, through discussion with research staff. In addition, the acceptability of randomization to clients and healthcare professionals assisting in recruitment is examined.

Clients holding negative attitudes may decline enrollment in the study; healthcare professionals with similar perceptions may decide to not refer clients to the study, jeopardizing accrual of the required sample size and the representativeness of the sample. The acceptability of randomization to clients is inferred from stated reasons for non-participation or from discussion with community leaders who are familiar with the values and beliefs of the target population. The acceptability of randomization to healthcare professionals' can be inferred by monitoring their referral. A meeting is scheduled with healthcare professionals with a low referral pattern to discuss their concerns. Alternative procedures for client assignment may be considered for the Phase 3 trial if randomization is a major issue for clients and healthcare professionals. Also, other sites and healthcare professionals, accepting of randomization, are invited in the Phase 3 trial.

Retention strategies are incorporated in an intervention evaluation study to minimize attrition, which is a major threat to internal validity. Different retention strategies can be used (see Chapter 9). However, it is useful to evaluate their applicability, effectiveness, and acceptability to clients in a pilot study. Applicability refers to the extent to which the retention procedures are implemented properly, with no difficulty. The nature of difficulty varies with the type of retention strategy used, such as delays in sending or receiving incentives and staff's schedule that precludes them from being flexible to accommodate clients' preferences. Information on applicability is gathered informally through discussion with research staff. Solutions are generated to facilitate the implementation of the retention strategies in the Phase 3 trial. Effectiveness refers to the contribution of the procedures to retention of clients. It is implied from the study retention rate, which is the percentage of consenting participants who complete the study. High retention rates are evidence of effectiveness. Acceptability refers to the relevance and appropriateness of the retention strategies to the target population. For instance, some clients may find it intrusive to identify and provide contact information of persons who know their whereabouts, which is a strategy used with hard to reach participants; others may be dissatisfied with the compensation provided. Acceptability is assessed by asking community leaders about the target population's view of the retention strategies, or by analyzing reasons for withdrawal given by participants who drop out indicative of dissatisfaction with the strategies. Retention strategies found to be applicable, effective, and acceptable are retained or modified as necessary, for future use.

The feasibility of data collection procedures is also tested in a pilot study. This involves:

1. Evaluation of the instruments measuring the variables (clients' characteristics, reactions to the intervention, moderators, mediators, outcomes, fidelity of treatment implementation) for comprehension (i.e., ease of understanding instructions, item content, response options) and relevance (i.e., applicability of the content to the target population). Clients who find the items' content and response options unclear and irrelevant may not complete the measures, resulting in missing data, or may randomly select a response option increasing the potential for measurement error. This in turn affects the power

to detect significant intervention effects. Cognitive interviewing techniques (Nápoles-Springer et al., 2006; Oremus et al., 2005) are recommended for assessing the measures' comprehension and relevance. These consist of semi-structured interview during which participants are asked to read each item, reiterate its content, read the response options, explain what the options mean, think aloud when formulating their response, identify words or sentences that are not clear, and comment on the relevance of the items' content (Sidani and Braden, 2011).

2. Variability of responses to instruments measuring all variables, with particular attention to those assessing the outcomes. The goal is to identify measures with floor or ceiling effects (i.e., the majority of clients select extreme values on the response scale), which may not capture the expected changes in outcomes post-intervention. Descriptive statistics are used to examine the distribution of the items' and measures' scores, administered at pre-test and post-test with the expectation that all possible response options are selected.

3. Estimation of the length of time it takes to complete the measures. Completing lengthy measures takes time and increases response burden, which affects the quality of data. Estimation of this indicator of feasibility is done by noting the start and end time of the data collection session.

4. Assessment of the data collection procedures for challenges in implementation. Issues with the administration of the instruments influence the quality of the data. These may relate to ease of carrying out the data collection procedure in the specified sequence, in the specified time frame and in a consistent way. Examples of challenges are: delays in sending specimens to the laboratory, inadequate space for conducting the walk test, and inability to hold the data collection session for busy clients at the right time. Challenges are inferred from discussion with research staff, complaints expressed by clients, and observation or recording of data collection sessions.

The information gathered may point to the need for adapting the measures to improve clarity, selecting other measures that are more relevant to the target population, using a short version of the instruments if available, to reduce response burden, and revising the data collection procedures to facilitate their implementation in the Phase 3 trial.

PHASE 3: EXAMINING EFFICACY OF THE INTERVENTION

Phase 3 of the systematic evaluation process aims at examining the efficacy of the intervention (Robey, 2004). Efficacy refers to the extent to which the intervention produces the hypothesized effects under ideal conditions (Streiner, 2002). The focus is on the causal relationship between the intervention and the outcomes. The goal is to demonstrate that changes in the outcomes, observed at post-test, are attributable to the intervention and not to any other factor. Therefore, the effects of the intervention are examined under the ideal conditions. These conditions control for factors that potentially influence outcome achievement and present alternative plausible explanations of the changes in outcomes. Accordingly, internal validity is of primary concern in Phase 3 trials. As explained in Chapter 1, the factors relate to the characteristics of clients, interventionists, context, actual implementation of the intervention, and the methods used in the evaluation. Control of the factors is exerted experimentally by:

1. Selecting clients on the basis of stringent eligibility criteria. The inclusion criteria ensure that clients who experience the health problem targeted by the intervention, indicated by the manifestations, determinants, and level of severity specified in the conceptualization of the problem (developed in Phase 1), are selected into the study. The exclusion criteria are set to exclude clients who have particular characteristics or experience the characteristics at certain levels, that are directly associated with the outcomes or that may interfere with the implementation of the intervention and adherence to treatment recommendations.
2. Carefully selecting interventionists who have the professional qualifications that enable them to deliver the intervention; intensively training them to refine their competencies required for implementing the intervention; and requesting them to strictly follow the intervention protocol in order to provide the intervention, with consistency, to all clients assigned to the intervention group.
3. Choosing the context that has the physical and psychological features expected to facilitate the implementation of the intervention and maintain the features constant when providing the intervention to all clients assigned to the intervention.
4. Randomly assigning eligible clients to the intervention and comparison groups to enhance the comparability of the two groups on measured and unmeasured characteristics with the potential to influence the outcomes, thereby minimizing selection bias and confounding; and concealing, to the extent possible, the treatment to which clients are assigned to reduce reactivity.
5. Implementing the intervention with fidelity, in a standardized and consistent manner, across all clients assigned to the intervention group, in order to reduce variability in the intervention activities, mode of delivery, and dose to which clients are exposed; and withholding the intervention from clients assigned to the comparison group.
6. Assessing outcomes with reliable and valid measures, before and after the intervention.
7. Incorporating strategies to minimize attrition and prevent contamination or dissemination of the intervention to the comparison group.

The RCT design is considered the most appropriate design for evaluating the efficacy of the intervention. Its features facilitate the application of all criteria for demonstrating causality, of which the experimental control of potentially confounding factors is the most important for making valid inferences about the intervention efficacy (see Chapter 4). The RCT may not always be feasible for different reasons. Modifications to the RCT design can be applied (see Chapter 6). If there is concern that the target population will not agree to withholding an intervention with some evidence of effectiveness, then a waiting-list control group design or stepped wedge design is appropriate. If the likelihood of treatment contamination within a particular site is high, then the cluster randomized trial is the alternative (Craig et al., 2008). If the intervention targets the community, and finding another community with comparable characteristics is not possible, then interrupted time series design is acceptable.

The results of Phase 3 efficacy trial provide evidence for making a valid inference that the intervention causes the changes in outcomes. However, the extent to which the causal effects are reproduced under the conditions of day-to-day practice is unknown but is investigated in Phase 4.

PHASE 4: DETERMINING EFFECTIVENESS OF THE INTERVENTION

Phase 4 of the systematic evaluation process aims to determine the effectiveness of the intervention (Campbell et al., 2000; Robey, 2004). Effectiveness refers to the extent to which an intervention with known efficacy produces the outcomes when delivered under the real world conditions (Streiner, 2002). The real world conditions are characterized by variability in the characteristics of clients, healthcare professionals responsible for delivering the intervention, and context that may lead to variability in the components, mode of delivery, and dose with which the intervention is implemented. Thus, the focus is on the reproducibility of the relationship between the intervention and the outcomes under different conditions reflective of day-to-day practice. Accordingly, external validity is of concern in Phase 4 studies.

The influence of different conditions is of substantive interest. The evaluation study is designed to examine:

1. How clients, presenting with a range of personal, health and clinical characteristics representing different subgroups of the target population, experiencing different levels of the health problem severity, and having varying levels of perceived acceptability of and motivation to apply the intervention, react to the intervention, adhere to treatment recommendations, and exhibit the expected improvement in the outcomes.
2. How healthcare professionals varying in their level of understanding and acceptability of the intervention, competencies in delivering the intervention, practical experience

with providing care to the target population, and interactional style or working alliance, deliver the intervention.

3. What contextual features facilitate or impede the implementation of the intervention by the healthcare professionals, and adherence to treatment recommendations by clients.

4. What variations in intervention implementation are applied and for what reasons (e.g., attempts to be responsive to clients' needs and preferences); specifically, what combination of treatment components is delivered and is effective in producing the outcomes, and what is the minimal and optimal dose level associated with the achievement of outcomes.

5. How effective the is intervention in resolving the health problem and in producing the outcomes, compared to alternative treatments available and used in day-to-day practice.

The research design and methods used to address these questions have to be flexible if they are to account for the variability encountered in day-to-day practice (Tunis et al., 2003). Practical or pragmatic clinical trials are considered appropriate for determining the effectiveness of the intervention (Thorpe et al., 2009; Zwarenstein and Treweek, 2009). In these trials, the client eligibility criteria are less restrictive, allowing representation of different subgroups of the client population; and the moderating influence of key client characteristics is examined. Healthcare professionals with diverse qualifications are entrusted with the delivery of the intervention, their performance and interactional style are assessed, and the contribution of interactional style to clients' adherence to treatment recommendations and outcomes is investigated. Multiple settings with varying features are selected; differences in intervention implementation and outcome achievement across settings are noted. Although differences in intervention implementation take place, deviations in the provision of the active ingredients are not permitted. The effects of the intervention are compared to treatments in current use (Borglin and Richards, 2010; Holtz, 2007). In addition, clients in the real world have preferences for treatment. Providing clients the treatment of their choice is an expectation in day-to-day practice. Partially randomized clinical or preference trials (see Chapter 7) are applied to determine the influence of treatment preferences on initiation and adherence to treatment, and outcome achievement (Kiesler and Auerbach, 2006; Sidani et al., 2009a).

The results of Phase 4 effectiveness studies provide answers to the questions of relevance to day-to-day practice: What subgroups of clients benefit to what extent from the intervention implemented in what format, at what dose, by healthcare professionals with which qualifications and in what type of context? These answers can be incorporated in guidelines for implementing the intervention; the guidelines are widely disseminated in Phase 5.

PHASE 5: TRANSLATING THE INTERVENTION

The systematic process culminates in Phase 5, in which the intervention is translated, implemented, and evaluated in the context of day-to-day practice. The overall goal is to evaluate the clinical utility of the intervention. Translation involves the development of guidelines to inform practice. The guidelines specify: the health problem amenable to remediation by the intervention and the aspects of the problem targeted by the intervention; the active ingredients of the intervention as operationalized in the components and respective activities to be carried out; the mode for delivering the intervention components; the range of the dose associated with beneficial outcomes; the mechanisms responsible for producing the outcomes (i.e., how and why the intervention works); potential moderators of the intervention effects; and ways in which the implementation of the intervention can be customized to be responsive to the individual clients' needs and circumstances. Implementation consists of disseminating the guidelines to healthcare professionals, providing training to enhance their competencies for providing the intervention and collaborating with others to overcome any barriers and to sustain intervention implementation in day-to-day practice. Several strategies can be used to foster initial and sustained implementation. Multi-component, multi-level strategies incorporating elements of a participatory-collaborative approach to research have been found most effective in promoting healthcare professionals' implementation of the intervention (Fixsen et al., 2005; Russell and Walsh, 2009). Evaluation in this phase represents an extension of the effectiveness research conducted in Phase 4. It is done using practical, pragmatic trials or non-experimental, observational designs (Nallamothu et al., 2008), with the additional analysis related to cost (e.g., cost efficiency). The results of the latter analysis inform practice and policy change.

ADDITIONAL THOUGHTS

- The systematic evaluation process is flexible. Although the phases are logically sequenced, the results of each phase drive the work forward to the next phase or backward to earlier phases. Favorable findings supporting the hypothesized effects of the intervention drive the work forward to expand knowledge related to the reproducibility of the causal relationship between the intervention and the outcomes under different conditions. Unfavorable findings require investigation of what went wrong, which may move the work backward, to the drawing board (i.e., reconceptualizing the intervention).
- Westen et al. (2004) suggested to start the process from the point of clinical practice. Interventions applied in the context of day-to-day practice and reported to be useful but for which there is limited knowledge, are isolated and subjected to rigorous testing. The claim is that such interventions are more clinically relevant and easier to implement and sustain than those developed following the systematic evaluation process described in this chapter.

Summary

- The process of evaluating interventions involves five phases, detailed in Table 3.1

TABLE 3.1 Summary

Phase	Goal	Methodology	Outcome	Validity
Phase 1	1. To understand the problem requiring remediation and targeted by the intervention	1. Critical review of theory 2. Review of quantitative and qualitative research findings 3. Validation of problem conceptualization using quantitative and/or qualitative methods	1. Conceptualization of the problem (nature, manifestations, level of severity, determinants)	Construct
	2. To develop the intervention	1. Review of theory 2. Review of evidence-based interventions 3. Participatory approach 4. Analysis and logical reasoning to specify the intervention and model the mechanism responsible for its effects	1. Conceptualization of the intervention (goal, components, activities, mode of delivery, dose) 2. Specification of mediating and outcome variables	
	3. To develop the intervention protocol	1. Analysis and logical reasoning to describe the components and activities that operationalize the intervention	1. Preparation of intervention manual	

(Continued)

TABLE 3.1   (Continued)

Phase	Goal	Methodology	Outcome	Validity
Phase 2	1. To examine acceptability of the intervention	1. Consultative, semi-structured interview with stakeholders 2. Quantitative, non-experimental, survey-type design 3. Mixed methods, quantitative and qualitative, design	1. Identification of intervention components, activities, mode of delivery, dose, acceptable to target population	Construct
	2. To examine feasibility of the intervention	1. Small-scale, mixed methods, quantitative and qualitative, design	1. Determination of aspects of the intervention that are feasible and those requiring revision	
	3. To examine intervention effects	1. Exploratory research designs: case studies, retrospective, pre-experimental or single group pre-test–post-test or repeated measures design, with quantitative and qualitative data collection methods	1. Determination of extent to which intervention triggers mechanisms responsible for its effects on ultimate outcome	
	4. To explore feasibility of research methods	1. Same design as the one to be used in Phase 3; often experimental or RCT	1. Determination of aspects of research study that are feasible and those requiring revision	

Phase	Goal	Methodology	Outcome	Validity
Phase 3	1. To examine efficacy of the intervention	1. Experimental or RCT, or variants (e.g., waiting list control group design, cluster randomized clinical trial, interrupted time series)	1. Demonstration of causal effects of intervention	Internal
Phase 4	1. To determine effectiveness of intervention	1. Practical or pragmatic clinical trials 2. Partially randomized clinical, or preference, trials	1. Delineation of who benefits, to what extent from intervention, delivered in what format and dose, by which healthcare professionals in what context	External
Phase 5	1. To translate the intervention and evaluate its clinical utility	1. Development of guideline for providing the intervention 2. Implementation of guideline in day-to-day practice 3. Evaluation of intervention effects and cost, using pragmatic trials or observational research design	1. Incorporation of intervention in day-to-day practice	Clinical utility

4

EXPERIMENTAL DESIGNS OR RANDOMIZED CONTROLLED TRIALS: CHARACTERISTIC FEATURES

The experimental or randomized controlled/clinical trial (RCT) design has been, and still is, considered the most appropriate for a Phase 3 efficacy trial, the goal of which is to determine the causal relationship between the intervention and the outcomes. The features of this design assist in controlling for potential confounding and are advantageous in demonstrating the direct effects of the intervention on the outcomes. In this chapter, the features of the RCT are explained. Some practical considerations for conducting an RCT are delineated.

FEATURES OF THE EXPERIMENTAL OR RCT DESIGN

The experimental or RCT design has features that facilitate the control of different aspects of the intervention evaluation study, with the goal of minimizing, and if possible eliminating factors that could potentially confound the intervention effects (Victora et al., 2004). The factors relate to the characteristics of the participants, the context of intervention delivery, and the assessment of outcomes. Identification of these factors and delineation of their influence are guided by the intervention theory that provides an understanding of the health problem targeted by the intervention, the intervention elements, the hypothesized outcomes, the mediators, and the moderators (see Chapter 1). By manipulating these factors and controlling their influence on intervention implementation and outcome achievement, changes in the outcomes observed following the intervention can be confidently attributed to the intervention, and not to the potentially confounding factors; this, in turn, helps ascertain the causal effects of the intervention (Chatterji, 2007).

The main features of the RCT design are conducive to the establishment of causality: careful selection of clients, random assignment of clients to the intervention and the comparison group, concealment of treatment allocation and outcome assessment, manipulation of intervention implementation, and assessment of outcomes before and after treatment. Random assignment, done at the level of individual clients participating in the trial (hereafter referred to as participants), is the feature that distinguishes the RCT from other designs used in intervention evaluation research.

Careful Selection of Participants

In an RCT testing the efficacy of the intervention, participants are carefully selected to obtain a sample that is representative of the target client population and to control for participants' characteristics that are known to confound the effects of the intervention on the outcomes. The inclusion criteria reflect the characteristics that define the target population. This population is identified relative to the experience of the health problem amenable to remediation by the intervention under evaluation. Specifically, individuals are deemed eligible for the trial if they report having the determinants, manifestations, and severity level of the problem that are addressed by the intervention, as delineated in the intervention theory. For instance, persons experiencing obesity are eligible for a dietary regimen if they report a high calorie food intake (which is the determinant of obesity targeted by the dietary intervention). Persons experiencing insomnia are included in an RCT of behavioral interventions if they experience difficulty falling asleep or difficulty staying asleep (which are indicators of insomnia), of at least 30 minutes per night, for a minimum of 3 nights per week, for 6 weeks or more (which represent the level of insomnia severity). The inclusion criteria ensure that participants belong to the target population and experience the health problem specifically addressed by the intervention.

The exclusion criteria represent client characteristics that may interfere with the engagement, enactment, and adherence to the intervention, and may be directly associated with the outcomes. These characteristics include: 1) personal or socio-demographic profile such as proficiency in the language used in delivering the intervention and in assessing outcomes; 2) health condition such as level of cognitive function which is necessary to understand the treatment recommendations, level of physical function which may be important for enacting the treatment recommendations, and presence of comorbid disorders that may limit treatment application, or for which the intervention may be contraindicated, or that may be correlated with the outcomes; 3) psychological status such as lack of motivation or readiness for changing behavior, and tendency for non-adherence to the intervention or the study protocol; and 4) current treatment for the health problem targeted by the intervention or for comorbid disorders, and unwillingness to stop or keep constant the type and dose of current treatment during the trial period. Of particular concern are treatments that may interact with the intervention under evaluation, strengthening or weakening its effects on the outcomes. In the example of an RCT for behavioral therapies for the management of insomnia, persons are excluded if they have cognitive impairment and psychological dysfunction, receive treatment for psychological conditions (e.g., antidepressant medication), and are diagnosed with and being treated for sleep apnea (which is a determinant of insomnia that is not effectively treated by the behavioral therapies; its treatment – use of CPAP (continuous positive airway pressure) – interferes with the application of the instructions comprising stimulus control therapy). The exclusion criteria eliminate individuals with characteristics that potentially confound the effects of the intervention. Persons expressing interest in taking part in the study should be screened to determine if they meet all eligibility criteria.

The careful selection of participants on the basis of strictly preset inclusion and exclusion criteria results in a homogeneous sample. Participants are comparable in their experience of the health problem, personal, health and clinical characteristics, as well as receipt of concurrent treatment (Hyde, 2004). This sample homogeneity promotes the comparability of participants assigned to the intervention and comparison groups at baseline, and contributes to the similarity in participants' response to the intervention. This implies that the latter participants react to the intervention in the same way and hence exhibit the same pattern of change in the outcomes following the implementation of the intervention. Similarity in response to treatment is demonstrated in achievement of the same direction and amount of change in the outcomes assessed at post-test, which translates in reduced variability in the outcome levels reported by participants in the intervention group. In contrast, participants assigned to the comparison group do not show changes in the outcomes. Comparisons of the post-test outcomes reveal large between-group differences relative to within-group variability, which increases the power to detect significant intervention effects (Lipsey, 1990). These effects are confidently attributed to the intervention because potential confounding participants' characteristics are controlled experimentally (i.e., through application of exclusion criteria).

Random Assignment

Randomization or random assignment of eligible participants consists of allocating them to the intervention or the comparison group, on the basis of chance. It is the key feature of the RCT design to prevent selection bias and therefore to establish the causal association between the intervention and the outcomes (Watson et al., 2004). Different randomization methods are available (see Chapter 10).

The application of randomization eliminates any human influence on the allocation of participants to the intervention and comparison treatment groups. The sources of human influence include: 1) the research staff, who have a vested interest in showing that the intervention works and therefore allocate participants with the greatest potential to benefit (e.g., motivated to comply with the treatment recommendations) to the intervention group;

2) the participants, who have a particular personal and health profile that contributes to their preference for treatment and therefore self-select into the respective treatment group; and 3) the healthcare professionals caring for clients participating in the trial, who believe in a treatment and hence use their clinical judgement to provide the treatment to those patients they consider most likely to benefit from it. The interference of human influence with participants' allocation to treatment leads to differences in the composition of the intervention and comparison treatment groups.

Randomization is believed to maintain comparability of participants in all groups included in an RCT, on all measured and unmeasured characteristics assessed at baseline encompassing personal, health or clinical factors, experience of the health or clinical problem addressed by the intervention, concurrent treatment, and pre-test level on outcomes (Kaul and Diamond, 2010). Baseline group comparability implies that the distribution of client characteristics, specifically those that potentially confound the intervention effects, is balanced between the intervention and comparison groups (Bottomley, 1997). By holding participants' characteristics constant across groups, they cannot contribute to the outcomes, that is, they cannot produce variability in the outcomes measured at post-test which is not associated with receipt of the intervention. Improvement in the outcomes reported by participants in the intervention group and no change in the outcomes shown by participants in the comparison group create between-group differences in the outcomes observed at post-test. No between-group differences in participants' characteristics and level on outcomes at baseline, and large between-group differences in outcomes at post-test represents the evidence required to confidently attribute the observed post-test outcomes to the intervention and not to participants' characteristics. Accordingly, randomization controls for selection bias and subsequent confounding introduced by participants' characteristics (Bamberger and White, 2007; Borglin and Richards, 2010; Stone and Pocock, 2010; Towne and Hilton, 2004).

Concealment of Treatment Allocation

Ethical conduct of intervention evaluation research requires provision of information on all treatments (intervention and comparison) included in the trial to participants. This is done as part of the process for obtaining informed written consent. The information pertains to the nature of treatment (i.e., experimental or comparison), what it consists of (i.e., components and activities), risks, and benefits. Such knowledge influences participants' perception and response to the treatment. For instance, participants assigned to the comparison treatment view it less attractive or less helpful than the experimental intervention, generating unfavorable responses. The responses entail: 1) withdrawal from the study which could compromise the composition of the comparison group and subsequently its initial comparability with the intervention group; and 2) a sense of resentful demoralization or negative reactions that interfere with the enactment and adherence to treatment, as well as outcome achievement. Accordingly, participants experience worsening in the outcomes observed at post-test, which yields an overestimate of the intervention effects when compared to the improvement in outcomes exhibited by participants who receive the experimental intervention. In contrast, participants assigned to the experimental intervention may view it favorably, get motivated to apply it, and demonstrate the hypothesized benefits.

Concealment of treatment allocation is a feature of the RCT design introduced to prevent participants' reactions to the allocated treatment that may affect their initiation, adherence, and satisfaction with treatment, and outcome achievement. These reactions may confound the treatment effects, resulting in biased estimates of its impact on outcomes. Concealment consists of not divulging to participants the nature of the treatments under evaluation. Thus, during the consent process, participants are informed of the treatments offered in the trial; however, the treatments are not labeled as experimental or comparison, and participants are unaware if they are allocated to the experimental intervention or the comparison treatment. Concealment is also applied to research staff responsible for outcome assessment. It is anticipated that staff who are unaware of participants' treatment assignment will be unbiased in their evaluation of outcomes achieved by participants in the two groups, that is, they will be less tempted to report improvement and no changes in outcomes for participants in the intervention and comparison treatment groups, respectively. If relevant, concealment of treatment should be maintained for healthcare professionals who are responsible for the care of clients participating in the RCT. Healthcare professionals aware of the allocated treatment may hold positive or negative attitudes toward the treatment which could affect their assessment of clients' condition (e.g., heightened sensitivity toward side effects, or disregarding reports of improvement in status) and their interactions with clients (e.g., prompt to monitor side effects or express uncertainty about utility of a treatment). As a result, participants' reactions and responses to the treatment are altered in ways that confound the intervention impact on the outcomes and bias the estimates of the intervention effects.

Manipulation of Intervention Implementation

Manipulation of intervention implementation involves the provision of the intervention under evaluation to one group of eligible participants and withholding it from the comparison group, control of the timing of intervention delivery relative to outcome assessment, and standardized and consistent implementation of the intervention. These RCT features are important for establishing causality.

Provision of the intervention to one group and withholding it from another generate the conditions required for demonstrating the covariation criterion of causality. Creating these two groups induces variability in the exposure and receipt of treatment. Obtaining outcome data prospectively (before and after implementation of the intervention) and concurrently (at the same points in time) from both groups allows examination of variability in outcome achievement that is expected of the intervention. Covariation is inferred from the following pattern of findings: 1) participants allocated to the intervention and comparison groups are similar on personal, health or clinical characteristics, experience of the health problem targeted by the intervention, and outcomes assessed at pre-test; 2) participants exposed to the intervention show improvement in the outcomes, of the hypothesized direction and magnitude at post-test; 3) participants in the comparison group exhibit no changes in the outcome at post-test; and 4) post-test outcomes differ between the two groups in the hypothesized direction. This pattern of findings indicates that changes in outcomes occur with the implementation of the intervention and do not occur in the absence of the intervention, and is evidence of covariation between the intervention and the outcomes.

Controlling the timing of the intervention delivery relative to outcome assessment is important for maintaining the temporality criterion of causality. This feature of the RCT design consists of measuring the outcomes before and after implementation of the intervention. The first outcome assessment describes participants' outcome level at baseline and serves as a reference point for comparison with the outcome level observed at the second assessment. This comparison determines the extent of change in the outcome that is attributable to the intervention. The confidence in attributing the change in outcome to the intervention demands 1) evidence of change in the outcome in the group of participants exposed to the intervention and no change in the outcome in the group of participants not exposed the intervention, and 2) careful selection of the points in time for outcome assessment (see section on assessment overleaf).

Standardized and consistent implementation of the intervention minimizes variability in intervention delivery across participants assigned to this group, and consequently increases the power to detect significant intervention effects and confidence in attributing the outcomes to the intervention (Westen et al., 2004). Standardized and consistent delivery implies that the same intervention components and activities are given in the same mode and at the same dose to all participants assigned to the intervention group, and that participants strictly comply with all treatment recommendations. Standardization and consistency in intervention implementation reduce variability in the intervention components, activities, mode of delivery and dose to which participants are exposed and actually receive; compliance also decreases variability in participants' enactment of treatment recommendations in daily life. Accordingly, participants are expected to respond in the same way to the intervention, manifested in the same pattern of change in the outcomes. This, in turn, is reflected in low within-group variability in the post-test outcomes which increases the power to detect differences in outcomes between the intervention and comparison treatment groups (Jo, 2002; Towne and Hilton, 2004). Implementing the intervention as designed minimizes the chance of 1) deviations in exposure to its active ingredients across participants which weakens its potency in producing the anticipated amount of change in the outcomes, and 2) contamination between the intervention and the comparison groups in that components of one treatment are incorporated in the other, resulting in overlap or the lack of a clear distinction between treatments and subsequent increase in within-group variability in post-treatment outcomes; this lowers the power to detect significant intervention effects.

Assessment of Outcomes

Assessment of the hypothesized outcomes is done before and after implementation of the intervention for participants assigned to the intervention and comparison groups. Outcome assessment should be concurrent for both groups, at carefully selected time points. The selection of the time points should be guided by the intervention theory, which delineates the anticipated pattern of change in immediate and ultimate outcomes and hence the most opportune points in time for detecting change. In general, it is recommended to schedule outcome assessment at close proximity before and after implementation of the intervention. A time lag from treatment completion to outcome measurement raises questions about the validity of the causal connection between the intervention and the outcome as several events could have occurred in this time interval and influenced, favorably or unfavorably, outcome achievement.

Outcome assessment must be conducted with reliable and valid measures in order to accurately capture the hypothesized changes in outcomes. Low reliability introduces measurement error, defined as unexplained variability in the responses to the measures. In intervention evaluation research, measures with low reliability contribute to increased error or within-group variability in the post-treatment outcomes, which decreases the statistical power to detect significant intervention effects (McClelland, 1997). Measures with no established validity do not accurately reflect the outcomes expected of the intervention and do not appropriately capture the anticipated changes in the outcomes. Such failures may lead to incorrect inferences about the intervention, claiming that the intervention is ineffective (type II error).

In an RCT design, analysis of outcome data is based on the principle of intention-to-treat and is focused on group comparisons. Intention-to-treat analysis involves the inclusion of all eligible participants randomized to the intervention and comparison groups in the outcome analysis. This means that participants who complete the study or withdraw from the study at any point in time (before, during, and after implementation of the intervention) are included in the analysis. The rationale for this decision is to maintain the comparability on characteristics and outcomes, measured at pre-test, of participants assigned to the intervention and comparison groups; this comparability is critical for minimizing selection bias resulting from attrition and controlling for potential confounds. The outcome analysis consists of examining differences in outcomes achieved by participants who do and do not receive the intervention. The intervention is considered effective if the between-group differences in the outcomes, favoring the intervention group, are larger than the within-group variability in the outcomes, implying that group (intervention vs. comparison) membership makes a difference in the outcomes above and beyond individual differences. Individual differences represent the within-group variability in the outcomes, and are often posited as error variance and therefore not attributable directly and solely to the intervention.

PRACTICAL TIPS FOR DESIGNING AN RCT

The design and conduct of an RCT require careful planning and execution of key research activities. Practical points to consider are listed for each activity.

Recruitment

- Recruitment involves informing the target population of the study. It is an important research activity contributing to the accrual of the required sample size.
- Several recruitment strategies are available and discussed in Chapter 8.
- The general recommendation is to use multiple strategies that are acceptable to the target population.

Screening for Eligibility

To be effective in identifying eligible participants and in controlling for potentially confounding participant characteristics, the following points are recommended:

- The inclusion and exclusion criteria are clearly defined at the conceptual and operational levels. The conceptual definition delineates the attributes that characterize the criterion and the operational definition specifies the level (i.e., range or cut-off score) at which the criterion is experienced to determine whether or not participants meet it. The definitions guide the selection of instruments for assessing the criteria and for interpreting the results of the screening.
- The content of the instrument should be congruent with and cover all the indicators of the characteristic set as a criterion. Single self-report items used to assess general eligibility criteria such as language proficiency, age, and presence of comorbid disorders must be easy to understand (use simple lay terms and avoid jargon) and evaluated for comprehension by individuals representing the target population. Multiple, self-report items of characteristics that manifest in different domains and dimensions, such as type and severity of insomnia or pain, should demonstrate acceptable psychometric properties. In particular, screening measures have to show high sensitivity and specificity to accurately and correctly identify eligible participants. Instruments used to assess objectively manifested eligibility criteria such as weight, blood pressure, or muscle strength should show precision, and must be calibrated throughout the study period. Participants' tendency for compliance is a selection criterion that is often assessed in a run-in period. Participants are asked to carry out some aspect of the study protocol such as completing a daily diary, over a pre-specified time interval. Participants exhibiting a pre-determined level of adherence (e.g., $\geq$ 70 per cent) are considered eligible (Rothwell, 2005).

- Screening is done as soon as clients indicate interest in taking part in the trial to avoid subjecting individuals to unnecessary and burdensome data collection procedures if they do not meet the main eligibility criteria (e.g., type of health problem targeted by the intervention), and only after obtaining their consent, in conformity with ethical con- duct of research. The time and location of the screening are determined by the level of intrusiveness of the measures to be administered. An initial screening is scheduled once interested individuals are informed of the study and provide oral consent. The initial screening covers the general eligibility criteria, including experience of the health or clinical problem, and is done over the telephone or secure website. Clients who meet the general eligibility criteria are subjected to additional screening, which often involves administration of intrusive measures such as those assessing cognitive or psychological impairment, in a face-to-face session held in a private room, and after securing the indi- viduals' written consent. Guidelines for scoring all screening measures, for interpreting the scores (e.g., cut-off or range of values indicating presence or absence of the criteria) on each measure, and for determining eligibility across all criteria, facilitate appropriate performance of this research activity.

Control of Experimental Condition

Control of the experimental condition relates to the selection of the setting in which the intervention is implemented, the selection and training of interventionists responsible for delivering the intervention, and the selection and training of research staff involved in screening and data collection. Careful attention to these aspects minimizes potential biases associated with the influence of environmental, human, and material factors on the imple- mentation of the intervention and the achievement of outcomes.

- The setting is selected on the basis of environmental features that may affect the fidelity with which the intervention is implemented and the outcomes are produced. Settings having features that facilitate intervention delivery and do not interfere with outcome achievement are chosen. For instance, the provision of behavioral therapy in a group format requires rooms that allow for group seating and for control of external noise. Specific aspects of the environment are kept constant across all participants receiving the intervention. For example, the room temperature is maintained at the same level when participants listen to relaxing music for the management of pain; uncomfortable tem- perature interferes with the response to music and hence the achievement of the desired outcome. The setting in which participants apply treatment recommendations (i.e., daily life) is not under the researchers' direct control. However, participants are informed of strategies to control for environmental features that influence treatment enactment.
- The interventionists are selected on the basis of well-specified professional qualifications such as licensing that enable them to deliver the intervention; experience of working

with the target population, which is useful to understand and address their needs; and the interpersonal skills required for a clear communication of treatment recommendations. The interventionists' characteristics are assessed either informally, during the hiring interview or by reviewing relevant documents (e.g., letter of reference), or formally by administering relevant measures (e.g., self-report measure of the working alliance). Selected interventionists are given intensive training in the competencies needed for an adequate implementation of the intervention (see Chapter 11).

- The research staff are selected on the basis of professional (e.g., research experience, skills in administering questionnaires, or in taking blood samples) and personal (e.g., communication skills) characteristics needed for performing the assigned duties. The didactic and hands-on training assists in 1) understanding the overall procedures and the principles of obtaining informed consent; 2) clarifying the conceptual and operational definitions of the study variables (screening, personal, health and clinical characteristics of participants, outcomes, fidelity of the intervention implementation by interventionists and participants); 3) learning the principles and recommendations for obtaining information with the selected methods of data collection (e.g., tips for conducting telephone interviews, storing samples); 4) developing competencies in administering the instruments measuring the study variables and computing and interpreting the scores; and 5) maintaining required documentation. For observational measures, the training involves assessment of inter-rater reliability. However, the study hypotheses and the nature of treatment allocated to participants are not divulged to research staff in order to maintain blinding and prevent expectancies or prejudice that may shape their assessment of the study variables, in particular post-test outcomes (Kaptchuk, 2001).

Selection of Comparison Group

In an RCT, the comparison group is essential for determining the causal effects of the intervention under evaluation. The comparison group represents participants who provide data on all study variables at all time points preset for the study (i.e., at the same time points at which participants in the intervention group complete the same measures); however, they do not receive the intervention.

- Different types of comparison treatments can be used in an RCT. These include: no-treatment control, usual care, waiting-list control, and placebo conditions.
- The selection of a comparison treatment is guided by the nature of the intervention under evaluation, the state of knowledge about the intervention, the target population's needs for the management of the health problem, and the ethical principle of not withholding treatment if needed.
- Participants' adherence with the comparison treatment should be monitored (see Chapter 11).

Allocation to Treatment Groups

In an RCT, randomization is used for allocating participants to the intervention or comparison group. Different methods can be applied in the execution of randomization; these are described in Chapter 10.

Treatment Implementation

Standardized and consistent implementation of the intervention and the comparison treatment is important to avoid variability in outcome achievement. Monitoring of treatment implementation is important to detect contamination or dissemination of the intervention to the comparison group, which reduces the power to detect significant intervention effects. Strategies for enhancing standardized treatment delivery and for monitoring fidelity of intervention implementation are discussed in Chapter 11.

Outcome Measurement and Analysis

Measurement of outcomes, on participants assigned to the intervention and comparison groups, before and after implementation of the intervention, and analysis of outcome data (i.e., comparison of changes in outcomes between groups) provide the empirical evidence of the intervention effects.

- Outcomes include the hypothesized immediate and ultimate consequences of the intervention. Both types are assessed before and after treatment delivery to examine their pattern of change in the intervention and comparison groups.
- Each outcome variable has to be clearly defined at the conceptual and operational levels to guide the selection of the most appropriate measure. The measure should demonstrate acceptable psychometric properties (see Chapter 12).
- Administration of the outcome measures is scheduled within a narrow interval (e.g., within 1 week) at the pre-specified time points in order to capture the hypothesized changes.

Summary

- The experimental or RCT design is considered the most appropriate for determining the causal effects of the intervention on the outcomes in Phase 3 trials
- The RCT features facilitate control of potential confounds

- Careful selection of participants → exclude those with characteristics that affect intervention implementation and outcomes
- Randomization → maintain comparability of intervention and comparison treatment groups before treatment delivery
- Concealment of treatment allocation → reduce selection bias and unfavorable reactions to allocated treatment
- Manipulation of intervention implementation → create the two groups needed to show covariation between intervention receipt and outcomes; enhance standard and consistent implementation of intervention which maintains fidelity of delivery, prevents contamination, and increases potency of intervention
- Assessment of outcomes before and after intervention delivery → detect changes in outcomes attributable to intervention

5

EXPERIMENTAL DESIGNS OR RANDOMIZED CONTROLLED TRIALS: LIMITATIONS

Careful selection of participants, random assignment, concealment of treatment allocation, manipulation of intervention implementation, and outcome analysis are features of the experimental or RCT design that makes it most appropriate for Phase 3 efficacy evaluation. The features are considered essential for establishing causality, defined as the direct connection between the intervention and the outcomes, and controlling for important sources of bias or threats to validity. This led to valuing the RCT design as the 'gold standard' for intervention evaluation research. Although advantageous in providing evidence for making valid inferences about the intervention effects, the RCT features have limitations that preclude their utility in evaluating effectiveness of the intervention and in generating knowledge of relevance to practice in a Phase 4 trial. Arguments pointing to the limitations of the RCT design, based on identified weaknesses inherent in its logic and on accumulating empirical evidence, are discussed in this chapter.

WEAKNESSES IN LOGIC

The superior, gold standard, status ascribed to the RCT design has been questioned on several grounds. Historically, many treatments in current use were widely accepted as effective on the basis of evidence that was not derived from RCT. Examples of these treatments include: surgical procedures, insulin for diabetes, blood transfusion for hemorrhagic shock, streptomycin for tuberculosis meningitis, defibrillation for ventricular fibrillation, closed reduction and splinting for fractures of long bones with displacement, and drainage for pain associated with abscesses (Glasziou et al., 2007).

The RCT features restrict the research questions that can be addressed in an intervention evaluation study. The features allow examination of a few questions related to the efficacy of the intervention, under controlled conditions; yet answers to these questions are not quite useful in guiding treatment decisions and implementation in the context of day-to-day practice (Stone and Pocock, 2010; US Government Accountability Office [GAO], 2009). Specifically, the emphasis on experimental control of potential confounds (e.g., those associated with characteristics of participants, interventionists, and settings, implementation of treatment) and the focus on demonstrating the direct and simple causal relationship between the intervention and each outcome yield knowledge about the effectiveness of the intervention that is counterproductive in clinical practice. In other words, the RCT design ignores all variables that could affect improvement in the outcomes such as adherence to treatment recommendations, presence of comorbid conditions, and receipt of other interventions to manage comorbidities which may interact with the intervention in inducing changes in the outcomes (Ablon and Marci, 2004; Horn et al., 2005; Pincus, 2002; Westen et al., 2004). Healthcare professionals should be aware of these variables and understand their contribution to outcome achievement so that they can assess for their presence and account for them when prescribing the intervention to clients assigned to their care and monitoring clients' progress toward outcome achievement. Further, most applications of the RCT design have been directed toward determining the impact of the intervention on outcomes, ignoring the examination of the mechanism responsible for producing its hypothesized effects on the ultimate outcomes (Ablon and Marci, 2004; Victora et al., 2004). This state of the science has the potential for reaching incorrect conclusions about the effects of the intervention on the ultimate outcomes. The underlying mechanism usually proposes an indirect relationship between the intervention and the ultimate outcomes, mediated by participants' reactions, enactment and adherence to treatment, and improvement in the immediate outcomes. Accordingly, the direct association between the intervention and ultimate outcomes is expected to be non-significant because it is accounted for by the series of mediators (MacKinnon and Fairchild, 2009). As presently conceptualized and applied, the RCT design is concerned with simple, direct causal intervention effects and hence does not provide answers to general questions of relevance to the context of day-to-day practice, including: Which clients, presenting with which personal, health, and clinical characteristics, benefit to what extent from the intervention? What is the optimal combination of components and dose to produce beneficial outcomes? How does the intervention produce the outcomes? How does the intervention interact with other treatments for the same health problem? And how effective is the intervention in producing the beneficial outcomes compared to alternative treatment in current use for managing the same health problem?

Careful selection of participants is done on the basis of a set of strict eligibility criteria to enhance the homogeneity of the sample on personal, health, and clinical characteristics that could influence their response to intervention and confound its effects on the outcomes. The application of stringent selection criteria, combined with non-consent bias, has negative consequences that limit the external validity of the RCT findings (Hyde, 2004). Stringent selection criteria 1) reduce the participant pool available at the sites participating in the RCT, often requiring recruitment at additional sites; 2) increase the demands for screening in terms of the human and material resources expended on this research activity and of the number of individuals subjected to screening; and 3) decrease the number of screened participants who meet all pre-specified eligibility criteria. The resulting sample size is rather small, often falling short of the sample size needed to attain adequate statistical power. A small sample size either lowers the power to detect significant intervention effects or yields unreliable estimates of the effects (Lindsay, 2004). Grapow et al. (2006) estimated that fewer than 10 per cent of screened participants are included in RCTs because of the strict eligibility criteria and the high rate of refusal to enroll in the study. Eligible clients may decline participation for different reasons (detailed in Chapter 8). Of concern here is their view of randomization; individuals who resent randomization tend not to enroll, whereas those who agree to randomization take part in the trial. Thus, this non-consent bias generates a sample that is not representative of all subgroups of the target population (Cook, 2006). Furthermore, eligible persons who volunteer for the trial have a homogeneous socio-demographic, health, and clinical profile; they represent a select subgroup of the target population. For instance, they may be highly motivated to change their health behavior or they may present with a less challenging condition (e.g., no comorbidity) than patients cared for in the context of day-to-day practice (Haaga, 2004; Horn et al., 2005; Lehman and Steinwachs, 2003; Pincus, 2002; Rohrer, 2000; Stone and Pocock, 2010). The RCT results, obtained from a selective subgroup may not be replicated in other subgroups of the target population (Cartwright and Munro, 2010). In other words, the reproducibility of the intervention effects in clients seen in the practice setting is constrained.

Randomization, done to equalize the intervention and comparison groups on participants' characteristics measured at baseline, has the following limitations:

1. Randomization does not secure valid inferences about the causal relationship between the intervention and the outcomes. It may enhance, but does not guarantee (as explained next) the comparability of participants allocated to the two groups on baseline variables and does not minimize the potential for selection bias. Randomization, however, does not prevent, address, or rule out other sources of bias (e.g., differential attrition, contamination, non-adherence to treatment, co-intervention) that are introduced following randomization and that confound the intervention effects (Cook et al., 2010; West and Thoemmes, 2010).

2. Randomization introduces bias associated with participants' unfavorable views of chance allocation and with their preferences for treatment. Participants resent randomization as it deprives them of a sense of control and active engagement in treatment decisions. They react negatively to the allocated treatment. The negative reaction is amplified in participants who have strong preferences for treatment. With randomization treatment

preferences are ignored, and participants may be assigned to the non-preferred treatment. This, in turn, contributes to their decision to withdraw from the treatment or the study; to dissatisfaction, non-initiation, and non-adherence to treatment; and minimal improvement in outcomes (Borglin and Richards, 2010; Lindsay, 2004; Rothwell, 2005; Sidani et al., 2009a). The distribution of participants with negative reactions to treatment within the experimental and comparison groups influences the estimates of the intervention effects.

3. Randomization does not ensure initial comparability of participants allocated to the intervention and the comparison groups, *within a particular study*. It increases the probability, but does not guarantee, that participants in the two groups are comparable on the characteristics assessed prior to intervention implementation (Cartwright, 2007). Therefore, randomization may not always, and with confidence, minimize selection bias and exclude possible, measured and unmeasured, confounding factors (Victora et al., 2004). Most importantly, the comparability on baseline characteristics is maintained at the group, and not the individual, level. Group level comparability is manifested in non-significant differences in the groups' averages on the baseline characteristics. However, individual participants within each group show variability in these characteristics, reflected in large within-group variance. Inter-individual differences in baseline variables are not controlled through randomization and therefore can still influence application of treatment and achievement of outcomes (Sidani and Braden, 1998).

4. Randomization is not acceptable to clients, healthcare professionals, and policy makers (Bamberger and White, 2007). It is not used to allocate treatment in day-to-day practice. In the latter context, clients and healthcare professionals consider alternative treatments for the management of the health problems, review treatments' benefits and risks, and collaboratively select the most appropriate treatment (Towne and Hilton, 2004).

Concealment or blinding of treatment allocation, applied to prevent the influence of participants' reactions and outcome assessors' bias, is not feasible in RCTs evaluating health interventions and is not easy to maintain throughout the study period. Concealment is possible when the intervention and the comparison treatment have a similar structure as is the case with active and placebo pills or solutions. Structure of a treatment has to do with its 'appearance' like pills of the same shape, color, and consistency. For health interventions, structure relates primarily to the mode of delivery and dose. The intervention and comparison treatments should be delivered in the same format (e.g., group discussion), the same length and number of contacts or sessions given at the same frequency over the same time period; they should also incorporate the same common or non-specific elements (e.g., homework assignment). Discrepancies in the structure of the intervention and comparison treatment may interfere with participants' perception of the treatments' credibility, which contributes to their ability to guess whether or not they received the experimental intervention. Accordingly, concealment is not feasible in studies comparing a health intervention to a no-treatment control condition, structurally unequivalent placebo condition, or structurally equivalent placebo condition that covers content unrelated to the health problem. Furthermore, participants should be informed of the allocated intervention so that they can make necessary arrangements (e.g., time off work, childcare, transportation) to attend the planned sessions of a health intervention (Shapiro et al., 2002), which could violate concealment. In addition, concealment is difficult to maintain once treatment is delivered because of participants' experiences. Participants receiving the intervention experience improvement in the health problem and in their general condition, as well as possible treatment side effects. In contrast, participants allocated to the comparison treatment report no changes in the health problem, as well as no side effects. Well-informed participants correctly guess the treatment they receive. Similarly, healthcare professionals caring for these clients and research staff assessing the outcomes can easily infer the treatment participants receive on the basis of reported changes in status.

Manipulation of the intervention, as described for the RCT design, is in contrast to what goes on in the context of day-to-day practice, which limits the ecological validity of the RCT findings (Horn et al., 2005) and therefore, their relevance to practice. The discrepancy between the RCT and the practice contexts relates to the nature of the experimental intervention, the implementation of the intervention, the characteristics of interventionists, the type of comparison treatment, and the setting for intervention delivery.

1. Nature of intervention: The experimental intervention evaluated in an RCT is often discrete, involving clearly defined and distinct sets of components and activities; it is provided in a specific mode and at a specified dose (Nallamothu et al., 2008). Interventions implemented in day-to-day practice tend to be complex, consisting of multiple components and activities that may reflect active ingredients and non-specific elements of various therapies. They are offered in different formats that fit the human and material resources available in the practice setting and that are convenient to clients, and at variable dose levels that are consistent with clients' needs and responses to treatment. The RCT features may not be appropriate for evaluating such complex interventions given in a flexible manner (Haaga, 2004; Hawe et al., 2004).

2. Implementation of intervention: In an RCT, the intervention under evaluation is provided under the researcher's control and implemented in a standardized and consistent manner for participants. In other words, treatment implementation is inflexible and rigid in that its components and activities are given, in the same sequence, in the same mode of delivery, and at the fixed dose, to all participants regardless of their individual needs, preferences, and improvement in outcomes. In the context of practice, patient-centred care is one dimension of high quality care (Institute of Medicine, 2001) and healthcare professionals are encouraged to tailor or individualize treatment. Tailoring or individualization involves customization of the intervention's components, activities, mode of delivery, and dose so that they are responsive to clients' characteristics, preferences, and lifestyles. Consequently, the standardized and inflexible intervention protocols applied in the

RCT are not compatible with the individualized implementation of treatment that is distinctive of day-to-day practice (Bamberger and White, 2007; Davidson, 2006; Horn et al., 2005; Moffett et al., 2005; Nallamothu et al., 2008; Pincus, 2002; Westen et al., 2004). The relevance of the RCT design to the evaluation of tailored or individualized treatments and the utility of a discrete, standardized, and inflexible intervention protocol in guiding practice are questionable.

3. Characteristics of interventionists: In an RCT, the implementation of the intervention is entrusted to carefully selected and intensively trained interventionists (Victora et al., 2004). Usually interventionists have specific professional qualities considered important in facilitating the delivery of the intervention, such as disciplinary preparation, level of education, licensing, and favorable perception of the intervention. Interventionists are subjected to intensive training that involves didactic content, covering explanation of the theory underlying the intervention and the operationalization of the intervention, as well as practical training, consisting of a review of the intervention protocol and of case studies, and a close and frequent supervision of interventionists' performance (Sidani and Braden, 2011). In the context of practice, the intervention is delivered by healthcare professionals who may vary in their disciplinary preparation, perceived acceptability of the intervention, and level of competency in implementing all components and activities of the intervention. They may not have the opportunity to receive intensive training that adequately prepares them for enacting the intervention with fidelity. Furthermore, the implementation of most, if not all, health interventions occurs within the context of interpersonal interactions between the interventionist and clients. The interactions serve to relay and clarify the treatment recommendations in a non-threatening way, and to motivate clients to engage, enact, and adhere to treatment. The influence of interventionist–client interactions or working alliance on intervention implementation and outcome achievement is either ignored, or isolated and controlled by using structurally equivalent placebo treatment for comparison in an RCT (Lindsay, 2004; Rothwell, 2005). Yet the healthcare professional–client interaction is acknowledged as an important element of high quality care and has been found to contribute significantly to patient satisfaction with care and outcome improvement (Tarlov et al., 1989).

4. Type of comparison treatment: A comparison group is included in an RCT to meet the covariation criterion of causality. A control group is often used; participants randomized to this condition are not given the intervention, and if ethical, any treatment they may be receiving for the health problem is withheld. Some argue that a no-treatment control group does not eliminate many biases (Pincus, 2002) but may even introduce a few, such as resentful demoralization. Others suggest that healthcare professionals are not interested in learning about the effects of the intervention compared to no-treatment, because no-treatment is not a viable option for many clients seen in day-to-day practice. Rather, they demand evidence of the effectiveness of the intervention relative to alternative treatments available to inform decision making.

5. Setting of intervention delivery: Most RCTs are conducted in settings that have the material and human resources needed to facilitate the implementation of the intervention. The settings tend to be highly specialized with advanced technology, highly qualified healthcare professionals, and a general culture of receptivity for research and innovation (Zwarenstein and Treweek, 2009). These settings may not be representative of those settings included in translating and incorporating the intervention into day-to-day practice, raising questions about the applicability of the intervention and the reproducibility of its effects. In addition, environmental factors inherent in the context of treatment implementation are controlled for experimentally (e.g., selection of environments with most suitable features, or keeping the features constant when delivering the intervention to all participants), or measured and accounted for statistically (e.g., using setting as a between-subject factor in the statistical analysis). Stripping the intervention effects out of context limits the ecological and external validity of the RCT findings (Chatterji, 2007; Kaufman et al., 2003).

The data analysis in an RCT produces findings of limited relevance to practice. The analysis is focused on the outcome performance of the intervention and comparison groups. Differences in outcomes observed at the individual participant level are considered a nuisance or error variance. However, these individual differences in outcome achievement are important in the context of practice, in which healthcare professionals deal with individual clients. Healthcare professionals need information on clients who benefit, to various extents, from the intervention in order to make informed treatment decisions (Ablon and Marci, 2004; Cartwright, 2007; Hyde, 2004). The logic of the intention-to-treat principle for data analysis has been questioned. It is believed to estimate the causal effect of 'treatment assignment' rather than the actual exposure and receipt of the intervention; further, it tends to underestimate the intervention effects, potentially leading to type II error (Horn et al., 2005; Victora et al., 2004; West and Thoemmes, 2010). Last, the data analysis is heavily based on demonstrating that the between-group differences in outcomes are statistically significant; this means they are reliable and not a chance occurrence. Less emphasis is given to the clinical meaningfulness of the findings (Hyde, 2004; Kaul and Diamond, 2010; Pincus, 2002). The magnitude of the intervention effects and the proportion of participants who show the hypothesized improvement in outcomes (e.g., reported resolution of the health problem) are useful in validating the benefits of the intervention.

EMPIRICAL EVIDENCE

There is increasing empirical evidence which questions the superiority or gold standard status ascribed to the experimental or RCT design in intervention evaluation research, and the utility of some of its features (participant selection, randomization, concealment of treatment allocation, intention-to-treat analysis). The evidence is synthesized next.

Superiority of RCT

The evidence questioning the superiority of the RCT over other designs in providing unbiased estimates of the intervention effects is obtained in single studies and systematic reviews or meta-analyses. These studies compared the results of RCTs to those of non-RCTs evaluating similar treatments (Table 5.1). The non-RCT studies applied quasi-experimental, observational, cohort, case control or historical control group designs, in which participants were not randomized to the intervention and the comparison groups. A range of interventions were examined, including educational, behavioral, psychological, medical (e.g., vaccine, anticoagulant), and surgical treatments. The comparisons involved determination of the extent to which 1) the results of statistical tests conducted on post-test outcomes converged, that is, were of the same direction in supporting the effectiveness of the intervention, and 2) the effect sizes (standardized differences in the means of the intervention and the comparison groups) for the post-test outcomes reported in RCT and non-RCT studies were similar in indicating the magnitude of the intervention effects.

TABLE 5.1 Empirical evidence comparing RCT to non-RCT studies

Author (year)	Study design	Context	Main findings
Ottenbacher (1992)	Systematic review of 30 studies that used randomization and 30 that did not	Variety of interventions	Significant effects were more frequently reported in non-RCT Weighted and unweighted mean effect size was comparable between RCT (d = .23) and non-RCT (d = .21)
Shadish and Ragsdale (1996)	Meta-analysis of 64 RCTs and 36 non-RCTs	Marital or family psychotherapy or enrichment	RCTs yielded larger effect sizes than non-RCTs, even after excluding outliers Effect sizes for post-test outcomes were predicted by publication status, effect sizes for pre-test outcomes, use of passive control condition Association between randomization and effect sizes for post-test outcomes was mediated by features of control group (other vs. self-selection, internal vs. external, passive vs. active)
Smith et al. (1980)	Meta-analysis	Psychotherapy	Mean effect size for RCT (d = .84) was not significantly different from mean effect size for studies that used other methods of assignment, including matching (.92), pre-test equation (.74), and other (.91)

(Continued)

TABLE 5.1   (Continued)

Author (year)	Study design	Context	Main findings
Shapiro and Shapiro (1982)	Meta-analysis	Psychotherapy	No difference in the mean effect size for RCT and non-RCT
Lipsey and Wilson (1993)	Review of meta-analyses (N = 302)	Psychological, behavioral, and educational interventions	In some areas of study, there was no difference in mean effect size for RCT and non-RCT studies; in other areas, mean effect size of RCT was larger than mean effect size of non-RCT; still in other areas, mean effect size was larger for non-RCT than RCT Overall, mean effects size was .46 for RCT and .41 for non-RCT
Heinsman and Shadish (1996)	Systematic review of meta-analyses	Variety of psychosocial interventions	Mean effect size was larger for RCT than non-RCT High effect sizes for post-test outcomes were associated with low attrition, use of passive control, high effect sizes for pre-test outcomes, allocation procedures that did not involve self-selection Randomization was not directly associated with effect sizes for post-test outcomes
Concato et al. (2000)	Systematic review of randomized and non-randomized trials	1) Vaccine for tuberculosis 2) Screening mammography 3) Cholesterol lowering medication 4) Anti-hypertensive medication	1) Mean OR was .49 for RCT and .50 for non-RCT 2) Mean OR was .74 for RCT and .61 for non-RCT 3) Mean OR was 1.42 for RCT and 1.40 for non-RCT 4) Mean OR for risk of stroke was .58 for RCT and .62 for non-RCT; for risk of heart disease was .86 for RCT and .77 for non-RCT
Ferriter and Huband (2005)	Review of 2 meta-analyses	1) Clozapine vs. chlorpromazine 2) Assertive vs. standard community	1) Mean OR was .46 for RCT and .52 for non-RCT 2) Mean OR was .59 for and .17 for non-RCT
Benson and Hartz (2000)	Review of studies that compared RCT and non-RCT results	19 treatments were compared	Overall, effect sizes of non-RCTs were comparable (within 95% of confidence intervals) to those of RCTs

Author (year)	Study design	Context	Main findings
Britton et al. (1998)	Review of 18 studies comparing RCTs to non-RCTs (using prospective design)	Variety of treatments	No difference in RCT and non-RCT findings
Kunz and Oxman (1998)	Systematic review of studies that compared RCTs and non-RCTs	Variety of treatments	In studies evaluating the same interventions, effect sizes of RCTs were larger than effect sizes of non-RCTs In studies evaluating different interventions, effect sizes of RCTs and non-RCTs were heterogeneous
Sacks et al. (1982)	Review of studies that compared RCTs and historical control studies	Variety of treatments	In 20% of RCTs and 79% of historical control studies, the intervention was beneficial
Sacks et al. (1983)	Review of studies that compared RCTs and historical control studies	Variety of treatments	In 11% of RCTs and 84% of historical control studies, the intervention was beneficial
Demissie et al. (1998)	Meta-analysis of RCTs and case control studies	Screening mammography	Results of RCTs and case control studies were of same direction but results of RCTs showed lower levels of intervention effectiveness
Wilson and Lipsey (2001)	Meta-analysis of 319 meta-analyses	Psychological, behavioral, and educational interventions	No significant difference in the effect sizes of RCTs and non-RCTs
Pallesen et al. (2005)	Meta-analysis of studies of RCTs and non-RCTs	Psychological interventions	RCTs had better outcomes than non-RCTs
LaLonde (1986)	Compared results of experimental and quasi-experimental studies	Training programs providing job, counseling and work experience	No particular pattern of difference in the effect sizes of RCTs and non-RCTs
Miao (1977)	Review of results of RCTs and non-RCTs	Gastric freezing for ulcers	Results of non-RCTs showed benefits, and of RCTs showed no benefits of the intervention

(Continued)

TABLE 5.1 (Continued)

Author (year)	Study design	Context	Main findings
Colditz et al. (1988)	Review of RCTs and non-RCTs	Variety of treatments (medical and surgical)	Effect sizes of RCTs were smaller than effect sizes of non-RCTs
Gilbert et al. (1978)	Review of RCTs and non-RCTs	Variety of treatments (medical and surgical)	Effect sizes of RCTs were smaller than effect sizes of non-RCTs
Becker (1990)	Review of RCTs and non-RCTs	Coaching for SAT	Effect sizes of RCTs were larger than effect sizes of non-RCTs
Aiken et al. (1998)	Examined effects of design (RCT vs. non-equivalent/matched control group vs. regression discontinuity)	Educational intervention	Findings of the three designs were consistent
Glazerman et al. (2003)	Synthesis of results of RCTs and non-RCTs	Variety of treatments	Results of RCTs and non-RCTs were not different
Bloom et al. (2005)	Synthesis of results of RCTs and non-RCTs	Variety of treatments	Results of RCTs and non-RCTs were not different
Wilder and Hollister (2002)	Reviewed results of 11 studies using RCTs and non-RCTs	Class size	Agreement in results of RCTs and yoked non-RCTs
Buddelmeyer and Skoufias (2003)	Compared results of RCTs and regression discontinuity designs in 12 studies	Variety of treatments	In 10 of 12 studies, the results of RCTs and regression discontinuity design were comparable
Agodini and Dynarski (2004)	Review of RCTs and non-RCTs	Educational programs	Results of RCT and non-RCT were comparable
MacLehose et al. (2000)	Review of RCTs and non-RCTs	Variety of treatments	The effect sizes of RCTs did not differ significantly from the effect sizes of non-RCT

Author (year)	Study design	Context	Main findings
Shadish et al. (2000)	Meta-analysis of RCTs and non-RCTs	Psychological interventions	Mean effect size of RCTs was larger (d = .52) than the mean effect size of non-RCTs (d = .20); the mean effect size of non-RCTs that used self-selection was -.03 and that applied other methods for treatment assignment was .46 (comparable to that of RCTs)
Kownacki (1997)	Review of RCTs and non-RCTs	Treatments for alcoholism	Mean effect size for non-RCTs (d = .57) was larger than mean effect size for RCTs (d = .35)
Miller et al. (1989)	Comparison of RCTs and non-RCTs results	New surgical therapies	The proportion of participants experiencing improvement in outcomes was smaller in RCTs than non-RCTs
Sørensen et al. (2006)	Reported on results of reviews that compared RCTs and non-RCTs		The effect sizes of RCT and non-RCT are comparable and correlated at .75
Ioannidis et al. (2001)	Review of meta-analyses that included RCTs (N = 240) and non-RCTs (N = 168)	Variety of treatments	Effect sizes of RCTs and non-RCTs were correlated at .75, which increased to .83 when historical control designs were excluded

RCT: randomized controlled/clinical trials; Non-RCT: non-randomized clinical trials; OR: odds ratio

A total of 32 investigations (individual, systematic review, and meta-analytic studies) were located, yielding 79 comparisons of RCTs and non-RCTs evaluating similar treatments. The majority (n = 56, 71%) of comparisons revealed convergence in findings, i.e., no significant differences in the mean effect sizes for the post-test outcomes reported in the RCTs and non-RCTs. Differences in effect sizes were found in the remaining (n = 23, 29%) comparisons: the results of 15 (19% of 79) comparisons indicated larger effect sizes in RCTs than non-RCTs, whereas the findings of 8 (10% of 79) comparisons showed larger effect sizes in non-RCTs than RCTs. Ioannidis et al. (2001) reported a strong correlation between the RCT and non-RCT results. The correlation coefficient was .75 when all types of non-RCT designs were considered, but increased to .83 when studies using a historical control design were excluded. This pattern of findings suggests that the results of RCT and non-RCT studies are comparable.

The influence of substantive (e.g., participants' characteristics, treatment dose) and methodological (e.g., type of comparison treatment, sample size) factors on post-test outcomes was examined in a few meta-analyses to understand the contribution of potential confounds. Shadish and Ragsdale (1996) focused on methodological factors, including effect sizes for the outcomes measured at pre-test (which reflects the extent of group comparability on baseline characteristics), attrition, type of control condition (i.e., passive, receiving no treatment vs. active, receiving some treatment like usual care), method of assignment (random vs. non-random), self vs. other selection of participants in treatment group, sample size, and method for calculating effect size (direct vs. derived). They found that effect sizes for post-test outcomes were higher in published studies, when pre-test outcome effect sizes were high, and when a passive control condition was used. All other methodological factors showed no association with the post-test outcome effect sizes. Using structural equation modeling, they found an indirect relationship between method of assignment (random vs. non-random) and post-test outcome effect sizes, which was mediated by features of the comparison groups (other vs. self-selection, passive vs. active). They concluded that post-test outcome values and features of the comparison group are more significant contributors to post-test outcomes than randomization. Heinsman and Shadish (1996) replicated the meta-analysis on studies that evaluated a wider range of treatments than those included in Shadish and Ragsdale's (1996) meta-analysis. Heinsman and Shadish reported that low attrition, use of passive control, higher pre-test outcome effect sizes, other selection of participants into treatments, and exact effect size computation method predicted higher post-test outcome effect sizes. Wilson and Lipsey (2001) indicated that participants' characteristics, treatment dose, outcomes examined, sample size, quality of the study, and type of comparison group each explained a small amount ($\leq$ 7 per cent) of the variance in post-test outcome effect sizes. Similarly, Pallesen et al. (2005) found that participants' diagnosis, type of trial, design, and number of treatment sessions were weakly related to post-test outcome effect sizes. Overall, the evidence clearly indicated that well-designed non-RCT (excluding the historical control group design) studies yielded estimates of intervention effects that were comparable to those reported in RCTs (Aiken et al., 1998; Benson and Hartz, 2000; Concato and Horwitz, 2004; Heinsman and Shadish, 1996), particularly when the same sample selection criteria were applied and prognostic factors were controlled (Concato et al., 2000; McKee et al., 1999).

Participant Selection

Several researchers commented on the potential for sample selection bias resulting from the application of stringent eligibility criteria in RCTs. The comments were based on two types of evidence: estimates of the percentage of the target population that meets the eligibility criteria and enters the trial, and comparison of the characteristics of enrollees and non-enrollees. For instance, Bottomley (1997) reported that at least 30 per cent of potentially eligible clients decline entry in trials of psychological interventions for persons with cancer. Grapow et al. (2006) estimated that fewer than 10 per cent of screened clients meet the eligibility criteria and are included in the trial; Pincus's (2002) estimate was ≤ 50 per cent. Vist et al. (2005) reviewed 55 studies that compared participants in an RCT with participants who received the same intervention outside of the trial, and found no differences in post-test outcomes achieved by the two groups of patients. Wiltsey-Stirman et al. (2003) examined the clinical characteristics of clients seen in a mental health clinic relative to the eligibility criteria set in an RCT of therapies for common adult mental disorders. The researchers rated whether clinic clients ($N = 347$) met the RCT eligibility criteria. They found that 67 per cent of clinic patients were considered ineligible because they either did not have the primary diagnosis studied in the RCT or had comorbid conditions identified as exclusionary criteria. Although limited and inconsistent, this evidence suggests that participants in RCTs are not representative of different subgroups constituting the target population.

Randomization

The limitation of randomization in maintaining comparability of participants assigned to the intervention and comparison treatment conditions at the group and individual levels is supported by results of a few systematic reviews. Sidani (2006) examined the results of baseline comparisons reported in 100 randomly selected RCTs. Of 87 RCTs reporting comparisons on demographic characteristics, 30 (34.5 per cent) indicated statistically significant between-group differences for up to 60 per cent of the variables compared. Of 70 studies reporting comparisons on outcomes assessed at baseline, 12 (17.2 per cent) revealed statistically significant between-group differences in up to 100 per cent of the outcomes examined. Shadish and Ragsdale (1996) and Heinsman and Shadish (1996) reported statistically significant correlation, of a moderate size, between pre-test and post-test outcome effect sizes. This correlation supports the point that randomization does not control for inter-individual variability in baseline characteristics, which contributes to variability in post-test outcome achievement. Further, randomization was not directly related to post-test outcome effect sizes, a finding that confirms the limitation of chance-based allocation to treatment in minimizing bias following pre-test assessment.

The extent to which randomization introduces self-selection bias was examined in two studies. McKay et al. (1998) compared participants who did and did not accept randomization in an RCT of rehabilitation for cocaine abuse. The results showed that randomized participants had less education, reported more days of cocaine use prior to entry into treatment, and had higher drug and psychiatric composite scores than those who refused random assignment. Westerberg et al. (2000) compared the characteristics of clients with alcohol use disorders who were 1) randomly allocated to treatment, and 2) assigned to treatment by the triage process followed in clinical practice. The two groups differed on several characteristics. Randomized clients reported fewer alcohol and emotional problems and lower readiness for change. Triaged patients had attended more support group meetings and reported more depression, unemployment, negative consequences of drinking, and alcohol consumption. Thus, the latter group of clients had more severe levels of the health problem. The findings are consistent in demonstrating that participants who accept randomization, and hence enrolled in an RCT, represent a select subgroup of the target population.

Concealment of Treatment Allocation and Intention-to-treat Analysis

The contribution of concealment to initial group comparability and to estimates of intervention effects was examined in a small number of systematic reviews. Chalmers et al. (1983) synthesized the findings of 145 studies evaluating treatments for acute myocardial infarction to determine the extent to which concealment of treatment allocation yielded a comparable distribution of prognostic factors between study groups. The results revealed an unbalanced distribution for at least one factor in 14 per cent of blinded RCTs, 27 per cent of unblinded RCTs, and 58 per cent of non-RCTs, confirming the importance of concealment in preventing selection bias. Kunz and Oxman (1998) and Schulz et al. (1995) conducted systematic reviews to evaluate the impact of concealment on post-test outcome effect sizes. The findings were consistent in showing larger effect sizes in inadequately concealed studies.

Horwitz (1987) reviewed the findings of 200 RCTs evaluating treatments for cardiac and gastroenterological conditions to evaluate the influence of intention-to-treat analysis on post-test outcomes. He reported inconsistency in the findings, which was related to the type of outcome analysis performed: results of RCTs that used the intention-to-treat analysis showed no beneficial effects for the treatment under evaluation, whereas results of RCTs that accounted for level of compliance with the treatment indicated better outcomes in participants reporting high adherence to the active or placebo treatment. These results question the utility of concealment and intention-to-treat analysis, which are highly recommended features of the RCT.

Summary

- The features of the RCT limit the utility of this design in evaluating the effectiveness of the intervention
- The limitations relate to the experimental control exerted in the RCT relative to participant selection and allocation to treatment, blinding, manipulation of intervention, and outcome measurement and analysis
- The experimental control constrains the research questions that can be addressed, resulting in findings that are not relevant to practice
- An accumulation of empirical evidence raises questions concerning the utility of the RCT design and supports the appropriateness of non-RCT designs in evaluating effectiveness of health interventions

6

ADVANCES IN INTERVENTION EVALUATION DESIGNS: EXTENSIONS OF EXPERIMENTAL DESIGNS

There are situations where it is not feasible to implement the experimental or randomized controlled trial (RCT) design because randomization may not be practical, acceptable, or desirable. Several designs have been proposed to evaluate interventions in these situations, to overcome the limitations of the RCT. It is beyond the scope of this book to discuss specific designs (for details, refer to Shadish et al., 2002). In this chapter, two general categories of advanced designs are introduced. The first category represents extensions of the RCT and the second involves quasi-experimental designs in which naturally occurring cohorts are compared. The rationale for considering them in intervention evaluation research and available empirical evidence of their utility are presented.

SITUATIONS UNSUITABLE FOR RANDOMIZATION

Randomization of participants to the intervention and comparison groups, the hallmark of the RCT design, is not always feasible or practical. This may be the case when the intervention targets clearly defined groups; for example, public health interventions such as immunization campaigns or multi-level, multi-component interventions to encourage physical activity provided to whole communities. Or it may be that the intervention must be delivered to pre-existing groups of people to avoid contamination of the intervention to the comparison group. For example, an inter-professional approach to discharge planning must be given to all clients admitted to the unit to which multidisciplinary healthcare teams, trained in the use of the approach, are assigned. It is difficult for the teams to refrain from applying some components of the approach to clients under their care but randomized to the comparison group. In such instances, randomization is done at the group, rather than the individual participant level.

In other situations, randomization is not acceptable. It may be viewed as unethical, clinically inappropriate, or unjustifiable by participants, healthcare professionals, and policy makers. Some client advocacy groups, such as those representing persons living with HIV/AIDS, have been vocal in protecting clients' rights for potentially beneficial treatments and have demanded that all clients are exposed to the experimental intervention. Healthcare professionals may favor and strongly believe in the benefits of particular interventions. They may not cooperate in studies involving randomization to interventions they do not favor. Therefore, they do not refer eligible clients to the trial; they refuse to implement the treatments or they deliver them with low levels of fidelity; or they undermine randomization by offering the intervention they favor to clients assigned to their care. For instance, radiologists still demand annual mammography for low risk women under the age of 50 years, despite evidence showing more harm than good because of the high false positive rate (e.g., Kerlikowske, 2012). Clients and healthcare professionals who agree to randomization form a biased sample, jeopardizing the generalizability of the RCT results. Policy makers formulate new health-related legislation and require its application to all institutions within a jurisdiction, which limits the availability of a concurrent reference group for prospective comparison, precluding the use of randomization. For example, legislation in one jurisdiction ordered that there be a utilization review of all inappropriate drug use; therefore, evaluation of an intervention to reduce the use of asthma-controlling medications in children necessarily had to include all those who met the study criteria (Lee et al., 2004).

There are situations in which randomization is not desirable. These involve Phase 4 trials aimed at determining the effectiveness of the intervention, and Phase 5 trials aimed at evaluating the clinical utility of the intervention under the conditions of day-to-day practice. Randomization is not congruent with the latter conditions, which are characterized by engagement of healthcare professionals and clients in treatment-related decisions. Alternative methods of treatment allocation are needed to enhance the relevance of these trials' findings to the context of practice.

EXTENSIONS OF THE RCT

Extensions of the RCT design have been proposed to address challenges encountered in the implementation of the RCT. Two general types of extension are considered in this section. The first type, cluster randomized trials, is used when the intervention under evaluation must be delivered to pre-existing groups of people; randomization is done at the group or cluster, rather than the individual participant, level. The second type, cross-over designs, is advocated when it is not possible or ethical to withhold treatment.

Cluster or Group Randomized Trial

Before discussing cluster randomized trials, it is necessary to differentiate it from multi-site RCT. Although both involve a number of sites (e.g., clinics, hospitals, communities, geographic locations), the rationale for selecting the design and the level at which randomization is done differ.

Multi-site RCTs

Multi-site RCTs are selected when the intervention targets individuals, but either of two situations is faced. The first situation is the inability to acquire the required sample size from one site only, due to the small pool of potentially eligible participants available or to a low enrollment rate. Low enrollment may be associated with healthcare professionals' limited cooperation in referring clients or clients' unfavorable perception of the study. In this instance, several sites with comparable characteristics (e.g., socio-cultural neighborhood, mix of healthcare professionals) are chosen for the RCT. The second situation demanding involvement of multiple sites in an RCT is the study's concern with examining the extent to which the intervention is implemented with fidelity and its effects are reproduced under different contexts. In this case, the site selection is done carefully to ensure representation of those with key characteristics hypothesized to influence the implementation and effects of the intervention. Once the sites are selected, the conduct of multi-site RCTs resembles that of the traditional RCT in that individual participants within each site are randomized to the intervention or comparison group, as illustrated in Figure 6.1.

The advantages of the multi-site RCT are: 1) accrual of the sample size needed to achieve adequate statistical power within a shorter time period than the traditional RCT, particularly for studies addressing health problems with low prevalence and incidence, or outcomes with low event rate (e.g., mortality or hospital-acquired complications); and 2) representation of sites with diverse characteristics of participants, healthcare professionals, and contexts (i.e., physical and psychosocial environment) to examine across-site differences in the implementation and effects of the intervention. The findings of these comparisons point to contextual factors that facilitate or hinder the delivery of the intervention and the achievement of outcomes, which enhances the applicability of the evidence to the practice setting. The multi-site RCT should be carefully planned and executed to either:

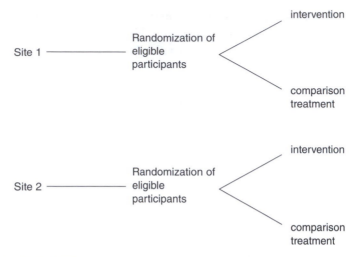

FIGURE 6.1   Multi-site RCT

1. Maintain comparability of the sample, treatments, context, and study methods across sites when the design is used to increase sample size (Weinberger et al., 2001). This can be achieved by developing a study protocol that details the participants' eligibility criteria, screening procedures, randomization methods, and data collection logistics, and treatment manuals that clarify and standardize the implementation of the intervention and comparison treatment; by subjecting all research staff and interventionists to intensive training; and by monitoring their performance on a frequent basis; or
2. Select sites to represent the range of contextual characteristics of interest to the study, obtain relevant data, and conduct appropriate analysis to delineate their contribution to the intervention's implementation and effects.

The multi-site RCT has limitations related to the potential for clustering effects (due to the nesting of participants within sites) and for dissemination of the intervention to participants assigned to the comparison group. The dissemination is due to possible interactions among participants within the same site or to the implementation of both the intervention and comparison treatment by the same interventionists within the same site. These limitations are addressed with the application of appropriate statistical techniques that account for clustering and the use of the cluster randomized trial that minimizes the potential for contamination.

Cluster randomized trials

Cluster randomized trials (CRTs) are used to minimize the likelihood of contamination in studies requiring the involvement of multiple sites and to provide the intervention to the targeted pre-existing groups. Examples are implementation of health promotion campaigns which should reach all members in a particular community or the application of best practice guidelines which should be followed by all healthcare professionals in a hospital. In a CRT, multiple sites housing the targeted groups are selected and the sites or clusters are randomized to the intervention or the comparison group. Thus, all participants in a given site are assigned to the same treatment; they are exposed to either the intervention or the comparison treatment (Donner and Klar, 2004; Eldridge et al., 2004) as illustrated in Figure 6.2. Since the site is the unit of randomization, it is essential to assign more than one site to each group in order to avoid confounding the site with the intervention effects. If only one site is allocated to the intervention and one site to the comparison group, and if each site has unique characteristics that influence the implementation and effects of the intervention, then it would be impossible to dismantle the contribution of the intervention from that of contextual site characteristics and it would be invalid to attribute the observed improvement in outcomes solely to the intervention. Although site is the unit of randomization, it is not necessarily the unit of analysis; the effects of the intervention are still examined at the level of individual participants. Therefore, outcome data are obtained from participants within the clusters (Murray et al., 2004). It is also conceivable to gather outcome data from the pre-existing groups forming the clusters, such as falls rate estimated for in-patient units within a hospital. Similar to the multi-site RCT, the nesting of individuals within clusters presents challenges for the planning and analysis of data.

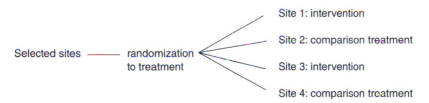

FIGURE 6.2 Cluster randomized trials

The nesting of participants within sites generates a clustering effect, which refers to the similarity of people within clusters. Persons belonging to the same cluster are likely to resemble one another in terms of personal, health, and clinical characteristics, exposure to contextual factors, and experiences, but differ from those in other clusters. Donner and Klar (2000) list three reasons for the non-comparability of the clusters:

1. Participants can choose the cluster to which they belong. For example, clients may select physicians because they come from the same cultural background, which makes the interactions comfortable as physicians understand and respect clients' beliefs and values. Clusters comprised of entire communities differ on geographic and political factors. For

instance, older people choose to live in warmer climates. Thus, clients in the different clusters are not comparable on some qualities.

2. Participants within a cluster have shared experiences related to their exposure to common physical elements and psychosocial features of the environment in which they reside. For instance, participants living in a particular geographic location are exposed to allergens prevalent in that area and to by-laws (e.g., smoking, helmet use) enforced in the area. Participants within a cluster receive care from common healthcare professionals who provide them with similar treatment. Variations in professionals' and hospitals' practices are well documented in the literature.

3. Participants interact within a cluster: The interactions among participants within a cluster facilitate the spread of germs and the adoption of attitudes, beliefs, norms, and behaviors or practices.

Briefly, participants within a cluster have similar characteristics and health and healthcare experiences; these influence their perception, enactment, and satisfaction with the intervention, and the achievement of outcomes. The outcomes observed for participants within a cluster are comparable. This clustering effect is reflected in the within-cluster correlation. A high correlation indicates that members of a cluster respond to the intervention in the same way, exhibited by the same direction and magnitude of improvement in the outcomes. A low correlation implies that the outcome of one person is independent of the response of others in the cluster. In addition to the clustering effect, clusters differ relative to the participants' personal, health or clinical characteristics, treatment experiences, and outcomes. Between-cluster differences in outcomes may be large enough to obscure the effects of the intervention whether evaluated at the individual participant or cluster level. The extent of across-cluster differences is estimated with the intra-class correlation (ICC) coefficient. In essence, the ICC is the ratio of the variance between the clusters to the variance within a cluster (Donner and Klar, 2000). A high ICC coefficient means that the clusters are not comparable, equivalent, or interchangeable. The clustering effect should be accounted for in the outcome data analysis when determining the impact of the intervention on the outcomes. If the clustering effect is ignored, then the intervention effects are overestimated, resulting in an inflated type I error. Mixed models or hierarchical linear models are appropriate statistical tests to analyze the data in CRTs (Raudenbush and Bryk, 2002). They account for the clustering effect and control for potential confounding variables measured at the individual and group levels, which reduces within- and between-cluster error variance (Jo et al., 2008).

The plan and conduct of CRTs have additional challenges:

1. Number of clusters and participants to include in the trial: The cluster is the unit of randomization. Therefore, a CRT should have an adequate number of clusters assigned to the intervention and comparison groups to tease out the effects of the clusters from those of the intervention. The challenge is to find enough clusters. It is often the case

that the number of participating clusters is low (due, for instance, to limited funding), which reduces the statistical power of the study (Eldridge et al., 2004). Furthermore, the number of participants within each cluster should be adequate and balanced, particularly when individual participants are the unit of analysis. The number of participants may be dependent on the expected level of within-cluster correlation. Consequently, sample size calculation accounts for the number of clusters, participants, and the inflation factor; the magnitude of the latter factor is based on the expected value of the ICC coefficient (Donner and Klar, 2000). Hussey and Hughes (2007) proposed the stepped wedge design in situations where the number of clusters is small. This is a CRT involving cross-over, whereby clusters are randomized to receive the intervention at different points in time (see Figure 6.3). The clusters are first randomized to the intervention or comparison group. Once post-test outcome data are collected from all clusters, those in the comparison group are randomized to receive the intervention or to continue with the comparison treatment; the latter clusters are offered the intervention following post-test. Stepped wedge designs require fewer clusters than parallel cluster randomized trials.

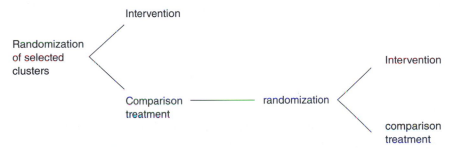

FIGURE 6.3 Stepped wedge design

2. Overlapping cluster membership: This challenge is encountered in CRTs with long follow-up periods (Donner and Klar, 2000). Overlapping membership means that participants who were in a specific cluster when the intervention was implemented may not be in that cluster, or may be in a different cluster when the outcome is evaluated, leading to changes in clusters' size and composition. For instance, movement of participants across clusters is likely among migrant workers. Large changes in cluster membership compromise the magnitude of the intervention effects. Overlapping cluster membership may not be controlled experimentally or statistically.

3. Heterogeneity of clusters: Clusters are expected to vary in the characteristics of participants, healthcare professionals, and context. This heterogeneity contributes to differences in the type of treatments applied, the fidelity with which the intervention and comparison treatment are implemented, and the level of reported improvement in the outcomes. Also,

the cluster heterogeneity presents challenges in the randomization, as it may yield an uneven distribution of cluster characteristics, between the two treatment groups, with the potential to confound the intervention effects (Kraemer et al., 2009; Murray et al., 2004). This is particularly true when the number of clusters is small. In this case, stratification or matching of the clusters on characteristics that are strongly associated with the outcomes is desirable (Murray et al., 2004). One stratification variable that is frequently used is the size of the cluster itself. The reasons are that statistical tests are often more robust when cluster sizes are similar and the size of the cluster is a surrogate for other important variables such as urbanicity (Donner and Klar, 2000). When the study involves clusters from many parts of a country, geographic area is usually a stratification variable because it is a surrogate for some cluster characteristics such as socio-economic status. The number of stratification variables should be limited to the key ones, known to influence treatment implementation and outcome achievement. Having too many stratification variables yields unequal allocation because some combinations of cluster characteristics are impossible to find. Kernan et al. (1999) recommend that the number of strata should be smaller than the number of clusters. Matching of clusters on key characteristics (similar to those used for stratification) before assigning clusters to the intervention and comparison groups is another strategy to address heterogeneity of clusters. Matching involves identification of pairs of clusters with comparable characteristics and allocation of the paired clusters to either the intervention or comparison group. Although matching results in a balanced distribution of clusters' characteristics, between the intervention and comparison groups, it presents some problems. Matching results in loss of degrees of freedom (Murray et al., 2004), and if one member of the pair is lost to follow-up, then both sites are lost from the study, which reduces the sample size. Matching also complicates the data analysis, especially if the interest is in the effects of the intervention on outcomes measured at the individual participant level (Donner et al., 2007)

4. Informed consent: Failure to appropriately identify the unit of analysis (i.e., individual vs. group) and the level at which the intervention exerts its impact and the outcomes are measured generates ethical issues: Who should be informed and from whom should consent be obtained? The issues are often encountered when the intervention targets the group but does not have a direct effect on individual participants within the cluster, as occurs in community-based campaigns, introduction of new policies, and implementation of best practice guidelines by healthcare professionals. McRae et al. (2011a) argued for exempting individual participants because they are only indirectly affected. However, there are instances where it is impractical to inform and obtain consent from individuals (e.g., changing smoking policies in a city), and others where it is not feasible to secure consent from the clusters (e.g., community; in this case, who would represent the community?). CRTs present ethical challenges that have been explored in a series of articles (McRae et al., 2011a, 2011b; Weijer et al., 2011), but have not been fully resolved.

5. Compliance with treatment and study protocols: Just like the multi-site RCT, cluster randomized trials are prone to variability in the implementation of the intervention and comparison treatment, and in the application of the study protocol related to recruitment, screening, and data collection within and across clusters. Whereas some variability in intervention delivery is necessary so that the protocols fit within the local context of the cluster, it should be documented and accounted for in data analysis and interpretation of the results (see Chapter 11). Differences in the application of the study protocol should be minimized. However, the differences are imposed by localized interpretation of research ethics (e.g., some research ethics boards consider administration of a screening test intrusive and should be done in a face-to-face session after obtaining written consent, and other boards do not), or required for logistical reasons (e.g., having the research assistant read the items and response options of an outcome measure for older adults vs. having participants complete the measure on their own). It is important to critically review the nature of the differences and analyze their potential impact on the validity of the study findings. Differences in protocol known to have no influence, based on theoretical and empirical evidence, can be accepted. Regular and close monitoring of research staff's performance, within and across clusters, is a useful strategy to track, document, and discuss non-compliance with the study protocol.

The plan, conduct, and analysis of CRTs demand clear and elaborate protocols to guide standard implementation of treatment and study procedures while identifying what can be tailored, and how, to the local context; collaboration and monitoring of the performance of research staff within and across clusters; and use of advanced statistics to account for the clustering effect and potential confounds operating at the individual participant and cluster levels. Although their use has increased in the evaluation of health interventions targeting communities, organizations, and healthcare systems, there is limited empirical evidence of the utility of CRTs, compared to the traditional RCT or other designs.

Cross-over Designs

Cross-over designs are often used when randomization of individual participants to the intervention and comparison groups is unethical or unacceptable. This happens when the experimental intervention demonstrates large benefits (exceeding those of standard care) in previous research; the target population is in need of treatment; and different stakeholder groups (patients, healthcare professionals, decision makers) find it inappropriate to with-hold treatment or to provide treatment on the basis of chance. The conduct of the RCT in these situations presents challenges: approval for the trial may be denied by the research ethics board and access to the target population may not be granted; healthcare profession-als may not refer their potential eligible patients to the study; and eligible patients may opt out, yielding a high refusal rate that exceeds 90 per cent in some studies (Amir et al., 2004).

Consequently, the ability to carry out the study and its external validity, if executed, are jeopardized. The cross-over design is a viable solution. In this design, participants are randomized to different treatments at different points in time; ultimately, all participants are prospectively exposed to all treatments. The treatments included in a particular study involve either an experimental intervention and a comparison treatment, or two or more experimental interventions.

Cross-over designs including experimental and comparison treatment

As illustrated in Figure 6.4, this cross-over design involves randomization of participants to receive the experimental intervention immediately following baseline data collection, or at a delayed point in time which takes place after post-test data collection. It has been labeled delayed start design (D'Agostino, 2009; Glasgow et al., 2005), deferred treatment design (Campbell et al., 2005), or waiting-list control group design. The features of this design are: 1) assessment of outcomes at baseline (time 1); 2) random assignment of participants to the experimental intervention or the comparison group (no-treatment or usual care) while ensuring a balanced number of participants in each group; 3) provision of the experimental treatment to participants in the intervention group (referred to as immediate treatment group) and withholding it from those in the comparison group; 4) measurement of outcomes on all participants following completion of the intervention (time 2); 5) delivery of the intervention to participants in the comparison group (referred to as delayed treatment group); 6) assessment of the outcomes after implementation of the intervention in the latter group (time 3). Some researchers choose to collect outcome data at time 3 from participants allocated to the immediate treatment group, which allows examination of the sustainability of the intervention effects.

The statistical analyses aimed at determining the effects of the intervention involve two stages. The first stage focuses on examining differences between the two groups in outcomes assessed at times 1 and 2, as is done in an RCT. The second stage expands the analysis in two

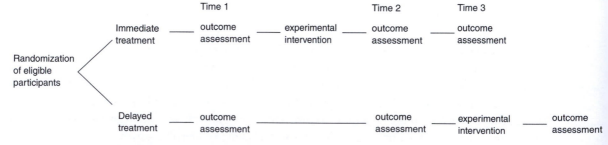

FIGURE 6.4   Cross-over design including intervention and comparison treatment

ways by conducting: 1) within-group analysis to determine the extent and timing of change in outcomes with the expectation to capture changes following implementation of the intervention in each group, and the sustainability of the intervention effects in the immediate treatment group, evidenced by no significant difference in the outcomes reported at times 2 and 3 in this group; and 2) a within group pre-test to post-test comparison, in which relevant outcome data are pooled from both groups to determine the extent of improvement in the outcomes after intervention delivery.

This type of cross-over design has several advantages. First, it addresses the ethical dilemma of withholding a potentially beneficial intervention, particularly for populations in great need of treatment (Schwartz et al., 1997). Second, participants' awareness that they will ultimately receive the experimental intervention has the potential to increase study participation rates. Delays in receipt of treatment are often anticipated in day-to-day practice; participants are accustomed to waiting for treatment and find this cross-over design acceptable. A third advantage is the potential for reduced likelihood of contamination (Campbell et al., 2005) or treatment compensation. Healthcare professionals are less compelled to disseminate the intervention or to improve usual care given to participants allocated to the comparison group as they know that the latter group will be exposed to the intervention at a later time. A fourth advantage relates to the types of analyses that can be performed, which combine between- and within-group comparisons. The between-group comparisons determine the causal effects of the intervention. The analysis within the immediate treatment group provides information on the sustainability of the intervention effects. The analysis within the delayed treatment group is useful in determining the extent of changes in outcomes while controlling for potential confounding of participants' characteristics (as participants serve as their own control). Last, the analysis done on the outcome data pooled from the immediate and delayed groups increases the number of cases available to examine the magnitude of changes in the outcomes immediately following implementation of the intervention.

The cross-over design has limitations. A high attrition rate is anticipated, and has been reported in the delayed treatment group. Participants allocated to the latter group may desire immediate attention to manage the presenting health problem and withdraw from the study to seek treatment elsewhere, resulting in differential attrition, which lowers statistical power and introduces non-comparability of the groups at baseline (see Chapter 9). In contrast, participants in the delayed treatment group may experience improvement in the outcomes prior to exposure to the experimental intervention (i.e., time interval between time 1 and time 2). The improvement is associated with: spontaneous, natural recovery, which tends to occur with acute, time-limited health problems (e.g., common cold); expectancy, that is, anticipation of improvement in the problem or changes in the perception of the severity of the problem with time; and seeking treatment outside the context of the study. The extent of changes in the outcomes within this time interval in the delayed treatment group reduces the magnitude of the differences between the groups at time 2, and therefore the power to detect a significant impact of the intervention.

Cross-over designs including two experimental treatments

This cross-over design is comparable to the one described in the previous section, with two exceptions. First, two interventions are evaluated, such as experimental interventions with distinct active ingredients (e.g., two types of behavioral therapy), or two components of complex interventions (e.g., sleep education and hygiene vs. stimulus control therapy for the management of insomnia). Second, a washout period is scheduled after participants receive the first intervention but prior to their exposure to the second intervention. In this period, participants are requested to withhold any treatment to allow any effect of the first intervention to dissipate and participants begin the second intervention with a clean state. The washout period prevents the carry-over effects of the first intervention, which has possible interaction with – or cumulative influence on – the impact of the second intervention. The length of the washout period is determined theoretically, based on available knowledge regarding the duration of the intervention effects. In the absence of such knowledge, it is logical to have the washout period equal to the period for providing each intervention. The features of this cross-over design entail: 1) randomization of participants to receive one (treatment A) or the other (treatment B) intervention first; 2) assessment of outcomes on all participants at pre-test; 3) delivery of the first allocated intervention (treatment A or B); 4) measurement of the outcomes on all participants at post-test; 5) allowance for the washout period; 6) assessment of outcomes on all participants, serving as baseline for the second intervention; 7) provision of the second experimental intervention, which is switched so that participants who receive treatment A first are given treatment B second and vice versa; and 8) measurement of the outcomes on all participants following completion of the second intervention, serving as the post-test for the latter treatment.

The statistical analysis of this cross-over design is complex. It is not sufficient to compare the two groups over time, or the two treatments provided either before or after the washout period, because the possibility of carry-over and order effects must be taken into account. The statistical methods to analyze cross-over designs can be found in Fleiss (1986) and Wellek and Blettner (2012).

The use of this cross-over design is based on three assumptions. The first is that the health problem targeted for treatment is stable; it neither improves nor deteriorates over time, at least within the study period. The second assumption is that the interventions have independent, fast-acting effects which are not sustained. The third is that the order of the interventions' delivery does not influence their impact on outcomes. Accordingly, the cross-over design involving two interventions is most appropriate for the evaluation of treatments that work quickly and provide short-term relief (Shadish et al., 2002). Its use is precluded with treatments expected to have permanent effects such as surgical procedures.

The advantages of this design are:

1. Provision of treatment to all participants, which addresses the ethical issue of denying or withholding treatment.
2. Efficiency in sample size, in that compared to the traditional RCT: only half of the number of participants is needed to produce the same precision in the estimates of the interventions' effects. This advantage is due to the use of the same participants and the application of within-subject comparison of the experimental interventions (Norman and Streiner, 2008).
3. Reduction of error variance, which also relates to the use of same participants, serving as their own control in the comparison of the two interventions. This minimizes any imbalance in the characteristics of participants exposed to the two interventions and the potential influence of participants' characteristics on treatment implementation and outcome achievement; this increases the statistical power to detect significant intervention effects.
4. Examination of possible order effects of treatments or components of complex interventions (Shadish et al., 2002), which is important in the evaluation of stepped treatment.

Some limitations are reported for cross-section designs. The first relates to attrition. The likelihood of attrition is high 1) when the treatment period is long; 2) if the first allocated treatment is effective in managing the health problem – participants who experience improvement are not interested in additional treatment; or 3) if the first treatment received has severe side effects. Experience of side effects may detract participants from further treatment. In contrast to the RCT in which withdrawal of one participant reduces the sample size of the respective group by one, in a cross-over design that dropout results in a loss of one person to both treatment groups, reducing the number of cases included in the data analyses. The second limitation is the high probability of carry-over effects; the effects of the first treatment do not dissipate prior to the introduction of the second treatment, resulting in possible interaction or cumulative influence on outcomes. The third limitation relates to the learning or testing effects, which occurs with repeated outcome assessments conducted within short time intervals. The fourth limitation is the order effects, that is, the possibility that the sequence in which treatments are delivered affects the outcome. For example, if the first treatment has many side effects, then participants are more aware of or sensitive to side effects with the second treatment. Consequently, participants who receive this treatment sequence report more adverse events to the second treatment than participants who receive the treatments in the reverse sequence. Randomizing the order of providing the interventions is a means for minimizing the order effect.

QUASI-EXPERIMENTAL DESIGNS

Quasi-experimental designs are used in situations when it is not possible to randomize participants to different treatments. Two general categories of quasi-experimental designs are available. The first involves between-subject studies, in which participants are allocated to the experimental intervention and the comparison treatment by non-random means. The second category consists of within-subject studies that do not include a comparison treatment group; the same participants are exposed to a comparison condition (e.g., no-treatment) and to the intervention.

Between-subject Quasi-experimental Designs

The main feature of between-subject quasi-experimental designs is the non-random allocation of participants to the intervention and the comparison group. The non-random allocation can be either under the control of the researcher or not (Norris and Atkins, 2005). Accordingly, the designs are subdivided into cohort, regression-discontinuity, and observational designs.

Cohort designs

This type of between-subject quasi-experimental design is also known as cohort, non-randomized (Norris and Atkins, 2005) or non-equivalent control group designs (Shadish et al., 2002). It is similar to the RCT. There are two groups of participants, one receiving the intervention and one the comparison treatment. Participants are selected from a common pool, using the same study eligibility criteria to ensure representativeness of the target population and control of potential confounding characteristics. The study is done prospectively in that outcomes are assessed for both groups before and after implementation of the intervention. The intervention is provided by trained interventionists and fidelity of treatment delivery is monitored. The major difference between the RCT and cohort design is that allocation of participants to groups, although under the control of the researcher, is done by non-random means. The researcher applies one of different schemes for treatment assignment (see Chapter 10).

The analysis in cohort design is concerned with comparing the post-test outcomes for participants in the intervention and comparison groups, while adjusting for between-group differences in variables measured at baseline. Baseline differences may confound the effects of the intervention on the outcomes. Adjustment can be achieved with the application of appropriate statistical techniques such as analysis of covariance, stratified or subgroup analysis, or hierarchical linear or mixed models. Alternatively, the analysis of cohort designs can be directed to model the process of selection into treatment and to represent the model in the examination of the intervention effects on the outcomes. The propensity score and the instrumental variable have been proposed to model the selection process; these incorporate covariates that best predict or are associated with treatment group membership. However, the utility of the propensity score and the instrumental variable is contingent on the availability of relevant covariates that correctly describe the selection process and the reliable and valid measurement of these covariates (Cook et al., 2010; Horn et al., 2005).

Although prone to selection bias and the potential confounding influence of baseline participants' characteristics on post-test outcomes, this design is considered most appropriate for the evaluation of interventions in situations not amenable to randomization. Results of individual and meta-analytic studies (Chapter 5) have provided empirical evidence supporting the utility of cohort designs in making valid inferences regarding the intervention effects. The application of the cohort design as described here, specifically in terms of using the same criteria for participant selection, yielded effect sizes that were comparable to those obtained in RCTs evaluating the same intervention (e.g., De Maat et al., 2007; Heinsman and Shadish, 1996).

Regression-discontinuity designs

This type of between-subject quasi-experimental design, also called cut-off experiment (Cook, 2007), has been used in fields such as economics, education, social welfare, and criminal justice. The regression-discontinuity design has the same features common to the RCT and cohort designs, with the exception of the method for assignment to groups. Allocation to treatment is under the control of the researcher but is based on participants' level on a specific variable measured at baseline (Glasgow et al., 2005; Shadish et al., 2002). The variable can be a personal, health, or clinical characteristic or an outcome; its identification is guided by the theory underlying the intervention and an understanding of the participants' needs. The process for allocating participants with different levels on the selected variable to treatments should be clearly delineated and faithfully applied. It can be specified in a protocol that indicates which participants, having what level on the selected variable, are allocated to which treatments. For instance, Shadish et al. (2011) used the regression-discontinuity design in a study involving mathematics and vocabulary training. They identified vocabulary knowledge assessed at pre-test as the variable guiding allocation to training. Participants having a score $\geq$ 20 on the vocabulary test (reflecting high vocabulary knowledge) were to receive mathematics training and those with a score < 20 were to get vocabulary training. Similarly, a regression-discontinuity design can be used to evaluate a new weight loss program, in which participants with a high body mass index (using a cut-off score of 30 for instance) are allocated to the program and those with a low index are assigned to a no-treatment condition. Having a clear cut-off score for the selected variable's measure makes it easy to apply the protocol for assignment to treatment. When a continuum is available, a more complex computational formula is required whereby assignment to treatments is a function of the score; this has been called 'fuzzy' regression-discontinuity design (Imbens and Lemieux, 2008). It is possible to use more than one variable to guide treatment allocation; this would introduce complexity in generating the scores to determine assignment, particularly if the measures of the variables are in different metrics. In these instances, assignment is based on the combination of cut-off scores set for separate variables or on an index representing a total score derived from all selected variables (Shadish et al., 2002).

The analysis in regression-discontinuity design focuses on comparing regression lines for the groups. The regression lines quantify the relationship between the pre-test and post-test outcomes. For more information on analysis of regression-discontinuity designs, refer to Imbens and Lemieux (2008). Error in the measurement of the variable guiding treatment allocation is a major threat to validity; it can lead to mis-assignment and subsequent risk of type II error of inference. The primary disadvantage of the regression-discontinuity design is that of power. This design requires a larger sample size than needed for an equivalent RCT. It is estimated that a study using a regression-discontinuity design requires 2.75 times the number of participants included in an RCT (Cappelleri et al., 1994). This is related to the nature of the design that introduces a high correlation between assignment to groups and the variables included in the regression. This problem is made worse in the presence of clustering effects (Schochet, 2008). The main advantage is that the regression-discontinuity design is nearly comparable to the RCT in terms of internal validity. There is accumulating empirical evidence showing that the regression-discontinuity design produces the same causal effects as those obtained in an RCT (Cook, 2006; Shadish et al., 2011). Accordingly, the US Government Accountability Office (2009) considers the regression-discontinuity design an acceptable alternative to the RCT when randomization is not possible.

Observational designs

In observational designs, the allocation to and the implementation of treatments follow a natural course (i.e., natural experiment). These designs are illustrated with studies evaluating the health impact of naturally-occurring events (e.g., earthquake, fire), changes in healthcare professional practices (e.g., implementation of best practice guidelines), or the introduction of new roles within the healthcare system (e.g., care coordinator). The researcher does not interfere with clients' assignment (Norris and Atkins, 2005). Allocation to treatment is done as part of usual practice, following healthcare professionals' clinical judgement or administrative guidelines. Healthcare professionals provide the experimental intervention and the comparison treatment and assess outcomes, at different points over time. Information on clients' characteristics, type and dose of treatment, and outcomes is documented in relevant databases maintained within particular healthcare institutions (e.g., databases for a health maintenance organization; Stone and Pocock, 2010). Analysis of available databases is directed toward describing the characteristics of clients who received different treatments and the implementation of these treatments; examining changes in the outcomes over time (if outcome data are recorded over time); determining the association between treatments and outcomes; or comparing the effectiveness of different treatments.

Observational designs are appropriate for Phase 4 and Phase 5 trials. The limitations of these designs relate to selection bias, which results in confounding and overestimate of treatments' effects (Dumbrigue et al., 2006), and to differences in the level of exposure to the intervention within each treatment group. Variability in treatment exposure may be associated with differences in participants' characteristics and the extent of outcome improvement (Jepsen et al., 2004). With data sets including a large number of cases, these limitations can be addressed by modeling the selection process (using propensity score or instrumental variable), examining the reproducibility of treatments' effects in different subgroups of the target population and in different contexts of day-to-day practice (Norris and Atkins, 2005), and determining the relationship between different levels of exposure to treatments and outcomes. Results of such analyses enhance external validity and provide answers to clinically relevant questions: Who would most benefit from which treatments given at what dose level?

Within-subject Quasi-experimental Designs

There are situations when it is not possible to form a group of participants, representative of the target population serving as comparison, or to randomize participants to treatments (Grimshaw et al., 2000). This is the case when the experimental intervention 1) is to be implemented globally, such as the World Health Organization's effort to eradicate poliomyelitis; 2) is specifically designed and provided to a particular subgroup of the target population; such interventions are tailored to the characteristics and needs of the subgroup, which may be unique, making it difficult to find a comparable subgroup for comparison; 3) is designed to fit within a local context, whereby its implementation relies heavily on the physical, psychosocial, or political characteristics of the context, which may not be available in other settings; and 4) cannot be withheld from participants for ethical or clinical reasons. In these situations, the intervention is delivered to all participants and outcomes are assessed before and after treatment implementation.

Within-subject quasi-experimental designs involve measurement of the outcomes for the same group, obtained repeatedly before and after implementation of the intervention (see Figure 6.5). The group consists of individual participants or a pre-existing cluster. Several assessments of the outcomes are made, at pre-specified time intervals, before delivery of the intervention. At least two outcome assessments should be planned for this no-treatment period.

Time 1		Time 2		Intervention		Time 3		Time 4
Outcome assessment	___	Outcome assessment	___	Intervention	___	Outcome assessment	___	Outcome assessment

FIGURE 6.5 Within-subject experimental design

The time intervals are selected either to be equivalent to the time period over which the intervention is given, or to reflect the time period over which changes in the post-test outcomes are expected to occur (e.g., within 3 months). No significant changes in the outcomes are expected over this no-treatment period. The intervention is provided to all participants. Several assessments of the outcomes are taken at the pre-specified time intervals (equivalent to those selected for the pre-intervention period) following the implementation of the intervention. Significant improvements in the outcomes are anticipated in the post-treatment period. Repeated measurement of the outcomes after implementation of the intervention is beneficial for examining the patterns of change in the outcomes and sustainability of the intervention effects (Glasgow et al., 2005). In this design, participants are subjected to both no-treatment and treatment conditions; comparison of these two conditions provides evidence needed to demonstrate covariation. Since participants serve as their own control, the potential confounding influence of their personal, health, or clinical characteristics is minimized (Lawlor et al., 2004). Further, the within-subject design requires a smaller sample size, in comparison to between-subject designs.

The within-subject, repeated measure design can be expanded to examine trends in the outcomes before and after implementation of the intervention. This is done in interrupted time series designs (Shadish et al., 2002), which are often used when the intervention targets a pre-existing group (e.g., introduction of a new health policy). The designs' features are:

1. Multiple assessments of the outcomes, at pre-specified time intervals, before and after implementation of the intervention. There is no clear agreement on the number of data points required for a time series design; 25–50 points for each period (i.e., 25–50 before and 25–50 after treatment) have been proposed. However, the number of data points is dependent on whether the time series is stationary or non-stationary. Stationary means that there is no trend over time, and that there is relatively minor fluctuation in values from one measurement to the next. In other words, the trend is fairly stable, with little variation around the line reflecting the trend. A non-stationary time series consists of values that vary considerably from one time point to the next, with little apparent pattern; such fluctuations represent seasonal variations or secular trends. Stationary time series require fewer data points to establish the patterns.
2. Delivery of the intervention to the targeted group.
3. Availability of outcome data across all time points before and after treatment implementation. It may be easier to use databases maintained by the pre-existing group (e.g., organization) than to prospectively collect the data within the context of a study with limited time and resources. The conceptual and operational definitions of the outcomes, and the instrument for outcome data collection, should be the same over time. Any change introduces error of measurement and hence fluctuations in values, which could yield invalid interpretation of the observed trends.

Time series have been used in behavioral studies including one participant and focusing on data amenable to repeated assessment such as objective data monitored continuously (e.g., pulse rate) and subjective data gathered with diaries. The administration of multi-item measures on multiple data points required in this design may not be practical and has the potential to introduce bias (testing effects).

The analysis in time series designs can take two forms. The first involves 'eyeball interpretation' and judgement of the outcome values plotted against time points, to determine if there is any trend before treatment implementation that is interrupted after delivery of the intervention, as depicted in Figure 6.6. Despite its simplicity, this form of analysis may not be reliable due to possible disagreement among judges on the extent of the observed effect. The second form relies on relatively sophisticated statistics to determine the effects of the intervention, quantified in the extent of change in the slope or intercept (disruption in the levels of outcomes) following the intervention. The statistical analyses (e.g., auto-regressive integrated moving average models, growth curve modeling, or linear mixed models) are complex and have to account for periodicity or seasonal variations.

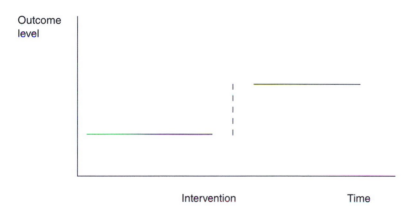

FIGURE 6.6 Visualization of interrupted time series

The advantages of the time series design relate to its use with a small sample, even in single case studies; inclusion and comparison of no-treatment and post-treatment outcome data, which reflects the counterfactual for determining causal effects of the intervention; and ability to examine sustainability of the intervention effects. History is a potential threat in time series design, which can be addressed by monitoring and documenting events that take place at different time points; these could be accounted for when interpreting the trends observed before and after implementation of the intervention.

Summary

- In some situations, randomization of participants to the intervention and comparison treatment may not be feasible, acceptable, or desirable
- Advanced designs that can be used in these situations are:

  o Cluster randomized trial: used to minimize contamination of the intervention, when the intervention targets groups. Randomization is done at the cluster level; more than one site is allocated to each study group to avoid confounding the effects of the intervention with those of the cluster
  o Cross-over design: used when evaluating different treatments in one sample, to address the ethical issue of withholding treatment when needed by participants; participants are randomized to different treatment at different points in time
  o Quasi-experimental design: used when randomization is not possible. They are of two types: 1) between-subject designs: involve intervention and comparison group but non-randomization of participants, and 2) within-subject designs: involve one group of participants who receive the intervention and repeated assessment of outcomes before and after its implementation

7

ADVANCES IN INTERVENTION EVALUATION DESIGNS: PRAGMATIC AND PREFERENCE TRIALS

The designs presented in Chapter 6 are an alternative to the RCT, used in situations when randomization is not feasible, acceptable, or desirable. They have features similar to those of the RCT, except the method of allocation to treatment. Thus, their findings may still be of limited applicability to the context of day-to-day practice. Pragmatic and preference trials are proposed to generate evidence of relevance to practice. In this chapter, the characteristics of these trials are described. The rationale for using them to evaluate the effectiveness of interventions (Phases 4 and 5) is explained. The empirical evidence supporting their utility is synthesized.

PRAGMATIC TRIALS

Pragmatic (Zwarenstein and Treweek, 2009) or practical clinical (Tunis et al., 2003) trials are advocated to overcome the limitations of the RCT design in evaluating the effectiveness of health interventions under the real world conditions of day-to-day practice (Karanicolas et al., 2009). Pragmatic trials provide empirical evidence regarding the effectiveness of interventions that is generalizable to the practice setting, is clinically relevant, and informs real world treatment decisions (Horn et al., 2005; Methodology Committee of the Patient-Centered Outcomes Research Institute [PCORI], 2012; Pincus, 2002). Pragmatic or practical clinical trials (PCTs) address questions that extend and expand the question dealt in RCT: Does the intervention, as compared to no-intervention, work? PCTs are concerned with practical questions related to the benefits, risks, and cost of the intervention compared to alternative treatments for the same health problem (Nallamothu et al., 2008), in patients seen in day-to-day practice and presenting with diverse personal, health and clinical profile and multiple concurrent health conditions (Methodology Committee of the PCORI, 2012). They are implemented with flexibility to account for contextual factors inherent in the life circumstances of clients and in the environment of day-to-day practice, by healthcare professionals with different competencies and interactional style. In general, PCTs represent a Phase 4, real world test of the intervention effects (Maclure, 2009; Oxman et al., 2009; Thorpe et al., 2009).

The current state of the science converges on delineating the features of the PCT that are important for addressing the practical questions about the intervention effectiveness. However, there is no consensus on the most appropriate designs and methods to use. A range of experimental, quasi-experimental or cohort, and observational designs are considered suitable for evaluating the effectiveness of interventions (Nallamothu et al., 2008; Sox et al., 2010). A mix of designs such as the cohort multiple RCT (Relton et al., 2010) and methods (quantitative and qualitative) may be necessary to provide relevant answers to the various practical questions of concern.

Features of the PCT

Five main features are distinctive of the PCT: sampling diverse patients, selecting a variety of practice settings, comparing clinically relevant alternative treatments, assessing a range of outcomes over a long follow-up period (Horn et al., 2005; Tunis et al., 2003), and involving all healthcare professionals in intervention implementation (Thorpe et al., 2009). The application of these features demands an in-depth understanding of the intervention theory, awareness of the real world practice setting, and a meticulous plan for data collection and analysis that takes into consideration the naturally occurring variability in clients, healthcare professionals, settings, and treatments that influences outcome achievement.

Sampling diverse patient populations

To enhance the relevance of the findings to the real world, the sample in a PCT has to be representative of the subgroups forming the target population seen in day-to-day practice. Sampling clients presenting with a range of characteristics is important to determine who or which subgroups of the target population engage in, comply with, and benefit to what extent from the intervention. The achievement of a representative sample is facilitated by pre-specifying a set of broad eligibility criteria (Glasgow et al., 2005; Zwarenstein and Treweek, 2009). These consist of general inclusion criteria that ensure selection of typical clients who experience the health problem, and minimal exclusion criteria that reflect characteristics of patients for whom the intervention is contraindicated. In fact, Pincus (2002) suggested the elimination of exclusion criteria in a PCT in order to obtain a sample that represents clients with different personal profiles, levels of severity and beliefs about the health problem targeted by the intervention, comorbid physical or psychosocial conditions, levels of motivation to engage in and adhere to the intervention, and concurrent treatments. The use of broad eligibility criteria increases the heterogeneity of participants' baseline characteristics, and exposure and response to the intervention. This heterogeneity is accounted for through subgroup or moderator analysis (using hierarchical linear models) aimed at determining the reproducibility or robustness of the intervention effects in theoretically and clearly defined subgroups of the target population (Lowenstein and Castro, 2009; Peduzzi et al., 2002).

Selecting a variety of practice settings

A variety of practice settings are selected for participation in a PCT (Glasgow et al., 2005; Horn et al., 2005; Tunis et al., 2003). The chosen settings have a range of physical and psychosocial features that facilitate the accrual of different subgroups forming the target population in adequate numbers and that represent contextual factors with the potential to influence implementation and effectiveness of the intervention. The setting features relate to factors such as geographic location, type of community served, type of services offered, mix of healthcare professionals providing the services, availability of physical resources, and organizational culture. The feature for which variability is sought depends on the characteristics of the target population and of the intervention, and on a thorough understanding of the extent to which the environment interferes with intervention implementation. Ensuring diversity in the contextual features and examining their contribution to intervention implementation and outcomes assist in the identification of those features (and the level at which they should be present) that facilitate or hinder the effectiveness of the intervention. This knowledge guides practice-related decisions regarding: 1) whether or not the intervention can be applied locally; 2) resources required for its implementation in day-to-day practice; 3) modifications to be made in the intervention to facilitate its translation into a particular setting in a way that fits with the setting's unique features; 4) the healthcare professionals who can deliver the intervention independently or collaboratively; and 5) the resources to make available to clients in support of their enactment and adherence to the intervention.

Comparing clinically relevant alternative treatments

Whereas comparing the intervention to no or comparison treatment is important for determining its causal effects on the outcomes, the results of such a comparison are not useful in informing treatment-related decisions in the context of practice. In the latter context, denying treatments is considered unethical and professionally unacceptable, unless no-treatment is a viable alternative (such as watchful waiting or monitoring of early stage benign prostate cancer). Healthcare professionals are expected to intervene by implementing treatments in common use, forming 'usual care'. Healthcare professionals want to know the effectiveness of the experimental intervention as compared to the treatments available and in current use, or the effectiveness of categories of interventions with theoretically different mechanisms of action (e.g., cognitive behavioral therapy vs. interpersonal therapy), or the effectiveness of the intervention as compared to similar alternatives (e.g., two behavioral interventions for the management of insomnia: stimulus control therapy vs. sleep restriction therapy). Accordingly, PCTs involve the comparison of clinically relevant alternative treatments. The comparison is done 'head-to-head' (Holtz, 2007) to determine the benefits, adverse effects, and cost of alternative treatments. The results inform clinical and policy decision makers of which treatment works best and is most cost-effective (Sox et al., 2010).

The clinically relevant alternative treatments evaluated in PCT need to be feasible and inexpensive, if they are to be translated and used in day-to-day practice (Glasgow et al., 2005; Grapow et al., 2006; Nallamothu et al., 2008; Tunis et al., 2003). This implies that the treatment protocol is rather simple to carry out by healthcare professionals with different levels of expertise, and is easy to implement within the reality of day-to-day operations that are often characterized as having limited physical and human resources; short and infrequent encounters between healthcare professionals and clients; and multiple competing demands. Further, the treatment alternatives are implemented with flexibility, as is usually done in practice (Thorpe et al., 2009; Zwarenstein and Treweek, 2009). Healthcare professionals, independently or in collaboration with clients, select the intervention components, activities, mode of delivery, and dose that are most appropriate to individual clients' condition. Similarly, variability in clients' enactment and adherence with the intervention is acknowledged as part of what happens in the real world. Thus, no additional remedial strategies are incorporated in the PCT to improve fidelity of treatment implementation by healthcare professionals and clients. However, fidelity of implementation is monitored and pertinent data are recorded. Analysis of these data provides information on 1) treatment alternatives that are easily applied in practice and well received by healthcare professionals and clients, yet have robust effects despite variability in implementation; 2) aspects of the treatments that can be modified without affecting their effectiveness and the reasons for those modifications; 3) client subgroups requiring adaptation of the treatment components, activities, mode of delivery, and dose; and 4) factors that influence treatment implementation and effectiveness. Ultimately, the information provides directions for developing algorithms that guide tailoring of the intervention to the needs of individual clients or subgroups of the target population.

Assessing a range of outcomes over time

In a PCT, the impact of the intervention on a range of outcomes is evaluated. The outcomes are of relevance to different stakeholder groups including clients, healthcare professionals, and decision makers (Sox et al., 2010; Tunis et al., 2003). Different outcome categories have been suggested and are described in Chapter 12. Whereas assessment of a range of outcomes is important for determining the utility of the intervention, the selection of outcomes is done carefully to capture the immediate and the ultimate effects, as hypothesized in the theory underlying the intervention. The selected outcomes also must be appropriately anticipated of all clinically relevant alternative treatments included in the PCT, forming the criteria in the comparison of treatment effectiveness and hence, in the identification of the most beneficial treatment (i.e., one demonstrating significant improvement in most immediate and ultimate outcomes).

Outcomes are measured before and after treatment implementation, as is done in an RCT. They are assessed at regular time intervals, over an extended follow-up period (Thorpe et al., 2009). The time intervals are specified based on the expected pattern of change in the outcomes (which indicates points in time at which change is anticipated), and the need to minimize measurement burden on healthcare professionals and clients (which implies that outcome assessment is planned at regularly scheduled healthcare visits). The follow-up period is extended reasonably to examine the sustainability of the effects and to explore possible adverse reactions that may arise with long-term application of the treatment. Outcome analysis is geared toward demonstrating not only statistical significance, but most importantly, clinical relevance of the intervention effects (Tunis et al., 2003). Clinical relevance is examined by: estimating the magnitude of the intervention effects (i.e., comparing the post-test outcomes for clients exposed to the intervention and the alternative treatment in a between-subject design; comparing the pre-test and post-test outcomes for clients who received the intervention in a within-subject design); reporting the percentage of clients who received the intervention and the alternative treatment and experience improvement in the outcomes; and socially validating the extent to which the observed changes in outcomes are meaningful (Hark and Stump, 2008).

Involving all healthcare professionals in treatment delivery

Healthcare professionals employed in the practice settings chosen for the PCT are involved in the implementation of the intervention and alternative treatments, in order to determine transferability of the intervention to day-to-day practice. Therefore, the healthcare professionals entrusted with treatment implementation in a PCT differ in their personal and professional qualities, interactional style, and awareness, beliefs, values and perception of the intervention and alternative treatments. The healthcare professionals are trained in the intervention. Often, the training is offered through continuing professional development workshops, which tend to focus on the conceptualization of the intervention more so than its hands-on application. Differences in healthcare professionals' characteristics yield variability in the implementation of the intervention, and in the style of the healthcare professionals interacting with clients. Variability in treatment delivery is associated with variability in outcome achievement. Therefore, the potential influence of healthcare professionals is examined in a PCT. The following are methodological issues to consider:

1. The number of healthcare professionals providing treatment should be adequate and balanced across treatment alternatives to attain sufficient statistical power and to obtain meaningful estimates of their influence on treatment implementation and their interactional style or working alliance.

2. The number of clients receiving treatment should also be balanced across healthcare professionals as well as treatment alternatives. Comparable numbers and characteristics of clients assigned to different healthcare professionals and treatment alternatives reduce selection bias and confounding (Lutz et al., 2007). Assignment has to reflect and to minimize interruptions to the process of client assignment followed in day-to-day practice.

3. The healthcare professionals are encouraged to provide all treatments in order to dismantle the influence of healthcare professionals from the effects of treatments. This is possible in a crossed design in which each healthcare professional is requested to offer the intervention and the alternative treatment to clients assigned to their care (Staines et al., 2006). This design creates variability in the intervention that is not confounded by variability in the healthcare professional. Each source of variability induces its unique effects on outcome achievement, which permits examination of the interventionist influence separately from the treatment effects on the outcomes. The use of a crossed design demands the availability of healthcare professionals who have favorable perception of the intervention and alternative treatments and are willing to gain the competencies needed for delivering all treatments (Sidani and Braden, 2011). In the practice settings, healthcare professionals may ascribe to a particular treatment orientation and develop expertise in its application. Therefore, the influence of healthcare professionals on outcome achievement is examined.

4. The allocation of patients to treatments and healthcare professionals may not be feasible at random (Glasgow et al., 2005), within the context of day-to-day practice. Different assignment methods (see Chapter 10) that are or are not based on client self-selection can be applied.

5. Implementation of the intervention and alternative treatments by healthcare professionals and clients is monitored, and pertinent information documented. The extent of variability in treatment delivery and the association between treatment implementation and improvement in the outcomes are examined using multi-level structural equation modeling.

Advantages and Limitations of PCT

The advantages of the PCT design relate to the generation of empirical evidence that maintains external and ecological validity and that addresses questions of relevance to clinical and policy decision making (Torgerson and Torgerson, 2004). The inclusion of a large sample representative of different subgroups forming the target population and the conduct of subgroup or moderator analysis provide information on the profile of patients who most benefit from the intervention. Inclusion of different practice settings points to the reproducibility of the intervention effects in contexts with variable human and material resources. Investigating complex, clinically relevant alternative treatments, delivered by different healthcare professionals, allowing flexibility in their implementation, and comparing their effectiveness in producing the outcomes over time determine the robustness of the intervention effects, the dose range that is optimal for producing the outcomes, the characteristics of healthcare professionals who provide the intervention competently and efficiently, and the utility (benefits vs. risks) of the intervention relative to alternative treatments (Methodology Committee of the PCORI, 2012; Relton et al., 2010).

Despite its advantages, the PCT design has limitations. The design and conduct of a PCT require large amounts of human and material resources, effort, and time to completion (Nallamothu et al., 2008). Explanation of the trial intent and negotiation of the support needed from the participating sites (e.g., release of healthcare professionals for training, uptake of the new intervention, referral of clients) are necessary but time consuming steps. Clarification of responsibilities ascribed to healthcare professionals and research staff is important. Healthcare professionals' awareness that their performance is monitored alters their actual implementation of the intervention and alternative treatments with the potential of Hawthorne effect. The need for research staff to track assignment of clients to treatment and healthcare professionals makes the staff aware of the treatment received, which increases the potential for ascertainment bias during post-test outcome assessment (Torgerson and Torgerson, 2004). Clients may have unfavorable perception of and thus refuse the treatments offered in a PCT (Relton et al., 2010). The clustering of patients within treatments and healthcare professionals affects estimates of the intervention effects if not accounted for in the statistical analysis. The alternative treatments may not be theoretically and operationally distinct, and therefore may be expected to yield small differences in levels of improvement in the outcomes. Last, the variability in treatment implementation across clients, professionals, and settings, if not appropriately accounted for in the data analysis, makes it difficult to detect significant, large intervention effects (Tunis et al., 2003).

PREFERENCE TRIALS

Preference or partially randomized clinical trials (PRCTs) overcome some limitations of the RCT in evaluating the effectiveness of interventions. They address clients' preferences for treatment, which if ignored, has the potential to introduce bias. Also, ignoring preferences does not reflect what happens in the practice setting: clients demand an active role in treatment decision making; they want to be informed of alternative treatments available for the management of the health problem, and to choose the treatment (Van der Wejden et al., 2010).

Role of Preferences

Preferences for treatment reflect patients' choices for treatment, that is, the treatment they desire and want to receive to manage the health problem (Stalmeier et al., 2007). Preferences affect the initiation, enactment, adherence, and satisfaction with the allocated treatment, and outcome achievement. If not accounted for, treatment preferences present threats that limit the external validity and weaken the internal validity of an intervention evaluation study (Howard and Thornicroft, 2006; Sidani et al., 2009a).

Preferences as threats to external validity

Preferences for treatment affect clients' enrollment in an intervention evaluation trial, resulting in a low enrollment rate and non-consent bias, which limit the representativeness of the sample and the generalizability of the findings. Clients contemplating entry into a trial are aware of different treatments available for the management of the health problem. They acquire treatment-related knowledge from different sources including written (e.g., websites, articles in newspapers) and oral (e.g., TV or radio health talk shows) media; discussion with significant others and healthcare professionals; personal experience with treatment; and the process of obtaining informed consent within the context of a trial (Mills et al., 2011). The ethical conduct of research requires informing eligible participants of the treatments under evaluation and describing the activities which comprise the treatment as well as their risks and benefits. This knowledge shapes participants' perception of the treatments under investigation. Treatments viewed as acceptable are favored and preferred (Epstein and Peters, 2009; Mills et al., 2011).

Evidence indicates that the majority ($\geq$ 100 per cent) of participants have clear preferences for the treatments under investigation. For instance, Raue et al. (2009) reported that 50–86 per cent of persons with depressive disorders prefer a psychosocial, as compared to pharmacological, treatment. The Preference Collaborative Review Group (2009) reviewed 11 trials and found the percentage of participants with a preference to vary between 16 per cent and 85 per cent, with a mean of 56 per cent. Participants with a strong preference for a particular treatment may decline enrollment in a trial in which allocation to treatment is done on the basis of chance (i.e., randomization) or other principles (e.g., assignment to next available healthcare professionals, which may be followed in the PCT design). When not involved in treatment selection, persons with a strong preference opt for not participating in the study because they are not willing to take the risk of being assigned to the non-preferred treatment (Ellis, 2000; Floyd and Moyer, 2010; TenHave et al., 2003). This point is well supported empirically. Concern with being allocated to the non-preferred treatment was the reason for refusing enrollment in RCTs evaluating different treatments including adjuvant therapy for breast cancer (Stevens and Ahmedzai, 2004), school-based sex education (Oakley et al., 2003), brief physiotherapy for back pain (Klaber-Moffett et al., 1999), early prostate cancer treatment (North West Uro-Oncology

Group, 2002), treatment for depression (Kwan et al., 2010), a support group for breast cancer survivors (Coward, 2002), and comprehensive treatment for mental health problems (Macias et al., 2005). Across these studies, the percentage of participants who refused randomization to treatment and therefore declined enrollment ranged from 10 per cent (Oakley et al., 2003) to 95 per cent (North West Uro-Oncology Group, 2002). In addition, King et al. (2005) estimated the percentage of persons who accept randomization to vary between 26 per cent and 88 per cent, further confirming that a large percentage (up to 74 per cent) refuses it. With the high percentage of persons refusing participation, the rate of study enrollment is low, potentially yielding a small sample size and reduced statistical power to detect significant intervention effects, particularly when resources for extending recruitment efforts are constrained. Sample size inadequacy and non-consent bias jeopardize the validity of inferences and their relevance to all subgroups of the target population.

With most persons with preferences declining enrollment for fear of allocation to non-preferred treatment, there is a high risk for non-consent bias. Non-participants differ from participants in at least two characteristics: preferences for treatment and unwillingness to be randomized. Thus, participants represent a subgroup of the target population that has no preferences for treatment and accept random allocation to treatment. An accumulation of empirical evidence demonstrates differences in personal and health characteristics of persons who do and do not enroll in an intervention evaluation trial. Results of multiple studies indicate that participants and non-participants differ in personal, psychological, and lifestyle characteristics, encompassing employment status, transportation difficulties, safety concerns, and poor health status (e.g., Harris and Dyson, 2001; Heaman, 2001). For instance, Dwight-Johnson et al. (2001) found that individuals who enrolled in an RCT comparing medication and psychotherapy for depression had higher levels of education, were more likely to be female and older, and perceived the treatment under evaluation as more acceptable than non-enrollees. Sidani et al. (2010) reported that enrollees in a trial of behavioral therapies for the management of insomnia presented with a lower level of insomnia severity than non-enrollees. Similarly, King et al. (2005) reported that, compared to those with no preferences for medical or surgical treatments, persons with clear preferences were more likely to be younger, women, well educated, white, and employed. In addition, emerging evidence suggests direct associations between participants' personal, clinical, and psychological characteristics, beliefs about the health problem, and preferences for treatment. For instance, the results of several studies (e.g., Bedi et al., 2000; Bluestein et al., 2011; Cooper et al., 2003; Gum et al., 2006; Heit et al., 2003; Vuorma et al., 2003) are consistent in showing a relationship between severity of the problem and treatment preferences. Participants experiencing high levels of problem severity tend to favor intensive treatments, even if intrusive, that may offer fast and effective relief.

Differences in the profiles of persons with and without preferences, who are and are not willing to be randomized to treatments, limit the representativeness of the sample. Participants form a subgroup of the target population, whose perception, initiation, enactment, adherence, and response to the treatment are unique. Therefore, the applicability of the study results to other subgroups of the target population and encountered in the context of day-to-day practice is constrained (Leykin et al., 2007).

Preferences as threats to internal validity

Persons with preferences may decide to enter the trial, even if the trial design does not account for their treatment preferences. They consider enrollment in the study as the only opportunity to receive the treatment of choice. Participants in an RCT realize that with randomization, they have a 50 per cent chance of being assigned to the preferred treatment (Bradley, 1993), whereas participants in studies not involving randomization have high hopes of getting the favored treatment. However, participants with preferences enrolled in a trial react to the allocated treatment differently. The reactions affect participants' initiation, engagement and adherence to treatment, and achievement of outcomes (Bottomley, 1997; Leykin et al., 2007), thereby weakening internal validity.

Through randomization or other assignment methods, participants are allocated to either the treatment of choice or to the non-preferred treatment. These two subgroups of participants exhibit different reactions. In the first subgroup, participants receive the preferred treatment; they are satisfied with the allocated treatment and respond favorably. They are enthusiastic and motivated to initiate and actively engage in treatment; they enact the treatment recommendations appropriately and adhere to them adequately. Appropriate enactment and adherence to treatment induce improvement in the immediate and ultimate outcomes (Lewis et al., 2006). In the second subgroup, participants are allocated to the non-preferred treatment; they are dissatisfied with the allocated treatment and respond unfavorably. The responses of participants deprived of their preferred treatment take two forms: withdrawal from the study or development of a sense of demoralization. Participants who do not get the treatment they want are disappointed and decide to drop out of the treatment or the study to seek treatment elsewhere (Kwan et al., 2010). Attrition is a major threat to internal validity (see Chapters 2 and 9). Of importance here is differential attrition associated with the withdrawal of participants with a particular personal or health profile or with strong treatment preferences (regardless of which treatment is preferred). It results in sample bias in that the sample represents a subgroup of the target population. The observed intervention effects may not be reproducible in other subgroups. Specifically, participants with preferences differ from those with no preferences on various baseline characteristics. Differential attrition introduces non-comparability on baseline characteristics which confounds the intervention effects, threatening the validity of the causal relationship between the intervention and the outcomes (Sidani et al., 2009a). Participants assigned to the non-preferred treatment develop a sense of demoralization. They feel 'hurt, disappointed and perhaps betrayed' (Floyd and Moyer, 2010) because they were deprived the power and control to make a choice, and hence to get the treatment they want (Leykin et al., 2007). They are no longer motivated to initiate, engage, enact, and adhere to treatment, and do not experience the hypothesized improvement in outcomes (Huibers et al., 2004). Further, this subgroup of participants report intolerance of treatment recommendations, particularly those requiring significant changes in behavior or lifestyle. They do not carry out all recommendations or at the pre-specified dose level. Last, demoralized participants may believe that the allocated treatment will not work. This belief may engender psychological reactions resulting in negative placebo effects (Floyd and Moyer, 2010), manifested in worsening of the outcomes over time.

The location of the two subgroups of participants (those who do and do not receive the preferred treatment) within the intervention and the comparison groups may bias the estimates of the intervention effects. When the number of participants receiving matched treatment (congruent with their preference) and the number of participants receiving mismatched treatment are balanced between the intervention and comparison groups, then the intervention effects are underestimated. The underestimation is due to the following mechanism: participants exposed to matched treatment are satisfied and motivated to enact and comply with the treatment; they report improvement in the outcomes. In contrast, participants receiving mismatched treatment are dissatisfied and do not enact the treatment; they experience no changes in the outcomes. The response to treatment of participants with matched and mismatched treatment differs, generating an increased level of variability in post-test outcomes within each of the intervention and the comparison groups. The high within-group variability reduces the power to detect significant intervention effects. When the number of participants with matched and mismatched treatment is unbalanced or unequal between the intervention and comparison groups, the following situations may arise:

1. If most participants in the intervention group receive mismatched treatment, then they may not demonstrate the hypothesized changes in the outcomes, or they may experience worsening of the outcomes, associated with a sense of demoralization. The intervention is claimed ineffective, potentially leading to type II error and abandonment of the intervention.
2. If most participants in the intervention group receive matched treatment, then they experience high levels of outcome improvement that result in large between-group differences. Therefore, the intervention effects are overestimated.
3. If most participants in the comparison group receive mismatched treatment, then they report no changes or worsening in the outcomes that can contribute to large between-group differences and possible overestimation of the intervention effects.
4. If most participants in the comparison group receive matched treatment, then they experience some changes in the outcomes that reduce the extent of between-group differences and decrease the power to detect significant intervention effects or yield an underestimation of the intervention effects.

Designs that Account for Treatment Preferences

Two general approaches have been used to determine the influence of participants' preferences for treatment on the intervention effects. The first approach focuses on assessing preferences, and examining or controlling statistically their effects on outcomes; this approach has been applied within the context of an RCT (Torgerson et al., 1996). The second approach accounts for preferences experimentally: participants are allocated to treatments on the basis of chance or preference, or a combination of both. This has been illustrated with the partially randomized clinical trial originally proposed by Bradley (1993) and the two-stage partially randomized clinical trial described by Rücker (1989).

Randomized controlled/clinical trial (RCT)

In an RCT, participants' preferences for treatment are assessed but are ignored in that all participants, regardless of their preferences, are randomized to the intervention or comparison group. The influence of preferences on treatment enactment, adherence, and outcomes is examined for participants who receive matched and those who receive mismatched treatment. The implementation of this design involves the assessment of treatment preferences after obtaining written consent and collecting baseline data, but before randomization. Eliciting preferences is done prior to randomization and exposure to treatment to identify participants' choice that is untainted by interventionists' and other participants' attitudes toward treatment expressed during treatment implementation (e.g., in group sessions) and by personal experience of outcomes. Sepucha and Ozanne (2010) stated that assessment of preferences upon treatment completion may result in bias introduced by reported improvement or no change in outcomes; that is, participants indicate preference for the treatment they receive if found effective in managing the health problem (e.g., Gum et al., 2006). Once the treatment of preference is identified and recorded, participants are randomized to the intervention and the comparison groups, and the RCT proceeds as usual. The effects of treatment preferences are examined at the stage of data analysis. Within each treatment group, participants are categorized as having a matched or mismatched treatment. The match variable is considered a between-subject factor in the statistical analysis aimed at determining differences in treatment enactment, adherence, and outcomes among the following four subgroups: 1) participants in the intervention group with matched treatment, who receive the intervention which is the treatment of their choice; 2) participants in the intervention group with mismatched treatment, who receive the intervention which is their non-preferred treatment; 3) participants in the comparison group who receive treatment (e.g., usual care) which is identified as their choice; and 4) participants in the comparison group who receive the treatment identified as non-preferred. Significant differences across the four subgroups (i.e., treatment-by-match interaction effect in a two-way analysis of variance) quantify the influence of treatment preferences. Participants with no preferences are either excluded or represented as a fifth subgroup in the analysis. The studies conducted by Torgerson et al. (1996), Klaber-Moffett et al. (1999), and Leykin et al. (2007) illustrate the application of this design to examine the effects of treatment preferences on outcomes.

The use of the RCT design to determine the contribution of treatment preferences is advantageous: with randomization of participants, selection bias is minimized, which reduces the potential for confounding and increases the confidence in attributing the outcomes to intervention and matching of treatment. The limitations of this design in investigating the influence of preferences are related to:

1. Ignoring preferences: the fact that participants are requested to identify the treatment of their choice, but ignoring this choice through the application of randomization, may not be well received by participants and researchers; it may be considered unethical.
2. Participants' reactions: as explained in previous sections, participants may be randomly allocated to the preferred or non-preferred treatment, inducing favorable or unfavorable reactions respectively; the reactions impact participants' enactment and adherence to treatment, completion of the study, and outcome achievement.
3. Sample size: the sample size calculation for an RCT focuses on attaining adequate power to detect significant intervention effects based on comparing the intervention and comparison treatments; the resulting sample size may not be large enough to detect a significant treatment-by-match interaction effect that reflects the influence of treatment preferences (Preference Collaborative Review Group, 2009).

Partially randomized clinical trial

In a partially randomized clinical trial (PRCT), participants' preferences for treatment are accounted for in the process of assigning them to the intervention and the comparison groups. Participants are actively involved in treatment selection which mirrors what happens in the context of day-to-day practice. Similar to the RCT design, assessment of treatment preferences is done systematically and prior to exposure to treatment. This timing is necessary because the results of this assessment guide allocation of participants to treatment. Participants are informed of the treatment options, and are requested to indicate whether or not they have a preference. Participants stating they have no preference for any treatment are randomized to the intervention and the comparison groups. Participants expressing a preference are asked of their choice (i.e., the treatment they want to have). They are allocated to the selected treatment. This process of treatment allocation yields four subgroups: 1) participants randomized to the intervention; 2) participants randomly assigned to the comparison group; 3) participants allocated to the intervention on the basis of preference; and 4) participants allocated to the comparison group on the basis of preference. As is done in a typical intervention evaluation study, data on the treatment implementation and outcomes are collected from all participants at the pre-specified time points. The treatment group (intervention vs. comparison) and the method of treatment allocation (random vs. preference) are included as between-subject factors in the data analysis. A significant treatment-by-method of allocation interaction effect supports the contribution of preferences. For instance, significant differences in the post-test outcomes between participants allocated to the intervention by chance or by preference indicate the extent to which accounting for preferences influences outcome achievement. The application of the PRCT is illustrated in Coward (2002).

Allocation to preferred treatment is the PRCT feature underlying its advantage. Providing participants the treatment of their choice induces favorable reactions, satisfaction, enactment, and adherence to treatment and improvement in outcomes. These reactions are also experienced by participants with no preferences and randomized to treatment; they are willing to receive any treatment. Accordingly, this pattern of assignment may mitigate unfavorable reactions such as resentful demoralization among participants randomized to what they perceive as the less desirable treatment. In addition, allocating participants to the preferred treatment offers the opportunity to model the context of practice in which patients make choices among available treatments and to determine the effectiveness of the intervention under this condition, yielding findings that are relevant to and potentially reproducible in day-to-day practice. It is an attractive design feature that enhances enrollment of participants with strong preferences (who may decline enrollment in an RCT because of unwillingness to be randomized to the non-preferred treatment); this reduces the potential for self-selection bias, unrepresentativeness of the study sample, and non-accrual of the required sample size. Finally the method contributes positively to initiation, enactment, satisfaction, and adherence to treatment and outcome achievement (Howard and Thornicroft, 2006; TenHave et al., 2003).

Two limitations of the PRCT have been identified. First is the high probability of having unbalanced sizes across the four subgroups (defined by type of treatment received and method of treatment allocation). This happens if the majority of participants indicate a choice; they will be assigned to treatment on the basis of preference, leaving a small proportion of participants to be randomized, as illustrated by the findings reported by Coward (2002). Similarly, the number of participants with preferences to particular treatments is not equal. For instance, 50–86 per cent of patients with depressive disorder prefer a psychosocial over a pharmacological treatment (Raue et al., 2009). Unbalanced numbers of participants across the subgroups preclude meaningful comparisons and limit quantification of the influence of preferences on treatment implementation and outcomes (TenHave et al., 2003). Second, the process of assignment to treatment followed in a PRCT introduces non-comparability of participants' characteristics assessed at baseline across subgroups; these baseline differences in personal and clinical characteristics, and in pre-test outcomes are due to known differences in the profiles of persons who do and do not have preferences, and who have preferences for particular treatments. Baseline differences, resulting in selection bias, serve as potential confounds of the treatment and preference effects on outcomes (Howard and Thornicroft, 2006).

Two-stage, partially randomized clinical trial

The two-stage partially randomized clinical trial is proposed to overcome the limitations of the PRCT. It combines the benefit of randomization in enhancing group comparability on baseline characteristics, and of accounting for preferences in allocation to treatment. The feature of this design is the two-stage process for assignment to treatment, which is initiated after collecting relevant data at baseline. In the first stage of this process, participants are randomized to one of two arms of the trial: random and preference. Randomization at this stage promotes the comparability of the participants on pre-test variables, in the two arms of the trial. In the second stage the process takes a different form within each trial arm. In the random arm, participants are randomized to the intervention or comparison group, as is done in an RCT. In the preference arm, participants' preferences are assessed and those with preferences are allocated to the treatment of choice. If some participants indicate no preference, then they are randomized to groups. The design yields four subgroups defined in terms of both the treatment option (intervention and comparison) and the method of assignment (random and preferences). The results of subgroup comparisons provide the evidence supporting the influence of treatment preferences. The application of the two-stage PRCT is illustrated in Floyd and Moyer (2010).

The advantages of the two-stage PRCT relate to the randomization of participants to the trial arms, which maintains balanced sizes and comparable characteristics of participants across the four subgroups. Balanced sizes allow for meaningful comparisons between participants in the random and preference arms, and baseline comparability increases the confidence in validly attributing differences in treatment implementation and outcomes to the intervention and the method of assignment. However, the two-stage PRCT is expensive. It requires human and material resources to recruit and enroll a large number of participants necessary to attain adequate power to detect significant main and interaction effects for intervention and method of assignment (Sidani and Braden, 2011). Additional limitations include:

1. Randomization to the random and preference arms in the first stage could be problematic. Through the process of obtaining participants' consent, participants may become aware of the two arms. Most may want to be allocated to the preference arm and may react unfavorably if this does not happen (Rücker, 1989).
2. Although a balanced sample is achieved at the first stage (assignment to the random and preference arms), this is not anticipated at the second stage in both arms. Whereas randomization yields an equal number of participants in the intervention and the comparison groups, preference allocation may result in unequal numbers.
3. The comparability on baseline characteristics of participants allocated to the intervention and comparison groups on the basis of preference may not be achieved due to differences in the personal and health profile of persons with preferences to particular treatments.
4. In the second stage, randomization to treatments may induce unfavorable reactions, attrition, non-adherence to treatment, and poor outcomes.

Empirical Evidence

Emerging empirical evidence supports the advantages of preference trials in promoting enrollment in an intervention evaluation study, in reducing attrition, in enhancing treatment enactment or adherence, and in improving outcomes. The evidence derives from individual studies and systematic reviews or meta-analyses, and is presented next.

Influence of preferences on enrollment

Persons participating in a preference trial are aware they may be given the treatment of choice. This method of treatment assignment is appealing to persons who would have declined enrollment in an intervention evaluation for fear of getting the non-preferred treatment. Accounting for preferences in treatment allocation is expected to enhance enrollment rate and the representativeness of the sample. However, the available evidence is inconclusive in supporting this claim. Janevic et al. (2003) examined the enrollment rate in the random and preference arms of a PCT that evaluated the effectiveness of two educational interventions for the management of heart disease. No difference was reported in the enrollment rate in the random (36 per cent) and the preference (38 per cent) arms. Sidani et al. (2010) found a higher enrollment rate in an RCT (92.4 per cent) than a PRCT (44.8 per cent) of behavioral therapies for the management of insomnia. In contrast, the findings of Awad et al. (2000) showed a significant difference in the refusal rates observed in the random (30 per cent) and the preference (3 per cent) arms of the trial of treatments for the management of endentulism (i.e., loss of teeth). Similarly, King et al. (2005) conducted a systematic review of 23 PCTs investigating medical and surgical interventions. The enrollment rate varied between 50 per cent and 100 per cent, which led the researchers to conclude that accounting for preferences in treatment allocation reduced barriers (related to fear of not getting the treatment of choice) and enhanced enrollment.

Whereas no study specifically examined the representativeness of the sample obtained in PCTs, a few compared the profile of participants in the random and the preference arms. The results of these comparisons are not consistent. In two studies, no differences were found in the demographic and health characteristics of participants in the random and preference arms (Floyd and Moyer, 2010; Janevic et al., 2003). The results of King et al.'s (2005) systematic review revealed differences between the two arms on at least one characteristic; such differences were reported in 9 of 20 trials. Sidani et al. (2010) evaluated the comparability on socio-demographic and clinical characteristics of persons with insomnia who did and did not enroll in an RCT or in a PCT of behavioral therapies for insomnia. The results showed statistically significant differences between enrollees and non-enrollees on one characteristic in the RCT and four characteristics in the PRCT; the differences on the remaining baseline variables were of moderate-to-high magnitude in the RCT and of a small magnitude in the PCT, which may reflect differences in the sample size (smaller in the RCT than PCT).

Influence of preferences on attrition

Participants assigned to the non-preferred treatment are disappointed because they are deprived of the treatment of choice. They may withdraw from the intervention evaluation study. Giving the treatment of choice is a means to mitigate the influence of preferences on attrition. Results of individual and meta-analytic studies provide evidence supporting, to some extent, this claim. Three individual studies and one systematic review found comparable attrition rates for participants who received matched and those who received mismatched treatment. Lewis et al. (2006) evaluated the effectiveness of motivationally tailored print and motivationally tailored telephone treatment to promote physical activity. They reported no difference in the study completion rates at 6 and 12 month follow-up between matched and mismatched treatment groups. In an RCT comparing the effects of antidepressants to those of cognitive therapy, Leykin et al. (2007) found no difference in the attrition rate, estimated at 15 per cent, for participants having matched and mismatched treatment. In a similar study comparing pharmacotherapy and psychotherapy for depression, Raue et al. (2009) reported dropout rates of 10 per cent in the matched treatment subgroup and 13 per cent in the mismatched treatment subgroup at post-test, and of 17 per cent and 23 per cent respectively, at 3 month follow-up. Furthermore, the attrition rates were estimated at 10.5 per cent for participants in the random arm and 8.8 per cent for those in the preference arm of the PRCTs included in King et al.'s (2005) systematic review. In contrast, the findings of one individual study and two meta-analyses demonstrated lower attrition rates in the preference than the random arm of PCTs. Kwan et al. (2010) examined the role of preferences within an RCT of pharmacotherapy and psychotherapy for depression. The dropout rate was 46 per cent for participants randomized to the non-preferred therapy, 18.5 per cent for participants expressing no preference, and 5 per cent for participants randomized to the preferred therapy. The odds ratio was 7.19, implying higher odds of withdrawal if participants were randomized to the non-preferred treatment. The Preference Collaborative Review Group (2009) conducted a meta-analysis of 17 studies and pooled the data obtained from eight studies of musculoskeletal problems (e.g., lower back pain) that accounted for preferences in treatment allocation. They found a higher study completion rate for participants who were allocated to the treatment of choice than those who did not. In a recent meta-analysis of 35 trials that investigated the contribution of treatment preferences, Swift et al. (2011) indicated that 18 of these trials compared the attrition rates for participants with matched and mismatched treatments. They estimated the odds ratio at .59, implying that participants who received the preferred treatment were between one-third and one-half less likely to withdraw from the trial than those receiving the non-preferred treatment.

Influence of preferences on treatment initiation, enactment, and adherence

Participants allocated to the preferred treatment are satisfied and motivated to initiate, enact, and adhere to the treatment. The results of six individual studies were consistent in supporting this claim. Raue et al. (2009) reported that all participants (100 per cent) in a trial of psychotherapy and pharmacotherapy for depression, who were assigned to the preferred therapy, initiated treatment; however, 74 per cent of participants allocated to incongruent therapy initiated treatment. Macias et al. (2005) found that participants assigned to the preferred intervention for the management of mental health problems, compared to those randomized to treatment, engaged in most intervention activities. Raue et al. (2009) also found higher adherence in matched than mismatched subgroups. Kwan et al. (2010) also reported a higher proportion of participants with matched, as compared to mismatched, treatment attended a large number of treatment visits. Similar findings were observed by Bedi et al. (2000), Hitchcock Noël et al. (1998), and Janevic et al. (2003): participants allocated to the treatment of choice attended a larger number of the planned intervention sessions.

Influence of preferences on outcomes

The direct influence of treatment preferences on outcomes has been examined by comparing the post-test outcomes for participants in the intervention and the comparison groups with matched vs. mismatched treatment in RCTs or those allocated to treatment on the basis of preference or chance in PCTs. The results of some individual studies showed no beneficial effects of giving the treatment of choice. For instance, Leykin et al. (2007) reported a small effect size (d = .31) comparing the outcomes of the matched and the mismatched treatment (antidepressant or cognitive therapy) subgroups. Thomas et al. (2004) found that receipt of the preferred treatment did not confer any additional benefit in the achievement of outcomes expected of pharmacotherapy or physiotherapy for the management of shoulder pain. Similarly, Lewis et al. (2006) observed no significant differences in the outcomes (physical activity) for patients with matched and mismatched treatment (motivationally tailored print or telephone intervention). Borradaile et al. (2011) found a relationship between preference and outcomes: participants who received the preferred treatment (low carbohydrate or low fat diets) lost less weight (mean = 7.7 kg) than those who did not receive the preferred treatment (mean = 9.7 kg). In contrast, the results of a few individual studies and those of three systematic reviews or meta-analyses indicated a small association between receiving the treatment of choice and improvement in outcomes. For example, Devine and Ferrald (1973) reported that psychology students assigned to the treatment of choice, compared to those randomized, showed significant improvement on outcomes. The results of King et al.'s (2005) systematic review indicated that seven (of 19) trials found a significant difference in outcomes between participants allocated to treatment on the basis of preference or randomly; in five of the seven trials, the hypothesized outcomes were reported in participants receiving the preferred treatment more so than those randomized to treatment. In their meta-analysis, the Preference Collaborative Review Group (2009) found greater improvement in outcomes for participants randomly allocated to the preferred, as compared to the non-preferred, treatment; the estimated mean effect size was .15. The findings of Swift et al.s (2011) meta-analysis were consistent with those of the Preference Collaborative Review Group. The overall mean effect size was .31, implying greater benefit for participants receiving the treatment of choice. The rather small direct effect of allocation to preferred treatment on outcome suggests the possibility of a mediated relationship: providing the treatment of choice enhances adherence to treatment, which, in turn, yields improvement in outcomes. Kwan et al.'s (2010) findings offer preliminary empirical evidence supporting the mediated relationship. The effect of receiving matched treatment on changes in level of depression was explained primarily by attendance at treatment sessions, which was higher in the matched than the mismatched subgroups of participants.

Summary

- Pragmatic and preference trials are proposed to generate evidence of intervention's effectiveness that is relevant to guide practice
- Pragmatic or practical clinical trials have the following features: sampling of diverse patient populations, selecting a variety of practice settings, comparing clinically relevant treatments, assessing outcomes over time, and involving healthcare professionals in treatment delivery. Results provide answers to questions of relevance to clinical and policy decision making: who most benefits from which treatment, given in what way and at what dose, by which healthcare professionals, under what context
- Preference or partially randomized clinical trials involve assessment of participants' preferences for treatment and accounting for these preferences in treatment allocation. This method of assignment mimics what occurs in the context of practice. Empirical evidence supports, to some extent, the benefits of preference allocation in enhancing enrollment in the trial, enactment and adherence to treatment, and outcome achievement, and in reducing attrition

8

SELECTION OF PARTICIPANTS

Obtaining a sample that is of an adequate size and representative of the target population and controlling for the potential confounding of participants' characteristics are essential for maintaining the validity of inferences in intervention evaluation research. The selection of participants plays a crucial role in accruing a sample of the required size and composition. The mechanisms through which participant selection poses threats to validity are explained in this chapter, supported with relevant empirical evidence. Strategies for effective selection are also described.

Selection consists of a process aimed at enrolling a sample of participants that is adequate in size and composition, in order to enhance statistical conclusion and internal and external validity. The process is multi-stage, involving: the pre-specification of eligibility criteria and the required sample size, the recruitment and selection of participants, and obtaining informed consent. Selection of participants should be carefully planned and executed to acquire a sample, of an adequate size, that is representative of the target population, to minimize the potential for confounding, and to reduce non-consent bias.

IMPORTANCE OF SELECTION

Selection contributes to the size and composition of the study sample, which are important for maintaining the validity of inferences regarding the effects of the intervention on outcomes. The sample size (i.e., the number of participants to enroll in the study) is a determinant of the study's statistical power to detect the hypothesized intervention effects. There is a tendency to find statistically significant intervention effects with large sample sizes, potentially yielding type I error of inference (concluding that the intervention is effective when in fact it is not). Conversely, it is likely to observe no differences in post-test outcomes with small sample sizes, potentially leading to type II error (inferring that the intervention is ineffective when, in fact, it is successful in producing the outcomes) (Lipsey, 1990). Therefore, the sample size should be large enough to validly detect the intervention effects. The sample size required for a study is best estimated on the basis of power analysis (Cohen, 1988) to achieve statistical conclusion validity.

The sample composition relates to the characteristics of participants. The sample should be representative of the target population to enhance external validity. Participants should have the personal, health, and clinical attributes, including the experience of the health problem addressed by the intervention, that are comparable to those representing the target population. This is essential so the results are applicable to the population (Larzelere et al., 2004). The sample also should be homogeneous relative to those characteristics hypothesized to influence participants' engagement, adherence, and response to the intervention, in order to minimize the potential for confounding the intervention effects (Pincus, 2002), which is a major threat to internal validity. The composition of the sample is affected by participants' right to self-determination, which is protected through the process of obtaining informed consent. The extent to which persons who agree to enroll in the intervention study differ on personal, health, or clinical characteristics from those who decline enrollment contributes to non-consent bias. This bias results in a sample that is not representative of all subgroups constituting the target population, limiting the generalizability of the study findings (Haaga, 2004). The sample composition is determined by the pre-specified eligibility criteria, the recruitment sampling strategies, and the consent process applied in an intervention evaluation trial.

DETERMINATION OF SAMPLE SIZE

Sample size is determined on the basis of power analysis. The analysis takes into consideration three main factors: the α-level, power, and the magnitude of the intervention effect. The α-level of statistical significance represents the rate of type I error. It is traditionally set at .05, implying that type I error will occur in 5, out of 100, times the same study is repeated. A liberal α-level (e.g., α = .10) is accepted for pilot studies focused on exploring the extent to which a new intervention produces improvement in the mediators and immediate outcomes. Conversely, a conservative α-level (α = .01) is set for efficacy and effectiveness studies aimed at confirming the intervention's impact on the outcomes. Power is related to the rate of committing type II error (i.e., β) and is estimated as $1 - \beta$. A power $\geq$ .80 is often set for most intervention evaluation studies. The magnitude of the intervention effect is usually specified for what is called the 'primary' outcome. Although there is no clear conceptual definition, the primary outcome appears to reflect the one of most interest to researchers or decision makers, such as quality of life. It is important to note that, for most health interventions, primary outcomes represent the ultimate effects, which are indirectly affected by the intervention. This implies that improvement in the ultimate outcomes is mediated by the changes in the mediators. Accordingly, the direct causal relationship between the intervention and the ultimate outcomes is expected to be non-significant or of a small magnitude. In contrast, the association between the intervention and the immediate outcomes, and between the latter and the ultimate outcomes is significant or of a larger magnitude, if the intervention is successful at inducing changes in the mechanism underlying its effects on the ultimate outcomes (MacKinnon and Fairchild, 2009). This point should be carefully considered when identifying the primary outcome to conduct a power analysis.

The magnitude of the intervention effect reflects the difference between the intervention and comparison groups on the post-test outcome. It is estimated on the basis of theoretical expectations, clinical judgement, and empirical evidence. A well-developed and specific intervention theory identifies the anticipated magnitude of the effects, which should be congruent with the nature and strength of the intervention. For instance, educational interventions are hypothesized to have a large impact on knowledge, whereas behavioral therapies are expected to have a large effect on performance of healthy behaviors. Clinical judgement indicates the amount of the difference between the groups, in the post-test outcomes or the amount of improvement in the post-test outcomes that healthcare professionals and clients consider meaningful in determining the benefits of an intervention. For instance, clinically meaningful changes in outcomes have been estimated for most objective outcomes such as blood pressure (through the specification of normal range values) and for well-established measures of some symptoms such as the Insomnia Severity Index and the one-item pain rating scale. Empirical evidence is derived from previous research. The effect size quantifies the magnitude of the intervention effects. It had been recommended to conduct a pilot study to estimate the effect size of a new intervention and to use the obtained effect size to do a power analysis for a subsequent efficacy trial. This practice is no longer endorsed because the effect size computed with data obtained in a pilot study involving a small sample size lacks precision, which gives inaccurate directions for the trial's power analysis. The pilot study effect size is unstable and is not replicated in subsequent trials (Leon et al., 2011).

The magnitude of the effect size used to conduct a power analysis for pilot studies is based on theoretical expectations and clinical judgement. For efficacy trials, it is based on empirical evidence obtained from full-scale studies that evaluated the same or similar intervention in different populations and contexts. Finally, for effectiveness and comparative effectiveness studies, it is based on empirical evidence reported in efficacy trials and clinical judgement. In addition to these factors (α-level, power, and magnitude of effects), the reliability of the outcome measure is also taken into account when conducting a power analysis. Reliability reduces error variance (i.e., variability in the post-test outcome that is not attributable to the intervention). Low error variance increases the statistical power and decreases the number of participants needed to detect significant intervention effects.

There are many statistical packages that can be used to do a power analysis. Whichever is used, the results of the analysis indicate the total number of participants needed. This number should be balanced across the intervention and comparison groups. However, the sample size required to detect significant intervention effects is not necessarily the number of persons to recruit and to enroll in the trial. The number of persons to recruit is inflated to account for refusal rate. The rate of refusal is estimated from previous research. For instance, about 45 per cent of persons with insomnia decline enrollment in studies of behavioral therapy; therefore, if the power analysis indicates that 100 participants are required, then the actual number of persons to recruit is 145. This number of persons to recruit accommodates the potential for non-eligibility and the total number to enroll should be estimated to take into consideration the anticipated attrition rate. Briefly, the number to recruit and enroll is much larger than the sample size required to detect significant intervention effects.

PRE-SPECIFICATION OF ELIGIBILITY CRITERIA

Eligibility criteria are pre-specified to select persons in the intervention evaluation study. The inclusion criteria ensure the selection of persons who are representative of the target population. They experience the health problem addressed by the intervention and hence, are likely to benefit from it; and have personal, health, and clinical characteristics comparable to those defining the target population. The exclusion criteria serve to control for participant characteristics that may affect implementation of the intervention (e.g., cognitive impairment) or may be directly associated with the outcomes (e.g., presence of comorbidity), as well as for participants' exposure to concurrent treatments that may interact with the intervention. In pilot studies and efficacy trials, a set of strict eligibility criteria is pre-specified to exclude persons who present with potentially confounding attributes and to increase the homogeneity of the sample. It is believed that participants homogeneous relative to key characteristics respond in the same way to the intervention, reflected in the achievement of the same post-test outcome level. Therefore, the within-group or error variance for most statistical tests is reduced. This, in turn, enhances the study's internal validity (as the outcomes are causally attributed to the intervention and not to participants' characteristics) and statistical conclusions validity (as the power to detect significant intervention effects is increased).

The application of strict criteria to determine eligibility limits the sampling pool and external validity. When several exclusion criteria are specified and these criteria represent characteristics that are prevalent in the target population, then the number of participants meeting the study criteria (i.e., sampling pool) is reduced. For instance, excluding patients with cardiac diseases who have hypertension or hyperglycemia (i.e., comorbid conditions with which half the patients present) will decrease the number of potentially eligible clients by almost 50 per cent. The reduced sampling pool, in combination with non-consent, decreases the number of persons who enroll in the study and thus, the sample size. The improvement in outcomes observed in a homogeneous sample may not be reproduced in other subgroups of the target population. The latter subgroups present with characteristics that are considered exclusionary for the trial.

Consequently, the applicability of the trial's results to real-world clients is questionable. In effectiveness studies, the eligibility criteria are relaxed and the effects of the intervention are estimated for different subgroups of the target population, defined in terms of key characteristics hypothesized to affect the implementation and outcomes of the intervention.

The pre-specification of eligibility criteria guides the selection of sites for participant recruitment and measures for screening. The sites that are most likely to have large pools of persons experiencing the health problem addressed by the intervention are chosen. However, it would be useful to gain information on the personal, health, and clinical characteristics of persons available at the sites. This information determines the extent to which the available pool is restricted to a particular subgroup or is representative of all subgroups of the target population. In the former case, additional sites are included in the trial in order to enhance the representativeness of the sample, especially if the trial aims at examining the effectiveness of the intervention. The eligibility criteria are clearly defined at the conceptual and operational levels, and the measures to screen for all criteria should be reliable and valid. Specifically, they should demonstrate good sensitivity and specificity to appropriately and correctly identify eligible persons. Failure of screening measures results in the selection of participants who may vary in their experience of the health problem, in their characteristics, and in receipt of concurrent treatment. Therefore, the accrued sample is heterogeneous and responds to the intervention differently, thereby weakening statistical conclusion and internal validity.

On a practical level, it is important to document and periodically review the results of screening. This practice assists in determining the most frequently reported exclusion criteria. These criteria may be revised if they are contributing to severe reduction in the sampling pool and interfering with the accrual of the required sample size. In a recent review of studies funded by two organizations, McDonald et al. (2006) found that in 63 per cent of the trials recruitment was slower than anticipated due to various reasons including fewer than expected number of persons meeting the study eligibility criteria. They called this phenomenon 'Lasagna Law'. Similarly, in an analysis of nearly 41,000 trials registered with the US government, nearly half failed to achieve the required number of participants (Califf et al., 2012). This highlights the importance of carefully pre-specifying the eligibility criteria in order to maintain a balance in enhancing internal and external validity.

RECRUITMENT STRATEGIES

Recruitment is the process of finding and informing potentially eligible persons of the intervention evaluation study (Butterfield et al., 2003). There are different strategies for recruitment, which may be appropriate to use with different populations, in different contexts. The strategies are categorized as active or passive (Cooley et al., 2003).

Active, also referred to as proactive, strategies usually involve direct contact between the research staff responsible for recruitment and potential participants. The direct contact consists of: face-to-face meeting with individual potentially eligible participants, such as approaching patients attending a clinic; presentations to a group of potentially eligible participants, such as explaining briefly the study to healthcare professionals present at a weekly case conferencing meeting or to persons present at a social gathering at a church; and attendance at social or health-related events targeting the population of interest, such as having a booth for the study at a health fair or at a shopping mall. The direct contact has the advantage of allowing interactions between research staff and potential participants to provide detailed information about the study, clarify any misperception about treatments and about taking part in the study, discuss the benefits of taking part in the trial, and address any concern persons may have about the treatments and the study, and barriers to enrollment. An additional advantage is that potential participants get to know the research staff. This familiarity contributes to the development of good rapport between the staff and eligible persons, which serves to promote participation in the trial, particularly for those of diverse ethnic backgrounds. Active recruitment strategies have some disadvantages. Their implementation is time consuming and expensive, as it requires the research staff's travel to the location and presence at the scheduled contact. Further, a small percentage of potentially eligible persons can be reached, confined to those available who may represent a select subgroup of the target population (Cooley et al., 2003). For example, setting a recruitment table in a shopping mall has the possibility of obtaining a biased sample. People who go to shopping malls are disproportionately female; they tend to be teenagers and elders, and to have the time and inclination to go shopping (Kang et al., 1996).

Passive, also called reactive, strategies involve indirect contact with potentially eligible persons. Different media are used to inform the public of the study and interested persons are asked to contact the research staff to get detailed information about the study. The information can be disseminated through:

1. Printed materials including distribution of brochures at centres visited by members of the target population (e.g., community health clinics, physician offices); posting flyers in strategic locations (e.g., public bulletin boards in hospitals or food stores); and placing advertisement in newspapers, newsletters, or magazines with wide distribution or those targeting the population of interest (e.g., newspapers for gays and lesbians), or in widely and freely accessed websites or those maintained by relevant associations (e.g., Sleep Society for the recruitment of persons with insomnia).
2. Media outlets including announcements on television or radio. The station and time slots for airing the announcement should be carefully selected to reach the target population at the most opportune time.
3. Word-of-mouth referral done by healthcare professionals caring for potentially eligible persons or community leaders who are well respected by the target population (e.g., religious figures are well respected by persons of African descent).

The advantages of passive recruitment strategies is the possibility of reaching large and diverse segments of the population at a cost lower than that incurred with the use of active strategies. However, the research staff has to respond to inquiries from a large number of interested persons to explain the study, which can be a demanding and time consuming task.

The effectiveness of recruitment strategies has been examined. Effectiveness was reflected in the number of persons informed of the study and showing interest in learning more about it. Harris et al. (2003) found that more people were enrolled using passive rather than active strategies, and that they were more likely to meet the eligibility criteria. Leach (2003) indicated that face-to-face contact, referral by healthcare professionals, media, and mailing letters to potentially eligible persons (e.g., letter signed by physicians and sent to their clients) were the most effective recruitment strategies. McDonald et al. (2006) reported the use of newsletters, mail shots sent to healthcare professionals and patients, and having a dedicated trial manager spearheading the recruitment effort, as effective strategies. Veitch et al. (2001) identified the following process as useful in recruiting general practitioners: 1) sending an introductory letter followed by 2) making a call to arrange for a discussion at a convenient time, and 3) holding a face-to-face or telephone meeting to discuss the details of the trial with the practitioners. The results of a systematic review suggested that active strategies are more successful than passive strategies in recruiting persons of diverse ethnic and cultural backgrounds (Ibrahim and Sidani, 2013).

The evidence presented previously and the experience of many researchers (Streiner and Sidani, 2010) clearly demonstrate that different strategies are required to recruit different populations and subgroups of the target population in different contexts. For example, if the trial includes people from the community, then passive approaches using the media may be appropriate options in order to reach as many people as possible. On the other hand, if the study targets clients with a particular illness, then active approaches involving direct contact with those attending a clinic are useful. Further, each recruitment strategy may reach a particular subgroup of the population. For instance, an advertisement in a newspaper will be read only by subscribers who have the time and are inclined to review every section of the newspaper. Therefore, it is highly recommended to implement multiple recruitment strategies in any trial to reach the largest proportion and diverse subgroups of the target population, which enhances the representativeness of the sample. In addition, the use of multiple strategies may help overcome barriers to recruitment.

Barriers to recruitment often relate to concerns of gatekeepers (i.e., agencies and healthcare professionals, who are intermediaries between the research staff and the potentially eligible clients) and potential participants. In many situations, recruitment is feasible only through entry into an agency such as a hospital or community health clinic. The cooperation of the agency must be gained in order to access and approach members of the target population served by the agency. Most agencies require approval from their research ethics board and from management or clinical directors of the program of interest (e.g., cardiology program). Approval may not be granted if there are concerns related to breeching the privacy and confidentiality of the institution (e.g., a trial requiring program level data on safety outcomes), the efficacy and safety of the new intervention under evaluation, and most importantly, the demands of conducting the study on the time and resources of the agency staff (e.g., nursing staff having to introduce research staff to in-patients; training healthcare professionals in the delivery of the intervention).

Healthcare professionals have long been described as gatekeepers, interfering with the recruitment of potentially eligible clients assigned to their care. Several issues have been identified as contributing to healthcare professionals' interference with recruitment. First is the healthcare professionals' attitude toward research, which is viewed as competing and in conflict with their role as healer; demanding in terms of effort and time spent on informing patients about the study, referring them, and obtaining their consent; and incompatible with clinical practice (Leach, 2003). Healthcare professionals feel a loss of clinical autonomy and decision-making power when they are requested to provide the treatment under evaluation. Often the treatments are inflexible, which contradicts the individualized approach to care to which they are accustomed. When recruiting patients to an intervention evaluation study, healthcare professionals are expected to relay a sense of uncertainty (i.e., equipoise) about treatments under evaluation. This sense of uncertainty is inconsistent with their beliefs, values, and preferences for treatment; it also jeopardizes their relationship with patients (Elander and Hermerén, 1995). Further, healthcare professionals consider the study protocol as incompatible with standard practice. They are not supportive of the randomization process and may not agree to withholding or keeping constant the dose of medications, to offering a no-treatment option, or to providing treatments of unknown benefits and risks (Cook Gotay, 1991). Lastly, healthcare professionals perceive their involvement in research, even if limited to recruitment, as financially burdensome and not rewarding because the time spent on research-related activities is not reimbursed; there is no incentive to or recognition of their involvement; and they lack the time, training, and resources to support research-related work (Leach, 2003).

Participants' concerns present barriers to their enrollment in a trial. The concerns relate to the study protocol, such as undergoing additional procedures (e.g., blood work, completing questionnaires) which are associated with discomfort, and aversion to randomization; they wish for more information and greater participation in treatment decisions. Participants are not comfortable with uncertainty of treatment and may decline entry into a trial if they have strong treatment preferences. Logistics, such as travel distance and expense, time commitment, and inconvenience of appointments for treatment implementation and outcome assessment, are additional barriers expressed by patients (Hicks, 1998; Leach, 2003; Ross et al., 1999).

Here are a number of practical tips that can be used to address the barriers to recruitment. The tips are applied at different levels.

1. Researcher:

   o Identify locations or sites where potentially eligible persons representing different subgroups of the target population can be found. This can be done in collaboration with healthcare professionals or other staff at the sites (Daunt, 2003; Montoro-Rodriguez and Smith, 2010; Spencer and Patrick, 2010).

   o Obtain data on the size and composition of the sampling pool. This assists in determining the type and number of sites to select for recruitment, with the goal of promoting the accrual of the required sample size and composition.

   o Discuss with the sites' leadership the relevance and applicability of recruitment strategies. Select those considered most appropriate for the local population. Use a combination of strategies.

   o Have a research staff member dedicated to recruitment at each site (McDonald et al., 2006).

   o Monitor the effectiveness of the recruitment strategies implemented at each site. This requires the sequential use of the strategies in the early recruitment period (e.g., put an advertisement in a particular newspaper in week 1; post flyers in one selected location or site in week 2) and recording in a log the number of persons approached or who called to inquire about the study after the use of the strategy. Alternatively, participants are asked how they learned about the study. Examination of the number of persons approached or the number of inquiries helps determine which strategy is most effective (i.e., has high yield).

   o Keep track of the screening rate (i.e., the number of persons who agree to screening; the number of persons found eligible), the number of persons not meeting each eligibility criterion, the enrollment rate (i.e., number of eligible persons who consented), and reasons for declining enrollment. Review these data, obtained at each study site, on a regular basis (e.g., monthly) to determine the need for modification of the eligibility criteria.

   o Train research staff in good communication skills. The skills include: making eye contact with participants throughout the interaction; appearing to have plenty of time (i.e., not rushing in relaying information about the study or in explaining any point as desired by the persons); listening and respecting concerns expressed by persons; responding to questions honestly; and personalizing the study information as needed (Steinke, 2004).

2. Gatekeepers (agencies and healthcare professionals):

   o Send a letter introducing the study to the gatekeeper; follow up with a telephone call to arrange a face-to-face meeting to discuss the study.

   o Provide details about the study and the gatekeepers' role in recruitment, at the scheduled face-to-face meeting.

   o Collaborate with the gatekeepers to select the recruitment strategies that are effective and appropriate to the target population, yet feasible and least intrusive to the gatekeepers' or their staff's work. Make their involvement in recruitment easy. For instance, Embi et al. (2005) used a clinical trial alert to remind healthcare professionals of the study and prompt them to refer potentially eligible patients. Also, ensure the staff are provided with all material needed for recruitment such as information sheets containing research staff contact numbers to hand to potential participants.

o Maintain contact with gatekeepers or their staff to discuss progress in recruitment, any issues that may arise and possible solutions (Butterfield et al., 2003). For instance, making weekly calls to the referring healthcare professionals or clinics may increase patient recruitment in a trial.

o Provide gatekeepers with incentive or support to maintain their interest and commitment to recruitment. The incentives can be monetary if allowable by the research funding agency. Non-monetary incentives vary from thank you notes, gift cards, a pizza party held for the in-patient unit with the highest recruitment rate, to offering in-service education to the agency staff on topics related to the health problem and its treatment (excluding the intervention under evaluation to avoid potential for dissemination) upon study completion.

3. Participants:

o Allow flexibility in scheduling recruitment and screening sessions, at a location and time that are convenient to potential participants.

o Provide accurate, non-judgemental information about the study activities including method of assignment to treatment, risks and benefits. Tailor the content and format of recruitment to the target population and to the individuals (Barrett, 2002). This is essential to enhance participants' understanding of the study and to help them set clear and realistic expectations, which contributes to enrollment and retention.

o Demonstrate respect and address any concern the persons may have. Do not rush the explanation.

SAMPLING STRATEGIES

Once identified, informed of the study, and found to meet general eligibility criteria (assessed with non-intrusive questions after obtaining oral consent), persons are selected into the study through the application of different sampling strategies. There are two general categories of sampling strategies: random and non-random.

Random Sampling

Random sampling strategies rely on chance in selecting participants into the intervention evaluation trial. There are two specific strategies: simple random and stratified random sampling.

In simple random sampling, each member of the population has the same chance of being included in the study. This is equivalent to putting each member's name on a slip of paper, mixing up the papers, and drawing the required number of names, one at a time and after returning the paper to the mix. The application of random sampling requires the availability of a list or database containing the names of all members of the target population. Such lists have been generated for some client populations (e.g., Canadian Cancer Registry); for healthcare professionals maintained by employing agencies or professional regulatory bodies; and for the general public (e.g., clinical database maintained by healthcare insurance agencies). Even if available, researchers may not have access to the lists or databases under strict privacy laws. An alternative procedure for simple random sampling is for the researcher to identify potential participants available at a recruitment site and time (e.g., in a hospital, on a day), and to select a number of these participants following a random process (e.g., every other participant or by drawing their names from a hat). Simple random sampling is claimed to reduce self-selection bias, and hence to improve the representativeness of the sample. In addition to limited availability and access of the lists or databases, simple random sampling has the following weaknesses: the lists or databases may not be complete or up-to-date or miss particular subgroups of the target population.

Stratified random sampling is used to ensure adequate representation in the sample of persons with specific characteristics. The selected characteristic can be one expected to influence the intervention effect, such as receipt of concurrent treatment. Strata are constructed to reflect different categories or levels of the characteristic and persons are randomly sampled within each stratum. The size of the strata can be either balanced, that is, an equal number of persons is selected within each stratum, which is often done for variables with the potential to influence the intervention effects, or proportional, that is, the number of persons in each stratum is proportional to the general population. Stratified random sampling yields a representative sample; however, it takes time to find and enroll persons, in the required numbers, within the strata.

Non-random Sampling

Non-random sampling strategies select potentially eligible participants on the basis of convenience, that is, persons who happen to be present at time of recruitment are sampled. These strategies are often used in health intervention evaluation research because they are feasible and easy. They involve taking in persons who show interest in the study. However, non-random sampling strategies may yield samples with limited representativeness of all subgroups forming the target population.

No matter what approach is used to recruit and sample potential participants, research ethics require that persons provide informed consent to enroll in the study. Obtaining consent affects the size and composition of the sample.

CONSENT PROCESS

The consent process consists of three steps. In the first, the research assistant informs potential participants about the study. The research assistant explains the purpose, the risks and the benefits of the study, clarifies the activities which participants are to perform (i.e., screening, data collection, attendance at treatment sessions), and describes the experimental and comparison treatments in terms of their goal, recommendations to be applied, side or adverse effects, and benefits. In the second step, the research assistant ensures the persons understand what the study involves and addresses any concerns they may have. In the third step, the persons are asked to sign the consent form to indicate their agreement to participate in the study.

Through the consent process, persons become aware of the treatment and the study demands. They may weigh them against their expectations and life or health condition; this weighing up contributes to their decision to enroll or decline enrollment. This decision results in self-selection or non-consent bias. This bias relates to differences in personal, health, and clinical characteristics between persons who participate in the trial and those who do not. Therefore, the accrued sample may not be representative of all subgroups constituting the target population (Haaga, 2004), as indicated by the empirical evidence presented next.

EMPIRICAL EVIDENCE

The selection process is supposed to yield a sample of an adequate size and representative of the target population. However, the application of its stages interferes with the achievement of this goal. Accumulating evidence indicates that a low percentage of individuals meet the trial eligibility criteria, an increasing number of persons decline enrollment in trials for different reasons, and the persons who participate differ from those who do not enroll in intervention evaluation studies, particularly those using an RCT design.

Percentage of Individuals Meeting Trial Eligibility Criteria

Evidence shows that a rather low percentage of recruited persons is found to meet the stringent eligibility criteria specified for an RCT. The percentage may vary according to the stringency of the criteria. For instance, Grapow et al. (2006) reported that < 10 per cent of all screened patients met the study criteria and were included in studies of percutaneous coronary interventions. Sellors et al. (2002) found that 48 per cent of screened people were eligible for an RCT of an expanded pharmacist role in providing consultation for multiple medications for older adults. Jolly et al. (2005) were able to include 26.3 per cent of the screened patients in an RCT comparing home vs. hospital-based cardiac programs. In one trial, 96 per cent of patients who were eligible for the treatment under evaluation, thrombolysis, were excluded because of other criteria (National Institute of Neurological Disorders and Strokes [NINDS], 1995). Barrett (2002) and Spiro et al. (2005) indicated that < 5 per cent of patients with cancer enter clinical trials, and about 40 per cent of those screened were considered ineligible. Charlson and Horwitz (1984) reviewed 41 RCTs and observed that 73 per cent of the recruited patients did not meet the eligibility criteria. Overall, Pincus (2002) estimated that < 50 per cent of patients meet the strict eligibility criteria set for RCTs, which limits the applicability of the treatment and the reproducibility of its effects in the subgroups of the target population not represented in the trial.

Percentage of Persons Declining Enrollment

The percentage of eligible persons declining enrollment in intervention evaluation trials appears to be generally decreasing over time, although it varies with the types of health interventions and target populations. Jenkins and Fallowfield (2000) found that 25 per cent of participants declined entry into an RCT of cancer therapy. In studies aimed at determining the effects of cognitive behavior therapy for insomnia, the rates of non-enrollment ranged between 26 per cent and 45 per cent (Edinger et al., 2007; Jacobs et al., 2004; Pallesen et al., 2005; Savard et al., 2005). Spiro et al. (2005) reported that 73.5 per cent of eligible patients with lung cancer refused participation in an RCT of chemotherapy. Understanding the reasons for non-enrollment in a trial is useful in making necessary modifications to the recruitment process or the study protocol with the goal of making participation attractive to large numbers of persons of different backgrounds.

Reasons for Declining Enrollment

Numerous and diverse reasons have been reported for declining enrollment in intervention evaluation studies. Some reasons are common across studies using different designs and others are unique to the RCT design:

1. Participant-related factors: Various personal, health, and clinical characteristics have been associated with the decision to accept or refuse enrollment. The characteristics contributing to the decision differ across target populations, types of treatments, and contexts. However, those commonly reported include:

   o Perception and attitude toward research: participants holding unfavorable attitudes, which are prevalent among some cultural groups, are highly likely to refuse enrollment in a trial.

   o Interest in the topic: participants not interested in the topic addressed in the study, such as those who believe the health problem targeted by the intervention is not severe or burdensome, or is a normal life process and therefore does not require treatment (e.g., some persons believe insomnia is a normal part of aging), decline entry into a trial.

- o Socio-economic status: there is a tendency for persons of middle and upper-middle class, and with higher levels of education to participate in research; these individuals may value the contribution of research and afford the personal costs (travel and childcare expenses) associated with participation in a study.
- o Employment status: many participants who are employed on a full-time basis are not able to take time off work or do not have time after work hours (due to competing demands such as family obligations) to engage in research-related activities.
- o Health status: persons experiencing overall poor health feel too ill to participate in a study (Barrett, 2002; DiMattio, 2001; Ganguli et al., 1998).

2. Study characteristics: Participants declining enrollment in RCTs have expressed concerns related to the safety and burden associated with the study (i.e., data collection procedures) and the treatment protocol; inflexibility of the treatment protocol (Connolly et al., 2004; Nystuen and Hagen, 2004); and being treated as a 'guinea pig' or experimental subject (Stevens and Ahmedzai, 2004). In addition, refusers appear to resent randomization to treatment, which they feel is unfair and decreases sense of control; they desire to be actively involved in treatment decisions or to leave treatment decisions to their attending physician (Jenkins and Fallowfield, 2000). Some participants fear that involvement in an RCT would change their relationship with their healthcare provider and may lead to loss of benefits to which they are, otherwise, entitled (Connolly et al., 2004; DiMattio, 2001). For instance, Robinson et al. (2005) found that lay people were reluctant to accept equipoise and considered it unacceptable for healthcare professionals to decide treatment at random. Also, they believed that randomization has no scientific advantage; they had preferences for treatment; and therefore they refused enrollment in a trial. In a systematic review of medical and surgical trials, King et al. (2005) estimated the percentage of participants who accept randomization to range from 26 per cent to 88 per cent. Similarly, Williams et al. (1999) reported a high rate of refusal for randomization in studies evaluating cognitive behavioral therapy for pain management.

3. Treatment attributes: There is a general tendency for persons to decline enrollment in RCTs examining the effects of treatments they perceive as unacceptable, demanding, or intensive (Haidich and Ioannidis, 2001). Participants have preferences for treatments. They may decline enrollment in an RCT to avoid being randomly allocated to the least or non-preferred treatment (see Chapter 7).

Differences between Enrollees and Non-enrollees

The reasons for non-enrollment in a trial contribute, to various extents, to differences in the personal, health, or clinical characteristics of enrollees and non-enrollees. For instance, Schwartz and Fox (1995) identified factors associated with participation in trials of psychological interventions. These included: age, functional status, desire to get the best care possible, belief that involvement in the trial would help fight the illness, judgement that the benefits of participation outweigh the risks, and thoughts that the condition will get worse without treatment. Man-Song-Hing et al. (2001) reviewed studies that examined differences between participants who enrolled and those who refused entry in RCTs. They reported that 1) the likelihood of enrollment is higher for persons with better health, younger age, higher socio-economic status, higher education, and previous experience with RCT; 2) transportation and availability of medical insurance influenced decision to enroll; 3) refusers have concerns about quality of life and research, are unwilling to take placebo, and desire an active role in treatment decisions. The evidence presented in Chapter 7 indicates that compared to enrollees, non-enrollees have clear preferences for treatments and are not willing to be randomized. Further, participants with preferences differ from those with no preference in their personal profile; those with preferences are more likely to be women, well educated, white, and employed (Dwight-Johnson et al., 2001; King et al., 2005). Consequently, persons who enroll in an RCT are not comparable to those seen in the context of day-to-day practice, limiting the generalizability of the RCT results to practice (Leykin et al., 2007; Millat et al., 2005). Two studies investigated the comparability of participants in RCTs to patients treated outside the context of the trial. The focus and the methods used in the two studies differed, which may explain the differences in findings. Stirman et al. (2003) had raters compare the clinical characteristics of patients attending a clinic to the eligibility criteria set for RCTs of psychotherapy, and determine the overall likelihood that the clinic patients would be eligible for an RCT. The results showed that 67 per cent of clinic patients ($N = 347$) were judged ineligible. The reasons for non-eligibility related to: clinic patients not having the primary disorder targeted in the RCT, reporting comorbid conditions, or experiencing the disorder at a subclinical level (i.e., the disorder was of insufficient severity or duration). Vist et al. (2005) reviewed 50 RCTs and 50 cohort studies of various treatments (e.g., surgery, drugs, radiotherapy, counseling, active monitoring) to determine if the outcomes of participants differ from the outcomes of similar patients, treated similarly, who do not enroll in the studies. The results showed no differences in the outcomes for patients treated within and outside a trial. Although reassuring, these results are based on small samples included in the studies.

Summary

- Selection of participants into an intervention evaluation study should be carefully done to acquire a sample of adequate size and composition. This is needed to enhance statistical conclusion, internal, and external validity
- Sample size is determined on the basis of power analysis; it takes into account the α (type I error), β (type II error), and effect size (magnitude of intervention effects)

- Adequacy of sample composition is achieved by:

  o Pre-specifying the eligibility criteria to ensure inclusion of participants representative of the target population and excluding those with potentially confounding characteristics; revising the criteria as needed (Resio et al., 2004)
  o Using a mix of active and passive strategies that are appropriate to recruit different subgroups of the target population; evaluating the yield of the strategies to determine the most useful
  o Implementing sample selection strategies that are feasible and minimize bias

9
RETENTION OF PARTICIPANTS

Obtaining a sample that is adequate in size and composition is important for maintaining the validity of inferences regarding the intervention effectiveness. However, the retention of the accrued sample is as critical for validity. Participants who complete all phases of the study (pretest and post-test outcome assessment, exposure to treatment) should have the socio-cultural, health, and clinical profile comparable to that characterizing the target population. The number of participants remaining in the study should be large enough to detect significant intervention effects. In this chapter the role of participant retention in enhancing statistical conclusion, internal, and external validity is clarified. Factors associated with attrition are identified, and strategies for preventing and managing attrition, together with evidence of their effectiveness, are discussed.

DEFINITION AND TYPES OF ATTRITION

Attrition, also called mortality, dropout, or loss to follow-up, refers to the withdrawal of eligible participants at any phase of the trial: before, during, or after exposure to treatment. Although the overall attrition rate, reflecting the total number of participants who withdraw, is of concern, it is worth exploring different categories of attrition as a means to elucidate the mechanism underlying participants' withdrawal. Understanding the mechanism is useful in the incorporation of strategies to prevent attrition and minimize its influence. Categorization of attrition is done on the basis of any or a combination of the following: the time at which withdrawal takes place (pre- vs. post-inclusion); the party initiating the withdrawal (participant vs. researcher); and the distribution and characteristics of participants who withdraw across treatment conditions (equal vs. differential).

Attrition is often categorized as pre-inclusion and post-inclusion dropout. Pre-inclusion attrition takes place when consenting participants withdraw from the study prior to the intervention phase. This group of dropouts is not exposed to treatment (either the experimental or the comparison treatment). Post-inclusion attrition happens at any point in time after the intervention phase begins. This group of dropouts may have been exposed to some or all elements of the allocated treatment or may have missed some or all of the planned post-test outcome assessments (Copeland et al., 2006; Young et al., 2006). The distinction between these two categories of attrition is warranted for two reasons. The first relates to the varying rates reported for the pre-inclusion and post-inclusion attrition. For instance, in a review of smoking cessation intervention studies, Curtin et al. (2000) found slightly higher pre-inclusion (range: 30–50 per cent) than post-inclusion (range: 10–50 per cent) attrition rates. Similarly, Sidani et al. (2007) observed higher pre-inclusion attrition rates in an RCT (30.6 per cent) and a PRCT (14.6 per cent) of behavioral therapies for insomnia than post-inclusion attrition rates (8 per cent and 2 per cent, respectively). The second reason has to do with the potential differences in the factors influencing participants' withdrawal before or after the intervention phase. For instance, concerns about medication, scheduling conflicts, access to transportation, low readiness to quit, and significant others not believing in the effectiveness of smoking cessation were identified as factors contributing to smokers' pre-inclusion attrition (Woods et al., 2002). Participants' income, gender, perceived health and number of cigarettes smoked daily were cited as the most influential factors in post-inclusion attrition in a study by Leeman et al. (2006).

In most instances, withdrawal from the intervention evaluation study is initiated by participants for various reasons related to their personal, health, or clinical condition, to their perception of the research study requirements, and to their appraisal of the treatments under evaluation (discussed in a later section). In a few situations, withdrawal is initiated by the researcher. Researchers may request participants to leave the trial or may exclude cases from the final analysis on the basis of some pre-specified criteria. The criteria may reflect participants' lack of cooperation in the implementation of some aspects of the study protocol (e.g., not completing a daily diary), limited or non-adherence to the allocated treatment (e.g., not engaging in physical activity at the recommended dose), poor response to treatment (e.g., showing no changes in short-term outcomes), or experience of treatment side effects (Baekeland and Lundwall, 1975). The various reasons for attrition contribute to differences in the profiles of participants who withdraw from and those who complete the trial.

Attrition is also categorized on the basis of the distribution and characteristics of dropouts across the treatment conditions. Equal attrition is inferred when 1) the number of participants who withdraw from the study is balanced between the intervention and the comparison groups; 2) the socio-demographic, health, and clinical characteristics assessed at baseline of participants who withdraw from the intervention and the comparison groups are comparable; and 3) the personal and clinical profile and response to allocated treatment of participants who drop out of the study are similar to the profile and response of participants who complete the trial. Differential attrition occurs when

1) the number of dropouts differs between the intervention and the comparison groups; 2) the profile of participants who withdraw from the intervention and comparison groups is different; 3) the reasons for withdrawal are not the same for participants in the intervention and comparison groups; and 4) the profile of dropouts differs from the profile of participants who complete the study. These patterns of attrition affect different types of validity.

Attrition results in missing data. Individual participants' data are not available for specific items within an instrument or for the total instrument measuring an outcome, at different points in time following treatment implementation. Data missing on outcome measures has been referred to as measurement attrition (Ahern and Le Brocque, 2005). Data missing for the extent of participation in the allocated treatment has been called treatment attrition (Valentine and McHugh, 2007). The distinction between measurement and treatment attrition has implications for the selection of strategies to address missing data. The missing data due to attrition are of two types, ignorable and non-ignorable (Hofmann et al., 1998; Valentine and McHugh, 2007), which are discussed in Chapter 12. All categories of attrition are of concern in an intervention evaluation study. They threaten the statistical conclusion, internal, and external validity.

EFFECTS OF ATTRITION

Attrition influences the validity of inferences related to the effectiveness of the intervention and requires the expansion of additional resources to complete the study. The effects of attrition on statistical conclusion, internal, and external validity are detrimental, making it the threat of utmost concern in intervention evaluation research.

Effects of Attrition on Statistical Conclusion Validity

With attrition, the number of participants with complete data across all time points before and after the implementation of the intervention is reduced. The distribution of participants with complete data across the intervention and the comparison groups determines the impact of attrition on statistical conclusion validity. When the number of participants with complete data is equal between the two groups, the total sample size is decreased and the power to detect significant intervention effects is low (Coday et al., 2005; Moser et al., 2000). The end result is increased likelihood of type II error and the abandonment of a potentially useful intervention. When the number of participants with complete data is unequal between groups, as may happen when a large proportion of participants assigned to the comparison group withdraw, there is a high chance of finding differences in the within-group variance; for instance, the within-group variance tends to be lower in the group with the larger number of participants with complete data. These differences violate the assumption of equal variance underlying some statistical tests (e.g., analysis of variance F-test) used to compare the outcomes between the study groups. If not accounted for with the application of the appropriate formula for the respective statistical tests, then the probability of detecting significant intervention effects is decreased.

Effects of Attrition on Internal Validity

Differential attrition, initiated by the participants or researchers post-inclusion, is most influential in weakening internal validity. When participants who are assigned to the intervention group and withdraw from the study differ on some characteristics from participants who are assigned to the comparison treatment group and withdraw, the comparability of the remaining participants in the two groups is compromised. With this pattern of attrition, participants with complete data in the two groups are not comparable on characteristics assessed at baseline. Differences in baseline characteristics are associated with variability in participants' reaction, enactment, and adherence to treatment, as well as outcome achievement. Therefore, the level of improvement in the outcomes observed following implementation of the intervention cannot be attributed, with confidence, directly and only to the intervention. Thus, differential attrition leads to between-group differences in baseline characteristics, which have great potential to confound the intervention effects (Dumville et al., 2006; Valentine and McHugh, 2007).

Effects of Attrition on External Validity

Attrition introduces differences in the characteristics and the response to treatment of participants who do and do not drop out. The socio-demographic, health, and clinical profile of participants with complete data varies, to some extent, from the profile of dropouts. The sample with complete data and included in the analysis is not representative of all subgroups of the target population (Ahern and Le Brocque, 2005). In addition, the characteristics of the sample may affect the way participants react, enact, and adhere to treatment, inducing a unique response to treatment. The latter response is reflected in improvement in the outcome level that may not be replicated in other subgroups of the target population. Accordingly, the intervention effects may not be reproducible, limiting the generalizability of the study findings (Coday et al., 2005).

Effects of Attrition on Study Resources

Attrition prompts researchers to expand additional study resources to account for the number of participants who drop out. This demands: 1) extensive recruitment that involves including new sites to increase the pool of potentially eligible participants, and using active strategies to inform and recruit more participants; 2) prolonged time to complete the study; and 3) increased funds needed to cover the expenses associated with human and material resources required for extensive recruitment. The goal is to increase the number of individuals who enroll, which will maintain an adequate sample size despite attrition (Lindsay Davis et al., 2002; Marcellus, 2004). An adequate sample size is necessary to attain statistical power to detect significant intervention effects.

EMPIRICAL EVIDENCE RELATED TO ATTRITION

Empirical evidence indicates that attrition occurs frequently and to various extents. It is usually attributed to characteristics of the participants, the study, and the treatments under evaluation, as well as the participants' status on the outcomes. Attrition is often non-random and results in non-comparability on baseline characteristics of participants assigned to the intervention and comparison treatment groups.

Frequency and Extent of Attrition

The occurrence of attrition is a certainty in intervention evaluation trials. In almost every study participants withdraw after providing consent, for a variety of reasons. This fact led to the concern about the extent of attrition, operationalized as attrition rates (i.e., the percentage of participants who withdraw from the study out of the total number who consented), as it reduces the sample size and the power to detect significant intervention effects. There are no clearly established criteria for determining what may be considered acceptable levels of attrition; however, the following ranges were suggested: an attrition rate < 5 per cent is of little concern in introducing bias; 5–20 per cent is a possible source of bias; and > 20 per cent has a great probability of bias (Dumville et al., 2006).

Systematic reviews have been conducted to examine attrition rates in intervention research. Dumville et al. (2006) reviewed 132 RCTs of different medical interventions; attrition was reported in 54 per cent of the trials but was not mentioned in the remaining trials. For trials reporting an attrition rate, the median rate was 7 per cent (range: .08 per cent – 48 per cent). In a similar review of 125 studies evaluating psychotherapy, Wierzbicki and Pekarik (1993) estimated the mean dropout rate at 47 per cent. Valentine and McHugh (2007) analyzed the results of 26 studies in the field of education and found an average attrition rate of 26 per cent (range: 1–30 per cent). High dropout rates are often observed in studies of smoking cessation interventions (up to 50 per cent; Young et al., 2006) and of cognitive behavioral therapies for the management of insomnia (up to 40 per cent; Ong et al., 2008). These results indicate that attrition is pervasive and its extent varies with the type of intervention under evaluation and the target population.

Factors Associated with Attrition

Attrition is not only pervasive in intervention evaluation research, but is often systematic (Shadish et al., 1998), being associated with a wide range of factors. Participants who withdraw differ from those who complete the trial on several factors, which alters the composition of the remaining sample and hence limits external validity, and compromises the comparability of the treatment groups and hence weakens internal validity.

Characteristics of participants

Ample evidence, obtained from individual studies and systematic reviews, shows that participants' personal, clinical, and psychological characteristics are related to attrition. Four reviews identified participants' characteristics contributing to attrition in studies evaluating different interventions. Harris (1998) mentioned that racial status, level of education, and income were commonly reported as the most significant predictors of attrition. Moser et al. (2000) listed the following factors as affecting attrition in a trial: perceived susceptibility to the health problem targeted by the intervention, perception of personal benefit from participation in the study or enactment of the treatment, age, psychological health (e.g., depression), and employment status. Lindsay Davis et al. (2002) stereotyped dropouts as older, non-white, men, with limited education, having multiple health problems and a pattern of erratic healthcare utilization, and experiencing increased life stress. Ahern and Le Brocque (2005) reported old age, loneliness, poor health, lower education and schooling, low socio-economic status, and low cognitive ability as factors contributing to attrition. Another five reviews highlighted the profile of participants who withdraw from studies evaluating different types of intervention. Graham and Donaldson (1993) found that participants with high levels of substance use at pre-test were more likely than others to drop out of treatment. Boyd et al. (1992) described participants who withdrew from a trial of dietary intervention as younger and lighter in weight than those who completed the study. Keller et al. (2005) identified that ethnicity, gender, severity of illness, age, psychological distress, lack of transportation, family obligations, and interference with work were associated with attrition in studies of interventions aimed at promoting physical activity. Coday et al. (2005) held focus group sessions with research staff involved in 15 studies of smoking cessation, physical activity, and dietary treatments to identify factors contributing to attrition. The results revealed the following participant-related factors: loss of interest in the study, being too busy, competing demand for time, poor health, transportation issues, family or life events (e.g., death or illness), financial difficulty, conflicts with job, and personality issues. In their systematic review of 125 studies evaluating psychotherapy, Wierzbicki and Pekarik (1993) found an increased risk of attrition for participants of an African American race, low level of education, and low socio-economic status. The investigators proposed a mechanism underlying the influence of these participants' characteristics on attrition. They explained that differences between the participants and the therapists in terms of education, value system, and expectations concerning the nature and duration of therapy account for withdrawal. Additional research is needed to understand how and why participants' characteristics contribute to attrition; such an understanding is necessary to design appropriate strategies to prevent attrition.

Characteristics of study

Different aspects of a research study have been reported to contribute to attrition. The aspects frequently mentioned as reasons for participants' withdrawal include: burdensome procedures such as completing a daily diary (Keller et al., 2005; Lindsay Davis et al., 2002); invasive procedures like taking blood samples; frequency and timing of data collection, where dropout rates are higher in studies involving frequent administration of measures at short time intervals (e.g., every month), over a long time period (e.g., over one year) (Lindsay Davis et al., 2002). Also noted are the type, amount, and appropriateness of incentives given for continued participation where monetary compensation adequate to cover costs of transportation, childcare, and time spent in research activities may be well received by participants of low socio-economic status (Keller et al., 2005; Lindsay Davis et al., 2002); a lack of flexibility in the application of research activities such as scheduling study visits (e.g., conflict between the working hours for participants and for research staff) and location at which the research activities are performed (e.g., a location requiring a long journey for most participants to receive the intervention) (Coday et al., 2005; Keller et al., 2005). The skills of research staff related to communication or interpersonal skills and empathy toward participants have also been mentioned (Coday et al., 2005; Harris, 1998).

The specific design used in intervention evaluation studies is emerging as a factor contributing to attrition. For instance, higher attrition rates are anticipated in waiting-list control group and RCT designs. In the waiting-list control group, the length of time on the waiting list (i.e., the time interval for participants in the delayed group to receive treatment) is believed to be associated with participants' withdrawal. Two mechanisms explain this association. The first is that participants waiting for a long time become dissatisfied, lose interest, and thus decide to withdraw (Harris, 1998). The second relates to participants' experience of spontaneous recovery or improvement in their condition during the waiting period; therefore, they no longer perceive the need for treatment and withdraw from the trial (Baekeland and Lundwall, 1975). However, Anderson et al. (1987) found no significant association between length of time on a waiting list and attrition. In an RCT participants with preferences randomized to mismatched treatment are more likely to withdraw from the trial than those allocated to the treatment matching their preference. Recent empirical evidence, presented in Chapter 7, showed lower attrition rates for the matched than mismatched participants within an RCT (e.g., Kwan et al., 2010; Ong et al., 2008; Preference Collaborative Review Group, 2009; Sidani et al., 2007; Swift et al., 2011).

Characteristics of treatment and outcome status

The characteristics of the treatments, whether actual or perceived, may prompt participants to withdraw from a trial. Actual characteristics reported to be associated with attrition
include:

1. Complexity and inflexibility of treatment protocols: Interventions that are complex,
   involving the application of multiple treatment recommendations, and requiring changes
   in different aspects of life are considered cumbersome, demanding, and difficult to enact.
   Similarly, interventions that are inflexible and ignore the participants' individual needs,
   values, and life conditions are not easily applied. Participants are not able to keep up
   with the treatment demands or to adhere to treatment recommendations. Faced with
   these challenges, some participants decide to withdraw from the treatment and the study
   (Keller et al., 2005; Wingerson et al., 1993).
2. Ineffectiveness of comparison treatment: Participants randomized to the comparison
   treatment become aware of the lack or low level of treatment effectiveness because they
   do not experience improvement in the outcomes. They withdraw from the treatment
   or study. This is often encountered in participants receiving a placebo treatment. In a
   systematic review of antipsychotic treatment trials, Kemmer et al. (2007) found higher
   attrition rates in two situations: 1) RCTs involving placebo treatment, compared to
   RCTs having active medication as comparison treatment, and 2) the group receiving
   placebo treatment, compared to those receiving the antipsychotic treatment, in placebo-
   controlled trials.

Perceived treatment characteristics reported to contribute to outcome are related to
participants' view of the intervention and the comparison treatment. Perceived desirability
and acceptability of treatment is acknowledged as a factor contributing to differential
attrition in a trial (Cook, 2007; Janevic et al., 2003). Acceptability refers to a favorable
attitude toward treatment (Tarrier et al., 2006). Participants perceiving the treatments in a
trial and to which they are allocated as ineffective tend to withdraw from the study (Moser
et al., 2000; Wingerson et al., 1993). In addition, outcome status has been mentioned as a
factor leading to attrition. Participants who do not experience improvement in the health
problem for which they seek treatment and participants who experience multiple and severe
side effects of treatment may withdraw from the study (Wingerson et al., 1993).

Baseline Non-comparability of Treatment Groups and Attrition

The impact of attrition that is of most concern is non-comparability of participants who
complete the study, in the intervention and comparison groups on personal, health, and
clinical characteristics, and outcomes measured at baseline. The non-comparability of the

study groups occurs primarily with differential attrition; it introduces selection bias and the potential confounding of the intervention effects, thereby weakening internal validity. Whereas the results of individual trials may indicate the presence of baseline between-group differences, the findings of one systematic review do not fully support the linkage between attrition and baseline non-comparability of the groups. Valentine and McHugh (2007) reviewed the results of 26 experiments in the field of education. The reports of these experiments presented data on attrition at the student level and data on baseline variables that allowed calculation of the effect size to quantify the magnitude of the between-group differences. A total of 34 comparisons on baseline characteristics were made and the respective effect sizes were estimated. Of these, 21 effect sizes were positive, implying higher scores for the intervention group; 12 effect sizes were negative, reflecting higher scores in the comparison group; and one effect size was close to zero. The mean effect size was .05. Although the mean effect size suggests a non-significant association between attrition and baseline group differences, the findings indicate that such differences, of various magnitude, were present in all but one of the comparisons. Therefore, baseline non-comparability is pervasive and should be managed to minimize confounding of the intervention effects.

STRATEGIES TO HANDLE ATTRITION

The potential impact of attrition on the statistical conclusion, internal, and external validity of an intervention evaluation study necessitates the application of strategies to handle it effectively. Two categories of strategies are used. The first consists of modifications that can be made to the study design and methods aimed at preventing attrition and promoting retention. The second involves statistical techniques to manage missing data related to attrition.

Retention Strategies

Numerous retention strategies have been proposed. Some strategies relate to the study design and conduct; others focus on the interaction with participants; and a few pertain to the treatment.

Strategies related to the study design and conduct

This type of strategy entails modifications in the study procedures to make participation convenient and rewarding, which encourages participants to remain in the study.

1. Creation of a project identity: The project identity can take the form of a study acronym or logo that reflects the essence of what the study is about. The acronym or logo can

be used on all forms to be administered and all correspondence with participants. The appearance of the acronym or logo on all correspondence materials assists participants in recognizing the materials (and hence to avoid ignoring or discarding it) and in self-identifying with the study (i.e., remembering they are enrolled in the study) (Lindsay Davis et al., 2002; Ribisl et al., 1996).

2. Distribution of a study newsletter: A newsletter can be produced to share information on the study progress (e.g., number of persons who enrolled and completed the study) and successes (e.g., unsolicited comments made by participants). The newsletter can also serve as a venue for answering commonly asked questions about the study (Salyer et al., 1998). The newsletter should be carefully crafted, short, and appealing; it can be distributed to recruitment settings, key stakeholders, and participants, electronically or in hard copy.

3. Extension of recruitment: This strategy consists of increasing the number of persons recruited for the study to account for attrition (Pruitt and Privette, 2001). This strategy can be implemented preemptively when calculating the study sample size, or reactively throughout the study period. An anticipated attrition rate can be estimated from relevant empirical evidence obtained from trials that evaluated the same or similar intervention as the one under evaluation, in the same or comparable target population. The additional number of participants to recruit is derived from the anticipated attrition rate and the required sample size. For example, if the power analysis for an intervention evaluation study indicates the need for 100 participants and the anticipated attrition rate is 30 per cent, then an additional 30 participants are recruited for a total of 130. This will yield the required sample size if 30 per cent of participants withdraw. This approach is efficient as recruitment resources are planned adequately and recruitment sites are approached and enrolled early on, thereby facilitating study completion in a timely manner. Alternatively, accurate and up-to-date recruitment logs are maintained throughout the study period, and reviewed periodically to determine the need for extending recruitment in order to account for the observed attrition rate.

4. Run-in period: Run-in periods are used to screen for potential non-adherence which is preset as an exclusion criterion in many RCTs (Lindsay Davis et al., 2002; Shumaker et al., 2000). The run-in periods are usually scheduled prior to baseline data collection. The periods extend over a few days or a few weeks, during which participants are requested to perform a research activity planned for the trial such as completion of a daily diary or to take a placebo treatment. Participants' compliance is monitored, and those showing an acceptable (e.g., $\geq$ 70 per cent) compliance level are considered eligible. Only this latter group of participants is enrolled in the trial, with the assumption that they will remain in the study and complete all the planned treatment and study activities. The selected participants have a low tendency to withdraw.

5. Tracking participants: Tracking participants involves monitoring their engagement in the phases planned for the study, as well as their behaviors associated with attrition

and non-adherence. A participant tracking log is used to document engagement in the research activities. The log lists the activities to be monitored (e.g., screening, baseline data collection, attendance at the treatment sessions, post-test and follow-up data collection). Documentation is done for whether or not the participants perform each listed activity, the date of performance, and the reasons for non-engagement in the activities if provided by participants. Periodical review of the recorded information is useful in identifying participants with missed appointments. Remedial strategies can be applied as needed. For instance, follow-up contacts are made with participants to explore reasons for the missed appointments and the possibility of rescheduling them. Analysis of the reasons for non-engagement in specific research activities may reveal issues or challenges experienced by participants and suggest ways to address them (e.g., scheduling conflicts, unclear treatment recommendations relayed by interventionists). Tracking participants' behaviors is done informally during any interaction with research staff and interventionists. Shumaker et al. (2000) reported the following cues as reliable predictors of attrition: rescheduling for data collection session; lateness to data collection or treatment sessions; difficulty reaching participants by phone; hesitancy expressed at the time of recruitment, data collection, or treatment delivery; grimaces made when staff explain the study at the time of recruitment, during the consent process, and the treatment sessions; and questioning the importance of the study. Close monitoring of these participants is highly encouraged; additional clarification is made or motivational strategies are implemented as a means for monitoring their interest in the study and promoting retention.

6. Follow-up: This strategy consists of following up with participants who missed appointments for data collection and attendance at treatment sessions. Participants who do not show up at a scheduled meeting are contacted to inquire about their status, the reasons for missing the session, and their interest in continued participation in the study (Coday et al., 2005; Pruitt and Privette, 2001). The follow-up contacts demonstrate interest and respect for the person and provide the opportunity to reschedule the meeting, if participants had extraneous circumstances that prevented their engagement in the planned research activity; thus, withdrawal is minimized. It is recommended to attempt a maximum of three to five follow-up contacts (Lindsay Davis et al., 2002) to avoid the perception of aggressive retention efforts. If participants do not respond, then they are considered to have dropped out or lost to follow-up.

7. Reduced participation burden: Reduced participation burden entails minimizing the demands and efforts expanded in engaging in the planned research activities. This can be accomplished by limiting data collection to key variables that are of direct relevance to the study and to the most significant time points at which changes in short- and long-term outcomes are anticipated to occur; and by simplifying data collection, that is, using short versions of measures if available, clear and easy to read items, and the most

appropriate yet simple method for obtaining data that is not time consuming (Coday et al. 2005; Veitch et al., 2001). Participants who perceive that the effort and time required for engaging in a research activity exceed the potential benefits of volunteering in the study, may withdraw (Pruitt and Privette, 2001).

8. Frequent contact: This strategy involves contacting participants at different time points to remind them of the upcoming research activity, of the need to complete the activity on a timely basis, and of the importance of full participation (Leach, 2003; Lindsay Davis et al., 2002; Lyons et al., 2004; Shumaker et al., 2000). The contacts are made verbally (in person or by telephone), in writing (postcard), or electronically based on available resources or preferences of the target population and individual participants. They are scheduled at key points, including 1) a few days or a week prior to the planned activity: this contact is made to remind participants of the date, time, and location of data collection or treatment session; 2) a few days or a week following the planned activity: this contact aims to inquire about the participants' status if they did not complete the planned activity, the reasons for non-completion, willingness for continued involvement in the trial, and the need to reschedule the activity within the required time frame – inquiry about participants' status is important to demonstrate respect for the person and not only as a research participant; 3) at the mid point within the time interval between two consecutive planned research activities (e.g., at 1.5 months within the 3-month interval between pre-test and first follow-up): this contact serves as a reminder of participants' involvement in the intervention evaluation trial; it can be used to express appreciation for their participation (e.g., thanking them for completing the post-test measures), to inform them of the type and date of the next research activity (e.g., questionnaire will be sent in about a month and a half), and to request an update on their contact information (e.g., changes in telephone number or mailing address). These frequent contacts provide opportunities to keep participants informed of the planned research activities and therefore to avoid missing engagement in these activities, and keep research staff informed of any changes in participants' status and contact information and therefore to avoid potential loss of contact.

9. Convenience: Making participation in an intervention evaluation study convenient is a commonly recommended strategy to promote retention (Leach, 2003; Lindsay Davis et al., 2002; Lyons et al., 2004; Ribisl et al., 1996; Salyer et al., 1998). This can be accomplished by allowing for some flexibility in the performance of the research activities in a way that accommodates for participants' life or health circumstances while maintaining study integrity. Convenience is reflected in selection of the location for delivering the intervention and for collecting data; the location should be accessible to most participants (by public transportation or having available parking spots), within reasonable travel distance, and easily recognized or identified (through a map and appropriate signage); yet, the setting should have the environmental features required

to facilitate the implementation of the treatments under evaluation. A convenient date and time for providing treatment and obtaining data is important also; the schedule for these research activities should be done at participants' convenience (e.g., early evening for working participants) to avoid any conflicts with the participants' usual activities; scheduling conflict is often reported as a reason for study withdrawal. Last, the mode of data collection or sending reminders must be acceptable and convenient to most participants. For instance, some participants indicate preference for phoning in their daily diary, others feel comfortable documenting the diary information on paper and faxing it to the study office; and others choose to complete an electronic copy of the diary and email it.

10. Incentives: Offering incentives to participants is a frequently used strategy for minimizing attrition (Coday et al., 2005; Leach, 2003; Lindsay Davis et al., 2002; Lyons et al., 2004; Veitch et al., 2001). Incentives are a means for rewarding participants and demonstrating appreciation for their involvement in the trial. The type, amount, and timing for giving the incentives should be carefully planned so that the incentives are appealing to participants yet not considered coercive. The type of incentives may vary with the target population and with the resources available to the study. For instance, making arrangements for childcare is of relevance to working women; reimbursement for travel and parking costs is appealing for persons with a low income; a gift card or movie pass may motivate young adults or adolescents to remain in the study. Monetary incentives, however, are not encouraged in studies involving substance abusers. The total amount of the incentives should cover expenses incurred by participants (e.g., travel costs). In addition, it may compensate for the time that participants put in to engage in some research activities, particularly those pertaining to data collection. It is usual to offer the treatment, whether pharmacological or non-pharmacological, free of charge, which serves as an incentive for some participants to remain in treatment and complete the study; therefore, participants are not compensated for the time spent in treatment. In some Phase 4 trials, the treatments under investigation are incorporated in best practice guidelines, and given to patients as part of the healthcare to which they are entitled. In such instances, participants may pay for the treatment they receive either directly (out of pocket) or indirectly (if covered by the healthcare insurance plan). Incentives are provided upon completion of the study or preferably at different points throughout the study period, such as upon completion of each data collection session or visit to the study office. The former option may not be approved from an ethical standpoint as it forces some participants to remain in the study. The latter option can serve as an immediate reward for participants' engagement in the research activity and to offset travel expenses associated with a particular visit, thereby maintaining participants' willingness to complete the study.

Strategies related to interaction with participants

This category of strategies focuses on communicating clear and accurate information about the study and treating participants with respect. The goals are to prevent misinformation and unrealistic expectations, and consequently disappointment, which may lead to withdrawal, and to convey a sense of appreciation for participants' involvement in the trial, which generates feelings of comfort and gratitude and hence willingness to complete the study. The implementation of these strategies requires the selection of research staff with good communication skills and appropriate interpersonal style, and adequate training in the performance of the strategies and in the skills for motivating and negotiating with participants (Lindsay Davis et al., 2002; Shumaker et al., 2000).

1. Clear explanation of the study: There should be a clear, comprehensive, and unbiased explanation of: what the study entails; the nature, sequence, timing, and length of time spent in the research activities; the method for treatment allocation; the burden, discomfort, or risks; as well as the incentives and benefits of taking part in the study. This should be done prior to participants' enrollment (i.e., during the consent process) and throughout the study as needed. The explanation ensures participants understand what their involvement consists of and can make necessary arrangements accordingly (e.g., taking time off work or arranging for childcare). Additional clarification is provided, in writing or orally, prior to the performance of an activity. For instance, participants are reminded of the number of treatment sessions, duration of each session, and frequency as well as the specific dates and times for giving the session by the interventionist at the beginning of the first session; and the approximate time it takes to complete the post-test outcome measures in a cover letter. Participants are encouraged to call the research staff to seek clarification on any aspect of the study or instructions for completing measures or applying treatment recommendations.

2. Benefits of participation: This strategy consists of emphasizing the significance of the study and the benefits of participation, during the consent process and throughout the study, as needed (Coday et al., 2005; Lindsay Davis et al., 2002). This may convince participants who are hesitant and question the utility of the treatment or the study, of the importance of their involvement, and motivate them to complete treatment or the study. For example, many persons who experience insomnia for a long period of time express their skepticism about the effectiveness of behavioral therapies. Reiterating the potential benefits of these treatments (i.e., they do not involve medications with known side effects; they help participants gain control of their sleep; they show long-term effectiveness and reduced daytime fatigue) and making the point that 'they have nothing to lose in trying the therapy' have been useful strategies in motivating this group of persons with

chronic insomnia to attend and adhere to the behavioral therapies. Experience of reduced insomnia severity contributes further to their retention in the trial.

3. Acknowledgement of participants' contribution: Acknowledgement of participants' contribution is done by expressing gratitude, orally or in writing, for completing measures of study variables (e.g., adding the words THANK YOU at the end of the self-report questionnaire or face-to-face interview) or for attending the treatment sessions; by sending them a card indicating receipt of the completed measures and thanking them for doing so; or by sending them a certificate of appreciation for their participation in the study (Lyons et al., 2004; Salyer et al., 1998). Acknowledgement of participants' contribution promotes a feeling that they are important (Leach, 2003) and hence sustains their involvement in the study.

4. Respect for participants: Conveying respect for participants can be done through the way they are addressed (e.g., with their last name) and treated which involves respecting their time by being prompt at scheduled sessions, not rushing them through when performing an activity, respecting and responding to their questions (Ahern and Le Brocque, 2005); using personal greetings and real signatures on correspondence with participants (Salyer et al., 1998); recognizing and addressing their individual needs and life circumstances when scheduling sessions; and acknowledging and respecting their right of self-determination. Respecting participants is a means for valuing them as human beings with meaningful contributions, which sustains their interest in the study.

Strategies related to the treatment

This category of strategy consists of a few suggestions to make the treatments appealing to participants. These include careful specification of the treatment dose: the advice is to have short treatment sessions (Pruitt and Privette, 2001) and the minimum required number of sessions, given over a short time period, which would make attendance manageable to various subgroups of participants, particularly those with potential scheduling conflict. A second strategy entails careful selection of the comparison treatment: the recommendation is to have an appealing comparison treatment (Lindsay Davis et al., 2002) in which participants are exposed to some form of therapy, even if it is inert (i.e., placebo) (see Chapter 11). Participants who receive some treatment recommendations, as compared to those allocated to the no-treatment control condition, are likely to remain in treatment and complete the study. Conducting a pilot study is critical for determining the feasibility and acceptability of the treatments; the results give directions for refining the design of the treatments to make them appealing.

Effectiveness of retention strategies

The empirical evidence supporting the effectiveness of the retention strategies described previously is very limited. No study was found that compared the utility of the strategies in reducing attrition and promoting retention rates in intervention evaluation trials. This may be related to the necessity to use multiple retention strategies in any particular trial, which makes it difficult to dismantle the effects of specific strategies on attrition or retention rates. The use of multiple retention strategies is advocated because they may target different subgroups of participants. Further, the strategies are complementary and supplementary, and expected to be highly effective when combined. In addition, the nature of some proposed retention strategies (e.g., respect for participants) may not lend to their measurement and quantification, which would be required to evaluate their impact on attrition. This may have led Coday et al. (2005) to conduct a qualitative study to explore the perceived effectiveness of retention strategies. The study consisted of focus group sessions held with research staff involved in 15 trials that examined the efficacy of health promotion interventions. The focus group sessions inquired about the research staff's perception of effective retention strategies. The results indicated that across the 15 trials, the research staff considered the following strategies as most effective in enhancing retention: flexibility in scheduling research activities with participants' input; provision of incentives; emphasizing the benefits of the trial to participants; and persistence which involved rescheduling of visits. The research staff advocated the use of multiple retention strategies in any intervention evaluation trial.

Management Strategies

Attrition yields data that are missing for some participants, on some treatment and outcome variables, at some points in time. Several strategies have been devised to handle missing data (McKnight et al., 2007). Four have been frequently used to address missing data associated with attrition in intervention evaluation trials: intention-to-treat, imputation, sensitivity analysis, and the use of an instrumental variable. The application of the strategies is preceded by preliminary analysis aimed at determining extent and impact of attrition.

1. Determining extent and impact of attrition: These preliminary analyses involve:

   o Estimation of the attrition rate (i.e., the percentage of consenting participants who withdraw) for the trial and for each of the intervention and comparison groups.
   o Content analysis of the reasons for withdrawal given by participants allocated to each treatment group, with particular attention to those reflecting dislike or dissatisfaction with the treatment received.
   o Comparison on characteristics and on outcomes assessed at baseline, of participants who dropped out and participants who completed the study; the results of this comparison shed light on the representativeness of the sample with complete data and assist in identifying variables contributing to attrition; these variables can be used to generate an instrumental variable.

    ○ Comparison on all baseline variables of participants who withdraw and participants who remain in the trial, and are assigned to the intervention or comparison group; the findings of this comparison indicate the presence of differential attrition and therefore, identify baseline variables with a potential confounding influence, which should be controlled for statistically.

2. Intention-to-treat: This strategy rests on the principle of maintaining group comparability at baseline to prevent selection bias and subsequent confounding. Accordingly, all participants randomized to the intervention and the comparison groups are included in the statistical analysis aimed at estimating the intervention effects, whether or not they withdraw from the trial. For participants who drop out, their missing outcome data are handled with different strategies (see Chapter 12).

3. Imputation: This strategy involves replacing the data missing on outcome variables on some time points, with some values (see Chapter 12).

4. Sensitivity analysis: This strategy calls for estimating the intervention effects using data obtained from participants who remained in the study and have complete data (i.e., excluding dropouts), and all participants included in the study with data missing for dropouts imputed. The intervention effects estimated with the two data sets are compared to determine appropriateness of the imputation technique used and extent of sample selection bias introduced with attrition.

5. Use of an instrumental variable: This strategy entails identifying the mechanism underlying attrition and accounting for the mechanism in the data analysis. Specifically, comparison on baseline characteristics of participants who complete and who withdraw from the study, and analysis of reasons for attrition, may indicate the variable or set of variables that contribute to attrition. An instrumental variable is generated to reflect the profile of dropouts, using appropriate statistical techniques (such as logistic regression). The instrumental variable is then included in the data analysis aimed at determining the intervention effects, for the purpose of controlling statistically its influence on the outcomes (Earle et al., 2001; Leigh et al., 1993).

The application of strategies to manage missing data resulting from attrition is useful in minimizing the impact of attrition on statistical conclusions (e.g., imputation of missing data maintains adequate sample size) and internal (e.g., control of potential confounds) validity, and in identifying the profile of patients (based on the profile of participants with complete data) who may benefit from the intervention. There is limited evidence of the effectiveness of these strategies in enhancing validity in intervention evaluation research.

Final note: prevention is better than cure!

Summary

- Attrition is prevalent in intervention research. It takes place before, during, and after treatment delivery and for various reasons related to the characteristics of participants, treatment, or study
- Attrition alters the size and composition of the sample, threatening statistical conclusion, internal, and external validity
- Retention strategies are incorporated in a trial to prevent attrition. They involve modification of study procedures to make participation convenient and rewarding; to convey clear and accurate information about the study and respect for participants; and to make treatments appealing
- Management strategies are used to handle missing data induced by attrition

10

ASSIGNMENT OF PARTICIPANTS TO STUDY GROUPS

Once selected and found eligible, participants are assigned to the intervention and comparison groups, using different methods. In this chapter, the logic underlying each method, as well as its strengths and weaknesses are discussed. Evidence supporting the points of discussion is synthesized. Practical issues encountered with the application of the treatment allocation methods are highlighted, as well as strategies for carrying out concealment of treatment allocation.

RANDOM ASSIGNMENT

Random assignment or randomization involves the application of chance-based procedures for allocating participants to the intervention and the comparison treatment (Borglin and Richards, 2010). The process of randomization is applied at the level of individual participants in RCTs or the level of the targeted group in cluster randomized trials. It is done in a way that gives eligible, consenting participants or clusters an equal chance of receiving the intervention, thereby increasing the likelihood that participants in the intervention and the comparison groups are comparable on personal, health, and clinical characteristics measured at baseline. There are different procedures and schemes for the application of the randomization process.

Randomization Procedures

Different procedures are available to randomly assign participants to the intervention and comparison groups. Some are more advantageous in providing an equal chance to all participants to receive the intervention and others are simpler and easier to apply. The selection of a procedure is based on a careful consideration of its advantages and disadvantages, as well as accessibility to required resources.

Flip of a coin

The simplest method is to make an assignment by flipping a coin. Research staff toss a coin to identify the group to which a participant is to be assigned, following a pre-specified decision guide such as: if the coin yields Heads, the participant goes to the intervention group, and if the coin toss yields Tails, the participant goes to the comparison treatment group. The coin flip can be done ahead and the results are recorded on a list to direct allocation of sequentially consenting participants. Alternatively, the coin flip is done by the research staff, in the presence of the participant. This randomization procedure is rather easy to apply and provides an equal (50 per cent) chance for each participant to get the intervention. However, this process breaks down if there are more than two treatments in the study. Flip of a coin has two disadvantages. First, the coin toss is under the control of research staff; it can be tampered with, in that the research staff can repeat the toss until the treatment desired by the participant or deemed suitable (i.e., consistent with participants' needs) by staff, is allocated. Second, there is a probability that the coin toss may yield, by chance, unbalanced numbers of participants in the groups.

Table of random numbers

This procedure involves random selection of a number from a table of numbers, to determine the treatment to which a participant is to be allocated. The tables are appended in most books on statistics. To use the table, one puts a finger on a randomly selected spot on the table; if the number listed on the spot is odd, then the participant would be assigned to, let's say, the intervention, and if the number is even, then allocation would be to the comparison group. One then moves in a randomly selected direction (e.g., upward, downward, right, or left) to randomly select another spot, and the corresponding number is used to assign another participant, based on the pre-specified rule. For instance, if the selected number is or ends with 0, 1, or 2, then the participant is assigned to one experimental intervention; if the number is or ends with 3, 4, or 5, then assignment is to the second experimental intervention (in studies evaluating two treatments); if the number is or ends with 6, 7, or 8, then allocation is to the comparison treatment; if the number ends with 9, it would simply be skipped. Similar to the flip of a coin, this randomization procedure is applied by the research staff in the presence of participants, or prior to enrollment. In the latter case, treatment assignment would be written on a card or paper and placed in a sealed opaque envelope. The advantages of using the table of random numbers are: ease of application and maintenance of chance allocation. Its disadvantage includes the possibility of being tampered with (if done by research staff at the moment of treatment allocation) and of generating unbalanced treatment group sizes (Padhye et al., 2009).

Sealed opaque envelopes

This randomization procedure consists of preparing envelopes containing a card or paper on which treatment group assignment is written. The envelopes are opaque and the card or paper is folded to conceal the group assignment. The group assignment is based on the selection of random numbers from the table as described in the previous section. Alternatively, the number of envelopes to be prepared is consistent with the total number of participants to be enrolled and is equally divided across the study groups. For instance, if the required sample size is 50 and the trial involves an experimental intervention and a comparison treatment, then 25 envelopes would indicate allocation to the intervention and 25 to the comparison treatment. All sealed envelops can be put in a box, and research staff can pick one when needed, as an additional strategy for maintaining concealment of assignment. The envelope can be opened in the presence of participants, which will illustrate the notion of randomization to participants. The advantages of this procedure are: it is simple and easy to apply; it maintains chance allocation and increases the probability of balanced group sizes; and it enhances concealment as it is less prone to human (research staff or participant) influence on allocation to treatments (Padhye et al., 2009; Watson et al., 2004). Its disadvantages relate to its limited practicality when the study sample size is large or when the study involves multiple sites that are geographically dispersed; in this case, computer-generated allocation is a more appropriate procedure.

Computer-generated allocation

In this procedure, the list of random numbers to be used for participants' allocation to treatment is generated through relevant computer software. The researcher stores the list in a computer and oversees the randomization process, or entrusts the process to a central coordination office led by a statistician. The advantages of computer-generated allocation include: maintenance of chance allocation, treatment assignment concealment, and balanced numbers of participants across study groups. In addition, this procedure makes easy the application of various randomization schemes, discussed in the next section. The disadvantages of computer-generated allocation relates to the resources needed to use this procedure and the logistics of exchanging pertinent information between the research and the central coordination office staff that may delay assignment of participants.

Random selection of participants into the intervention group

This procedure, also called Zelen randomization, consists of randomly selecting participants, from the pool of all those eligible, to receive the experimental intervention. The remaining participants continue to get treatment as usual. Zelen (1979) advocated this treatment allocation procedure to overcome the non-consent bias and the low enrollment rate prevalent in RCTs evaluating interventions in the practice context. The Zelen randomization procedure mitigates this problem by randomly selecting eligible patients and obtaining consent only from those allocated to the experimental intervention. It has the advantage of eliminating the possible feelings of disappointment and demoralization among those in a traditional RCT who give consent for a trial, hoping to get the experimental intervention but end up in the comparison group. The application of this randomization procedure is appropriate in trials involving comparison of an innovative intervention with usual care; no participant is denied treatment to which they are entitled. There are some ethical and practical issues that have limited the use of Zelen randomization (Homer, 2002). From an ethical perspective, there are serious concerns regarding enrolling patients and collecting data on their treatments and outcomes, without their consent, even if nothing new is being done to them. McLean (1997) raised concerns that this randomization procedure disregards the fundamental tenets of research ethics: respect for the individual and right to self-determination. On a practical level, this procedure implies that no additional information can be gathered from patients receiving treatment as usual, particularly data on outcomes not assessed on a regular basis within the context of day-to-day practice, such as patients' beliefs and behavior performance. Although Zelen randomization has been used in intervention evaluation research (Adamson et al., 2005), the British Medical Research Council and the National Institutes of Health in the US have prohibited this procedure (Schellings et al., 2006).

Pseudo-randomization

Pseudo-randomization, also referred to as 'quasi-random' (Schulz and Grimes, 2002a), involves the application of simple procedures for allocating participants to the intervention and comparison groups. The procedures include:

1. Alternating group allocation from one participant to the next, that is, the first eligible participant is allocated to the intervention, the second to the comparison treatment, the third to the intervention, and so on.
2. Assigning to the intervention and the comparison groups on alternate days or weeks, that is, patients admitted to in-patient unit or attending an out-patient clinic on a particular day or week are assigned to the intervention, and those admitted to the unit or attending the clinic on the next day or week are assigned to the comparison group.

3. Using the participants' date of birth, initial letter of the last name or hospital identification number for allocation; for example, participants with birth date or identification number ending with an odd number are assigned to the intervention and an even number to the comparison group.
4. Assigning participants to the intervention group until the number of cases required for this group is attained, with all subsequent participants placed in the comparison group.

The advantages of quasi-random allocation procedures relate to their simplicity, which makes them easy to apply in studies conducted within the context of day-to-day practice; their acceptability to patients and healthcare professionals; and their potential for reducing the likelihood of contamination. The limitations are: 1) the procedures do not give an equal chance to all participants to receive the intervention; 2) the allocation scheme is transparent and can be easily tampered with by research staff or healthcare professionals referring patients to the study (e.g., clinic appointments may be rescheduled for patients considered in need of the intervention); and 3) there is a potential for selection bias if different subgroups of the target population are available at alternating times.

Randomization Schemes

The simple, unrestricted randomization procedures described in the previous section may not always yield groups with balanced sizes and composition. Alternative randomization schemes are used to mitigate these potential problems: block randomization, stratified randomization, minimization, and adaptive randomization.

Block randomization

Block randomization is used to decrease the potential for unequal numbers of participants in the intervention and comparison groups. Imbalance in group sizes may occur when studies are ended early for various reasons such as low enrollment rate and demonstrated superiority of the intervention that would make unethical allocation of subsequent participants to the comparison group. Rather than assigning participants one by one, block randomization allocates blocks of people to groups. The size of the block is a multiple of the number of groups included in the study; for example, if there are two groups (groups A and B), the block size could be four, and there are six possible schemes of assigning participants to groups:

1. AABB   2. ABAB   3. ABBA   4. BBAA   5. BABA   6. BAAB

A random sequence of block assignment is generated, and participants within a block are allocated to groups according to the scheme specified for the block. For instance, if the sequence of the block assignment is 5, 1, 2, 3, 4, 6, then the first four consenting participants are assigned according to the scheme specified for block 5: BABA, in that the first and third participants are allocated to group B and the second and fourth participants to group A; the next block of four participants are assigned according to the scheme specified for block 1: AABB, in that the first two participants are allocated to group A and the rest to group B. This randomization scheme guarantees if the study has to end early that the imbalance in group size does not exceed two participants.

Stratified randomization

Stratified randomization is used to balance the composition of the intervention and comparison groups relative to patient characteristics known to confound the effects of the intervention. This randomization scheme is done in two steps. In the first step, participants are stratified or matched on baseline characteristics hypothesized to be highly associated with the outcomes, whereby those with the same or similar level on a particular characteristic (e.g., level of depression) or profile on a set of characteristics (e.g., gender, smoking history, and level of depression) are grouped in one stratum. In the second step, participants within each stratum are randomly allocated to the intervention or the comparison group. This randomization scheme results in balanced distribution of participants with comparable characteristics in the groups; this in turn, minimizes the potential for selection bias and subsequent confounding. The application of stratified randomization has logistical challenges. It is often impractical to stratify on two or more characteristics; it takes time to find participants with comparable characteristics and in adequate number prior to randomizing them, particularly when the sample size needed for the study is small. Stratification is easier for dichotomous or categorical than continuous variables; in the latter case, it is important to clearly specify what is considered a similar level, that is, what width of the score interval reflects an acceptable level of comparability. For example, if participants are to be stratified on age is a 1, 2, or 5 year interval acceptable to determine comparability (i.e., are a 70 and a 65 year old comparable)? These challenges along with the availability of statistical techniques to adjust for baseline differences may have limited the use of stratified randomization.

Minimization

Minimization is an alternative randomization scheme for enhancing the comparability of participants in the intervention and comparison groups. It is conceptually similar to stratified randomization; its goal is to minimize between-group differences in participants' characteristics measured at baseline. It is appropriate to use when the number of characteristics to control for is large, exceeding what could be handled with stratification. Minimization begins by using the simple, unrestricted randomization procedures to assign the first five to ten participants to the intervention and comparison groups. After that, allocation is based on minimizing the differences in baseline characteristics (that may confound the intervention effects) between the groups. This implies that:

1. The distribution of the characteristics of the first five to ten participants allocated to the groups is identified. For instance, if the groups are to be balanced on sex (female vs. male), socio-economic status (low, middle, high), and education ($\leq$ high school vs. > high school), then the number of participants belonging to the different categories reflecting these characteristics assigned to the intervention and comparison group is determined as: two females, three middle socio-economic status, and four with > high school education, and three females, two middle socio-economic status, and three > high school education, respectively.
2. The status on these characteristics of subsequent participants is assessed prior to randomization.
3. The participants' status indicates to which treatment group they are to be assigned to maintain a balanced distribution on the characteristics between groups.

The application of minimization is facilitated with computerized programs run by the investigator or statistician at a central coordination office, and requires clear and prompt communication between research staff (who assess and report the status of participants on the selected characteristics) and the researcher or statistician (who enters the data and reports group assignment).

Adaptive randomization

Adaptive, also called urn, randomization was introduced to minimize the ethical problem of participants in the comparison group being denied a useful treatment, or those in the experimental group being given a useless or harmful intervention. In this scheme, the allocation for a given participant is determined by the success or failure of the previously enrolled participants. If the previous participant receives the intervention and demonstrates a good outcome, then the next participant is allocated to the intervention group. Conversely, if the outcome for the previous participant is not beneficial, then the next participant is assigned to the comparison group. Alternatively, allocation is based on the number of successes and failures in each treatment, thereby reducing (to < 50 per cent) the probability of being assigned to the poorer treatment (Rosenberger, 1999). The advantage of adaptive randomization is that a large number of participants receive the successful intervention. However, there are some difficulties with the application of this scheme. The first is that the change in the outcome has to appear within a fairly short time period following treatment so that assignment of the next participants can be done in a timely way. The second is the need to have a clear-cut definition of what constitutes a successful outcome and a failure. The third is the possibility of having unbalanced sizes of groups, or having all participants assigned to one treatment group (i.e., the most effective treatment).

Role of Randomization

Random assignment has been considered the most critical safeguard of internal validity. It is believed to minimize selection bias associated with the process of assigning participants to the intervention and comparison groups (Porter et al., 2003; Towne and Hilton, 2004; Weinberger et al., 2002a, 2002b). The chance-based allocation to groups eliminates human influence on treatment allocation (Kaptchuk, 2001). Human influence relates to the participants' desire to receive the new, experimental intervention or preferences for treatment, and to the researchers' expectancies for demonstrating the benefits of the intervention. Human influence may result in non-comparability of participants in the intervention and comparison groups on characteristics measured at baseline, such that participants assigned to the intervention may be those most in need for treatment. For example, they experience the health problem targeted by the intervention at a high level of severity, they are of low socio-economic status, or they do not have health insurance to cover the treatment expenses. Needy participants may benefit from the intervention, showing high levels of improvement in the outcomes; this in turn may yield an overestimate of the intervention effects or show that the intervention is not effective if participants in the comparison group start better off and experience no change in the outcomes over time. Alternatively, participants may be assigned to the intervention group who have a profile that predisposes them to favorable reactions and responses to the intervention (Kraemer and Fendt, 1990), resulting in an over-estimate of the intervention effects.

Randomization minimizes selection bias and resultant confounding of the intervention effects through the following mechanisms:

1. Chance-based allocation implies that participants have an equal chance (50 per cent) of receiving the intervention, without the interference of the participants or the researchers.
2. Randomization creates a situation in which participants with given idiosyncrasies (i.e., personal, health, and clinical profile) assigned to one group will, on the average, be counterbalanced by participants with comparable idiosyncrasies allocated to the other group (Cook and Campbell, 1979). The end result is a balanced distribution of participants with similar, measured and unmeasured characteristics before implementation of the intervention (Kaul and Diamond, 2010).
3. This baseline comparability is indicated by non-significant between-group differences in participants' characteristics, at least in the characteristics actually measured prior to intervention delivery. This means that the average scores on the characteristics of participants in one group do not differ from the average scores reported for participants in the other group (Abel and Koch, 1999; McKee et al., 1999).

4. The initial comparability between the groups reduces the variability in the post-test outcomes that is not attributable to the intervention, which increases the chance of detecting significant and unbiased estimates of the intervention effects (Borglin and Richards, 2010). In other words, participants randomly assigned to the groups have comparable characteristics; if those who receive the intervention exhibit the hypothesized improvement in the outcomes, and those in the comparison group report no change in the outcomes from baseline to post-treatment, then the differences between groups in the outcomes observed at post-test can be confidently attributed to the intervention and not to any participant characteristics.

Limitations of Randomization

Despite its anticipated advantage in minimizing selection bias and confounding, and in enhancing internal validity, randomization has limitations. Recent arguments based on logic and emerging empirical evidence have challenged the previously uncontested advantage of randomization. The arguments are:

1. The baseline comparability of the groups, achieved by randomization, is probabilistic. This has two implications. The first implication is that random assignment does not guarantee that participants in the intervention and comparison groups are exactly matched on all characteristics and outcomes assessed at baseline, which may be associated with post-test outcomes (Cook et al., 2010; Watson et al., 2004). Accordingly, it has been recommended to check the comparability of the groups after randomization (Worrall, 2002). Any observed difference is due to chance and is considered of minimal consequence to internal validity if the characteristic for which a difference is found is weakly correlated with post-test outcomes (Peduzzi et al., 2002). However, even if the between-group differences are of small magnitude, they cannot be ignored; they may be clinically meaningful and may occur in characteristics that may influence engagement, adherence, and reactions to treatment, immediate outcomes, or mediators. The second implication of the probabilistic comparability is that randomization maintains comparability at the group, and not the individual participant level. As Cook and Campbell (1979: 340) stated: random assignment 'does not, of course, remove the idiosyncrasies from any one unit'. Therefore, inter-individual differences in baseline characteristics are not controlled for with randomization. The characteristics may still exert their influence on reactions to treatment and outcome achievement; they contribute to error variance, that is, variability in post-test outcomes that is not attributable to the intervention. Increased error variance reduces the power to detect significant intervention effects (Victora et al., 2004).

2. Randomization enhances group comparability prior to implementation of the intervention. However, it does not guarantee the maintenance of this comparability at post-test, particularly if differential attrition takes place. Yet comparability of participants

remaining in the intervention and comparison groups and providing outcome data at post-test is critical for making valid inferences regarding the effectiveness of the intervention (Chatterji, 2007).

3. Randomization poses threats to validity. This is related to participants' perception of randomization and of the treatments under evaluation. Many participants resent random assignment. They are not willing to leave the choice of treatment to chance alone; they prefer to be included in treatment decision making. The percentage of eligible participants who agree to randomization has been reported to be low across different fields of study. For instance, O'Reilly et al. (1999) found that 1 out of 20 participants accepted randomization to either of two treatments for prostate cancer. Coward (2002) reported that 6 of 41 women were willing to be randomly allocated to a support group for breast cancer survivors or a control group. Rothwell (2005) estimated that fewer than 10 per cent of participants agree to have their treatment chosen at random. Individuals who are not willing to be randomized may decline enrollment in the trial. Thus, participants differ from non-participants, at least in terms of acceptance of randomization, which is associated with personal, health, and clinical characteristics. Differences in the characteristics of participants and non-participants limit external validity, that is, the generalizability of the trial findings to all subgroups constituting the target population (Cook, 2006). For instance, McKay et al. (1998) compared male veterans seeking treatment for cocaine abuse who were and were not willing to be randomized to an in-patient rehabilitation program. They found that as compared to non-enrollees, participants were less educated, reported more days of cocaine use, and had more severe drug and psychiatric problems at baseline. In addition, eligible individuals may have strong preferences for the treatments under evaluation. If aware of random allocation to treatment, these individuals may decline enrollment in the study because they realize that they have a 50 per cent chance of getting the non-preferred treatment. Alternatively, they take part in the study with the hope to receive the preferred treatment. However, with randomization, some participants receive the non-preferred treatment and react unfavorably, whereas others receive the preferred treatment and react favorably, as described in Chapter 7. Their reactions influence their engagement, satisfaction, and adherence to treatment, and experience of improvement in the outcomes.

4. Randomization is not acceptable, and is not part of day-to-day practice (Bamberger and White, 2007; Towne and Hilton, 2004). In the latter context, patients and healthcare professionals expect careful consideration of alternative treatments for the prevention and management of health problems, and selection of the treatment that is responsive to patients' needs. Patients' needs and preferences are respected and healthcare professionals' expert opinion is sought throughout this collaborative effort. Random assignment is not consistent with the way in which treatment is allocated in the context of practice, raising questions about the applicability and utility of RCTs' results in guiding treatment decision making in day-to-day practice.

5. Randomization is not applicable, well received, or practical in some situations raising ethical concerns. Randomization rests on the state of equipoise. There are practical difficulties in ensuring a reasonably high level of compliance with random assignment when equipoise cannot be maintained. The latter situation includes the availability of evidence supporting the effectiveness of the intervention; in this case, it is unethical to deny some participants access to a potentially beneficial treatment; also patients and healthcare professionals perceive the treatments under investigation as unequally attractive and useful; therefore, they view randomization as an unfair method of allocation to treatment (Ong-Dean et al., 2011).

Additional empirical evidence supports the previously presented arguments, highlighting the limitations of randomization. As presented in Chapter 5, several individual and meta-analytic studies compared the effect sizes for the same intervention, given to the same target population, obtained in studies that did and did not randomize participants to the treatment groups. The results of most studies indicated that the mean effect sizes were similar for randomized and non-randomized studies (e.g., Concato et al., 2000; Ferriter and Huband, 2005). These findings suggest that aspects of the trial, other than randomization, contribute to the outcomes. These aspects include retention, participant selection of treatment, statistical control of confounding variables, and type of comparison treatment. The congruence in effect sizes of randomized and non-randomized studies weakens the claimed superiority (relative to other methods of treatment allocation) of random assignment in enhancing internal validity.

The extent to which randomization maintains comparability of the treatment groups on baseline characteristics has also been determined. Sidani (2006) examined the effect sizes for baseline characteristics in 100 randomly selected reports of RCTs evaluating a variety of interventions. The effect sizes quantified differences in demographic and outcome variables assessed at pre-test between the intervention and comparison groups. The absolute mean effect size, across the selected studies, was .24 for demographic characteristics and .20 for outcome variables. Shadish and Ragsdale (1996) reviewed 100 trials of marital or family psychotherapy using randomized and non-randomized designs and estimated the effect sizes for outcome variables measured at pre-test. They reported no statistically significant differences in the mean pre-test effect sizes between the randomized and non-randomized designs. Although the pre-test effect sizes estimated in these reviews were small, they reflect differences between groups that could potentially be clinically meaningful. This finding supports the argument that baseline comparability is achieved at the group level and that inter-individual differences in baseline characteristics are present and exert their influence on post-test outcomes. In fact, Sidani (2006), Heinsman and Shadish (1996), and Shadish and Ragsdale (1996) found a statistically significant, low-moderate, positive correlation between the effect sizes for outcomes assessed at pre-test and the effect sizes for the same outcomes assessed at post-test. Further, Shadish and colleagues reported that the effect size for the pre-test outcomes was the best predictor of the effect size for the post-test outcomes; this association was always significant, regardless of the presence of other predictors, such as method of assignment, attrition, or type of comparison, in the regression model.

The limitations of randomization identified on the basis of logic and empirical evidence raise questions about the utility of this method for treatment allocation in maintaining the validity of the inference regarding the causal effects of the intervention. Non-randomized methods of assignment are explored in the following section.

NON-RANDOM ASSIGNMENT METHODS

Two types of non-random methods for treatment assignment have been used in intervention evaluation research: others' selection of participants into treatment and participants' self-selection of treatment.

Others' Selection of Participant into Treatment

This method for allocating participants to groups is used in regression-discontinuity designs, pragmatic trials, observational studies, and in trials evaluating tailored or individualized interventions. In regression-discontinuity designs and in studies of tailored or individualized interventions, assignment to treatment is based on participants' status relative to a selected characteristic and follows a pre-specified algorithm. The algorithm delineates: 1) the specific characteristic guiding treatment allocation; 2) the instrument administered at baseline to measure the characteristic; 3) the procedure to compute the score that quantifies the participants' status on the characteristic; 4) the interpretation of the score obtained for individual participants relative to the available cut-off score or range of values; and 5) the rule directing the selection of treatment. The rule clarifies the linkage between the participants' status and the respective treatment. In regression-discontinuity designs, the rule is rather simple, taking a form, for example, that participants with a score above the cut-off value are allocated to the intervention and those with a score below the cut-off are assigned to the comparison treatment. The algorithm for allocating tailored or individualized treatments is rather complex stating which specific treatment or component of an intervention is given to participants whose scores fall within different ranges.

In pragmatic trials and observational studies, the researcher does not control or interfere with participants' assignment to treatment. The healthcare professionals are responsible for treatment decision making. However, the process used in treatment allocation is not clearly described; it may be based on the professionals' expert judgement or on a collaborative effort involving participants in treatment selection. Therefore, there is variability in the treatment assignment process, which may be associated with variability in participants' reactions and adherence to treatment, and consequently experience of improvement in outcomes.

Variability in outcome achievement reduces the statistical power to detect significant intervention effects. The empirical evidence presented in previous chapters show similarity in the findings of RCTs compared to non-randomized, observational studies and to regression-discontinuity designs, respectively. The evidence suggests that the method of assignment to treatment is not the only aspect of an intervention evaluation study with a critical contribution to the validity of causal inferences. Thus, others' selection of participants into treatment is a useful treatment assignment method that reflects what goes on in the context of day-to-day practice, without affecting internal validity. Further, it has the potential to enhance enrollment in the study, particularly for individuals who are not willing to receive treatment on the basis of chance.

Participant Self-selection of Treatment

Participant self-selection of treatment is represented in the allocation to the preferred treatment. The application of this type of assignment requires assessment of participants' preferences and allocation to the selected treatment. Two general approaches have been used to assess preference, direct and indirect, with variable utility in capturing participants' choice. The approaches are not guided by a clear conceptualization of treatment preferences and do not follow a rigorous procedure that yields well-informed and accurate reflection of participants' choice of treatment (Bowling and Rowe, 2005).

Conceptualization of treatment preferences

Treatment preferences refer to the participants' choice of treatment. They represent the specific treatment option they want to have (Stalmeier et al., 2007) to address the presenting health problem. Preferences are generated from the interplay of individuals' understanding of and attitudes toward the treatment options (Sidani et al., 2009b). Understanding is developed through exposure to information about each treatment option, prior to enrollment in the trial (e.g., through discussion with friends and healthcare providers, or review of material available on websites), or upon explanation of what is involved in the study during the consent process. Learning about the nature, benefits, risks, and the treatment recommendations contributes to the formulation of preferences. Attitudes toward treatment reflect participants' appraisal of the treatment options as acceptable or unacceptable (Van der Berg et al., 2008). Acceptability is based on a careful consideration of the following treatment attributes: appropriateness in addressing the presenting health problem, effectiveness in managing the problem, severity of side effects, and convenience or ease of applying the treatment recommendations in day-to-day life. Treatments are judged acceptable if they are perceived as appropriate, effective, convenient, and having minimal side effects (Sidani et al., 2009b; Tarrier et al., 2006).

This conceptualization has implications for the method to assess participants' treatment preferences. Participants must have an understanding of each treatment option and they need the opportunity to appraise the options for acceptability, before indicating which they prefer. Therefore assessment of treatment preferences should be systematic, involving three steps: 1) informing participants of the treatment options under investigation to ensure they have a clear, comprehensive, and accurate knowledge of the options; 2) engaging them in the evaluation of the treatment's acceptability; and 3) inquiring about their treatment of choice, to which they are allocated.

Approaches for assessing treatment preferences

Preferences for a variety of medical, surgical, and non-pharmacological (educational, psychological, behavioral, physical) treatments have been examined in a large number of studies. In most published reports, the method used to assess treatment preferences is not explained. Where described, there is limited indication that participants were given information about the treatments (e.g., Givens et al., 2007; Gum et al., 2006); if given, the content and format for relaying the information were not specified. Yet the content and format for providing treatment-related information influence participants' understanding and perception of the treatment options, and consequently their choice of treatment (Koedoot et al., 2003; Say and Thomson, 2003). Unclear presentation of information interferes with understanding what the intervention involves and how to apply it, whereas incomplete and biased presentation of information influences treatment appraisal which potentially results in inappropriate choices.

Two general approaches for assessment of treatment preferences have been reported: direct and indirect. The direct approach involves asking participants which treatment option they want to have, using single items. The content covered in and the wording selected for the item varies. Some inquire about participants' preference (e.g., which of the treatments you prefer) or choice (e.g., which treatment you would choose; Givens et al., 2007); agreement or willingness to receive the treatment (e.g., which treatment you are willing to have; Hazlett-Stevens et al., 2002); or rank ordering of the treatments under investigation from the most to least preferred (e.g., Tarrier et al., 2006). The simplicity of the direct approach in eliciting preferences is appealing. It may not be cognitively taxing to participants and mirrors the methods used to assess patients' choice in day-to-day practice. Nonetheless, the most appropriate wording and cognitive tasks (i.e., selecting vs. rank ordering) to be used in capturing, accurately, participants' preferences have not been determined. Further, the direct approach does not provide participants the opportunity to explicitly appraise the treatment options, which is a necessary step prior to making an informed choice.

The indirect approach consists of assessing participants' perception of the treatment options, rather than asking about their choice. Two types of measures have been used. In the behavioral and social sciences, self-report scales have been administered to measure participants' perceived acceptability of each treatment. The scales request participants to rate each treatment relative to a set of attributes, and a total score is computed as a function of the individual items (pertaining to a particular attribute) to reflect participants' overall acceptability of each treatment. The attributes most commonly captured in the scales include: appropriateness, suitability, tolerability, expectation of positive benefit, credibility, efficacy, reasonableness, justifiability, and discomfort (Deacon and Abramowitz, 2005; Tarrier et al., 2006). These self-report measures of treatment acceptability are simple, easy to use, and useful in quantifying perceived acceptability of treatment. However, the treatment attributes are not explicitly defined and participants may interpret their meaning differently from what is intended. The attributes may overlap (e.g., efficacy and positive benefits), potentially leading to confusion. In addition, the scores quantifying perceived acceptability have different ranges, which are functions of the response options used, resulting in some difficulty in interpreting the level of treatment acceptability. Finally, the self-report scales measure treatment acceptability, thereby offering participants a structured means for appraising the treatments, but they do not inquire about participants' choice of treatment.

In the medical sciences, the trade-off technique for utility assessment has been applied for eliciting participants' treatment preferences, albeit less frequently than the single items. The trade-off technique is illustrated by the standard gamble, time trade-off, and conjoint analysis or choice experiment (e.g., Fraenkel et al., 2007; Guentner et al., 2006; Schwartz et al., 2004). The standard gamble and time trade-off techniques consist of engaging participants in a series of treatment comparisons in which the types of treatments and their attributes are altered purposefully by the researcher. The treatments and favorable (e.g., effectiveness and survival rate) and unfavorable (e.g., side effects) attributes are presented in hypothetical scenarios. Participants are asked to weigh the alternative treatments, presented within and across scenarios, in terms of the selected set of attributes. Conjoint analysis is based on a similar trade-off technique but the focus is on determining the importance of the attributes in influencing preferences. The application of these techniques in research has encountered challenges. The weighing of different treatments is time consuming and cognitively burdensome. Many participants reported cognitive fatigue and difficulty in deciding on the importance of the attributes and on the trade-offs to make. Consequently, participants' responses were missing because of fatigue and unwillingness to continue, and inconsistent across scenarios (Osoba et al., 2006; Sinnot et al., 2007), limiting the quality of the responses. Additional disadvantages of the trade-off technique are: reliance on hypothetical scenarios which may not be of relevance to participants; manipulation of treatment attributes that may not be consistent with those of importance to participants; and high likelihood that scenarios with favorable attributes are preferred, which potentially leads to biased expression of treatment preferences (Douglas et al., 2005). Accordingly, the trade-off techniques are of limited feasibility and utility in assessing treatment preferences within the context of intervention evaluation research, and definitely in the context of day-to-day practice.

A mixed approach, involving elements of the direct and indirect techniques, has been proposed by Sidani et al. (2009b) and Sidani et al. (2006) to obtain a well-informed and accurate assessment of treatment preferences. The mixed approach is guided by the conceptualization of treatment preferences presented previously. It is systematic and involves four steps.

In the first step, participants are presented with information on one treatment (i.e., intervention or comparison) in order to enhance their understanding of the treatment. The information is synthesized from available literature and the treatment's protocol. Conceptual literature assists in identifying the active ingredients of the treatment and in specifying its components and activities. Empirical literature is useful in determining its benefits (i.e., the extent of effectiveness in resolving the health problem and in improving general health) and risks (i.e., the type and severity of side effects or discomfort experienced with the receipt of treatment). The treatment protocol provides details on how the treatment is implemented (mode of delivery, dose, role of interventionist and participants in applying the treatment). The information obtained from the literature and the protocol is integrated to cover the following points, in clearly labeled sections: treatment name, goals, components and activities, schedule (i.e., mode of delivery and dose), benefits, and risks, as recommended by Dwight-Johnson et al. (2001) and Zoeller et al. (2003). The information is presented, in writing, with clear, non-technical, and simple to understand terms that are at the 6th grade reading level. The information should be factual and pertain to the treatment being described only, i.e., comparisons between the treatments are excluded. Factual descriptions of treatment minimize bias in relaying information and ensure preferences are based on facts, not misconceptions about the treatment (Say and Thomson, 2003). Comparisons between treatments influence participants' perceptions of the treatment options (Tarrier et al., 2006). Participants are requested to read carefully the treatment description.

In the second step, participants are involved in critically appraising the treatment relative to the following attributes: 1) appropriateness, that is, viewing the treatment as logical, reasonable, and suitable for addressing the health problem; 2) effectiveness, that is, the extent to which the treatment is perceived as helpful in addressing the problem in the short and long term and in improving general well-being; 3) the severity of side effects, that is, rating of the extent to which the side effects or discomfort experienced as a result of treatment are 'bad'; and 4) convenience, that is, the perceived ease and willingness to apply and adhere to treatment recommendations. The four attributes represent those identified as relevant and important to participants in appraising treatments' acceptability (e.g., Lambert et al., 2004; Miranda, 2004; Tacher et al., 2005). Participants rate the treatment on the four attributes by responding to multiple items, with five-point response options ranging from *not at all* to *very much*.

In the third step, participants are given the description of the alternative treatment under investigation and requested to read it and rate the treatment on the same four attributes. In the last step, participants are asked two questions to identify their preferences. One question inquires whether or not they have a preference for any of the treatments they reviewed and rated, and the other question focuses on determining the preferred treatment. These two questions facilitate a valid assessment of treatment choice.

The mixed approach has been used in a few studies. It was well received by participants. It provides them with balanced and unbiased information about the treatments and the opportunity of appraising the treatments' acceptability, before identifying the preferred one, and without inducing cognitive fatigue.

CONCEALMENT OF TREATMENT ALLOCATION

Concealment of treatment allocation is applied to minimize the potential for research staff's influence on participants' assignment to the intervention and the comparison groups; such influence may result in non-comparability of participants in the two groups on baseline characteristics, which can confound the effects of the intervention. Hiding the randomization scheme from research staff is accomplished by putting the treatment allocation in an opaque envelope or keeping the allocation list with the investigator or statistician. Treatment allocation should also be concealed from healthcare professionals referring patients to the study and for providing treatments within the context of the trial. Despite all efforts at maintaining concealment of allocation, experiential evidence indicates that research staff and healthcare professionals engage in what can be described as 'gaming the system', in order to allocate a specific person to one treatment or the other.

Schulz and Grimes (2002b) has documented many of the ingenious ways that research staff and healthcare professionals have used to try to undermine randomization, ranging from opening up unsealed envelopes that contain the allocation sequence; to holding up sealed, opaque envelopes to an intense light source; looking for slight differences in the appearance of labels on bottles of the active drug and the placebo; to rifling through the filing cabinets of the principal investigator, searching for the randomization list. Horwitz (1987) reported that in one of the studies included in the review, the physicians managing the care of patients participating in a drug trial correctly suspected the use of the active drug 84 per cent of the time the drug was given, and correctly identified the use of the placebo 71 per cent of the time. This finding was explained by the patients' experience of prompt and profound effects with the use of the active drug and of no change in the clinical problem with placebo.

The contribution of allocation concealment to the validity of inferences regarding the intervention effects has been examined in several meta-analyses or systematic reviews. The results of some studies indicated that lack of adequate concealment led to overestimates of the intervention effects (e.g., Kjaergard et al., 2001; Kunz and Oxman, 1998; Schulz et al., 1995). In other meta-analyses, no relationship was found between allocation concealment and the magnitude of the effect sizes quantifying the intervention effects (e.g., Balk et al., 2002; Hyde, 2004; Jüni et al., 1999; Linde et al., 1999; Lindsay, 2004). Part of the discrepancy between the findings may be explained by differences in the reporting of concealment in the reviewed trials and in the adequacy of the coding of concealment in the meta-analyses. The discrepancy was also examined in the review done by Wood et al. (2008). They found that allocation concealment was related to larger effect sizes when the post-test outcomes were subjectively assessed by participants or healthcare professionals (e.g., rating scales for assessing pain) than when the outcomes were objectively assessed (e.g., laboratory tests); the reason for this difference is unclear. The inconsistency in the findings weakens the importance of allocation concealment in intervention evaluation research.

Summary

- Randomization of participants to the intervention and comparison treatment is believed to balance the number and characteristics of participants in the two groups (i.e., minimize selection bias) and to enhance internal validity
- Several randomization procedures and schemes can be used; the computer-generated allocation is highly recommended
- Randomization has limitations: the baseline group comparability is maintained at the group level and is probabilistic; participants resent randomization; empirical evidence questions the utility of randomization
- Other methods of allocation to treatment include: 1) researchers' or healthcare professionals' selection of participants into treatment, and 2) participants' self-selection into treatment, based on preferences

11

IMPLEMENTATION OF THE INTERVENTION

The intervention must be implemented with fidelity, in a standard and consistent manner, across all participants in order to produce the hypothesized changes in outcomes. Variability in implementation of the intervention presents a threat to the validity. This chapter looks at the mechanisms responsible for the influence of variability in implementation on the validity of study conclusions and synthesizes supporting empirical evidence. The chapter also discusses strategies for monitoring treatment implementation. In addition, the type of comparison treatments selected for a study affects the magnitude of the intervention effects, and the chapter examines the conditions under which different types of comparison treatment are used, on the basis of logic and available evidence.

IMPLEMENTATION OF INTERVENTION: AN OVERVIEW

Implementation of the intervention involves 'carrying out the components and specific activities of which it is comprised, through the selected mode and at the specified dose' (Sidani and Braden, 2011: 85). The implementation of most health interventions is the responsibility of both the interventionists and the participants. The interventionist represents the medium through which the treatment recommendations are relayed to participants. The interventionist facilitates the discussion of the health problem targeted by the intervention, explains strategies to manage it, engages participants in finding ways to address barriers to carrying out the treatment recommendations, and assists in learning, monitoring, and maintaining appropriate skill performance. The interventionist interacts with participants to clarify information and provide instrumental support in the application of treatment recommendations. Interactions between interventionists and participants occur whether the intervention is given in an individual or group, face-to-face, telephone, or electronic (e.g., chat room) format. Therefore, the interventionist plays a central role in the implementation of health interventions. Participants are exposed to the treatment recommendations as explained by the interventionist during the sessions. They have to gain a clear and comprehensive understanding of the treatment recommendations in order to enact and adhere to them within the context of daily life. Accordingly, the interventionist should successfully implement the intervention, and participants are expected to appropriately apply the treatment recommendations, to induce changes in the outcomes.

The successful implementation of the intervention demands that the interventionists and participants are adequately prepared and carry out its components with fidelity. Preparation is directed at making human and material resources available for delivering the intervention.

The human resources include primarily the interventionists responsible for and support staff facilitating the implementation of the intervention. The interventionists are professionals and/or lay persons ascribed the function of providing specific or all components and activities of the intervention. Individual interventionists are capable of delivering simple interventions, whereas a team of interventionists may be required for delivering complex, multi-component interventions. For example, the components of diabetes self-management are often given by different professionals: dietitians provide the component addressing nutrition; and nurses assisted by lay persons lead the discussion on general self-management strategies. All interventionists are carefully selected on the basis of pre-specified personal and professional qualifications, and trained in the intervention delivery. The training of interventionists should enable them to carry out the intervention as originally designed and to a high quality. Support staff are persons in particular positions within the setting in which the intervention is implemented and able to provide additional services needed for intervention delivery. The type of support staff and the extent of their involvement vary with the nature of the intervention and its mode of delivery. For instance, information technology (IT) staff members ensure the availability and proper functioning of hardware and software required for computer-assisted implementation of interventions; or technicians may be on-call (stand-by) to manage any malfunction of bio-feedback equipment. The support staff are informed of the intervention and their specific function, and subcontracted for proper, prompt, and uneventful implementation of the intervention.

Material resources must be readily available for the uninterrupted performance of the intervention activities as planned. The particular resources required vary with the nature of the activities and are delineated in the intervention protocol. Resources include: 1) measures that participants have to complete during the intervention sessions (e.g., to assess characteristics guiding treatment tailoring); 2) supplies and equipment needed to complete these measures (e.g., hard copies, pens, laptops or tablets) or to carry out some intervention activities (e.g., laptop and projector for showing videos demonstrating performance of a skill such as muscle relaxation); and 3) printed materials such as booklets that summarize treatment recommendations and describe appropriate procedures for carrying them out in the context of day-to-day life.

The specific setting for delivering the intervention is carefully selected to possess the main features that facilitate implementation of the intervention and control for extraneous factors that may interfere with the quality of implementation and hence, achievement of the outcomes. The features vary with the nature of the intervention; for example, educational interventions might require a room allowing for group seating arrangement, good acoustics, and control of extraneous auditory and visual stimuli that may distract participants.

The actual delivery of the intervention is done with fidelity. This is accomplished by requesting interventionists to carry out the components and activities as delineated in the protocol and detailed in the treatment manual, and asking participants to apply the treatment recommendations as explained during the intervention sessions and described in any accompanying material. Interventionists are requested to strictly adhere to the protocol instructions when implementing the intervention across all participants assigned to the intervention group. Participants are frequently reminded to apply the treatment recommendations; they may be asked to monitor and record performance of the recommendations, and to identify and address barriers to implementation.

Adherence to the intervention protocol by interventionists and to the treatment recommendations by participants is critical to maintain fidelity and consistency in implementation. As such, all participants are exposed to and enact the active ingredients characterizing the intervention, in the same format, and at the same dose; hence, they exhibit the same amount and pattern of change in the outcomes. This constant change in outcome observed in participants assigned to the intervention group generates the difference in the mean values on the post-test outcomes between the intervention and comparison groups. The difference is the evidence of the intervention effects. This ideal implementation of the intervention with fidelity and consistency may not always be possible or feasible in efficacy or effectiveness trials. Variability in treatment implementation is an expectation. Despite intensive training and request to follow the protocol, interventionists may drift in carrying out the intervention activities. Participants may not adhere to treatment, for a variety of reasons. Variability in intervention implementation affects the validity of inferences about its effects.

VARIABILITY IN INTERVENTION IMPLEMENTATION

Variability in intervention implementation is frequently encountered, though not always reported, in efficacy and effectiveness trials (Spillane et al., 2007). Variability occurs for various reasons, at different levels, including the operationalization of the intervention, the implementation of the intervention by interventionists in different contexts, and the engagement in the intervention by participants. Variations in treatment implementation weaken construct, internal, statistical conclusions, and external validity.

Variations in Operationalization of the Intervention

This type of variation represents a lack of correspondence between the conceptualization and the operationalization of the intervention. It takes place when specifying the intervention components and activities, and results in a discrepancy among the theoretically identified intervention's goals, its active ingredients, and non-specific elements, and the respectively derived components, activities, and mode of delivery. Therefore, what is planned to be implemented and specified in the intervention protocol is not fully congruent with the active ingredients characterizing the intervention and responsible for producing improvement in outcomes. Examples of discrepancies are educational interventions that aim to change health behaviors but that are not comprised of a behavioral component involving instrumental support for initiating the target behavior; and self-management interventions that aim to enhance self-efficacy but do not incorporate activities that operationalize the four sources of mastery as proposed in social cognitive theory.

The lack of correspondence between the conceptualization and the operationalization of the intervention is related to: 1) unclear or inadequate conceptualization of the health problem and the respective intervention, resulting in the misspecification of the intervention's active ingredients; 2) time constraints due to socio-political pressures to find solutions to health problems that limit engagement in the systematic process for designing interventions; and 3) limited experience in the application of the systematic process for intervention design.

Variations in the operationalization of the intervention present a threat to construct validity. They produce deviations of what is to be implemented from what is intended with the potential for delivering the incorrect intervention, an intervention that overlaps with the comparison treatment, or an intervention that misses some of its active ingredients. Such an intervention falls short of triggering the mechanism underlying its effects and of producing the hypothesized changes in outcomes (Mihalic, 2002).

Variations in Implementation of Intervention by Interventionists

This type of variation takes place when the interventionists actually carry out the intervention components and activities. The variations can take two forms: deviations from what was originally planned and deviations across participants.

Deviations in the implementation of the intervention from its original design consist of drift in the components, activities, mode of delivery and dose that are provided to participants. A discrepancy between what is delivered and what is designed yields lack of clarity about the specific activities performed and the intervention elements that produce the changes in the immediate and ultimate outcomes. This type of deviation poses a threat to construct validity (Shadish et al., 2002). Four situations contribute to this form of deviation:

1. Lack of clarity about the intervention. The intervention is not well defined in that its active ingredients are not elucidated, and the components and activities operationalizing the active ingredients are not clearly identified. The interventionists are not aware of the specific intervention activities that must be performed and of the most appropriate way of doing so, leaving much room for interpretation of what the intervention comprises. The interventionists use their own frame of reference in articulating the specific elements and in delivering the intervention, resulting in deviations from the intended treatment. For instance, provision of instrumental support, which may be a component of a behavioral intervention, can be interpreted in different ways by different interventionists if not clearly specified in a protocol; for some, it means provision of positive feedback related to behavior performance, and for others, it means discussion of barriers to behavior performance and of strategies to address the barriers.

2. Lack of availability and clarity of the intervention protocol. The protocol guiding the delivery of the intervention may not be available or its content is not clear, comprehensive, or written in a way that facilitates understanding of what is to be accomplished, how, and in what sequence. Lack of a well-prepared manual increases the likelihood of deviations in interventionists' performance of the intervention activities and incorporation of specific elements characterizing other treatments (Waltz et al., 1993).

3. Inadequate training of the interventionists. Inadequate training tends to occur in multi-site efficacy trials, in which the sites are geographically dispersed and investigators with different levels of expertise provide the training, and in effectiveness trials in which various healthcare professionals and lay persons are trained to assume the responsibility of delivering the intervention in the context of day-to-day practice. In this instance, it is often the case that training is condensed to fit within the time period (usually short) during which professionals are pulled from the practice setting; thus, the close supervision of actual intervention implementation by trainees is omitted or shortened. Consequently, interventionists may not have gained and retained the cognitive knowledge related to the intervention's active ingredients and mechanism responsible for its effects; and may not have had the opportunity to learn and apply correctly the practical skills required for a successful performance of the intervention activities. With limited skills, interventionists may not carry out the intervention appropriately and accurately.

4. Differences in context. This situation is encountered in multi-site effectiveness trials, in which the intervention is provided in different settings. The features inherent in these settings may demand modifications in the intervention delivery (Damschroder et al., 2009; Mowbray et al., 2003). In particular, the beliefs of the healthcare professionals and the cultural values of the community influence the acceptability of a specific intervention component or activity, or its mode of delivery. The availability of the number and type of healthcare professionals as well as the availability of material resources required for providing the intervention affect decisions to alter some aspects of the intervention and

its delivery. Although the modifications are justifiable and congruent with the resources and demands of local contexts, they represent deviations from the planned intervention, which have the potential of moderating its effects on the outcomes.

Deviations in the implementation of the intervention across participants take the form of inconsistency in carrying out the intervention with different participants. There is variability in the components or specific activities to which participants are exposed, and in the mode of delivery and dose at which the intervention is provided. In other words, participants differ in their exposure to the intervention, which deviates from what was originally planned in efficacy and effectiveness trials. It affects the reliability of intervention implementation (Shadish et al., 2002) and results in differences in the outcome level achieved by participants at post-test. This increased within-intervention group variance decreases the power to detect significant intervention effects (Borrelli et al., 2005; Dumas et al., 2001).

Inconsistent implementation is observed when providing standardized and tailored interventions. Although well-trained interventionists are requested to strictly follow the protocol when delivering a standardized intervention to all participants assigned to the intervention, they may not do so because of the belief in the importance of patient-centred care (Waller, 2009). Patient-centred care focuses on giving treatment that is responsive to the needs and preferences of individual clients. Interventionists trained in the patient-centred approach to care may modify elements of the intervention to fit with the circumstances of individual participants. These modifications result in variability in intervention exposure and the associated reduced statistical power to detect significant effects. Such alterations in intervention implementation, made in consideration of individual patients' contexts, strengthen the therapeutic alliance, which may impact the outcomes. The therapeutic alliance may confound the intervention effects, weakening the internal validity of the study (Dumas et al., 2001).

Deviations in the implementation of tailored interventions are often due to a lack of clarity on the process followed in customizing the intervention to the characteristics of participants. The algorithm for tailoring the intervention may not be well delineated and interventionists may not have a good grasp of how to apply it. Therefore, the aspects of the intervention (i.e., components, activities, mode of delivery, dose) that are tailored and how exactly they are customized differ across participants. The resulting variability in exposure to the intervention reduces the power to detect significant intervention effects.

Variations in Engagement in Intervention by Participants

Even when interventionists provide the intervention with fidelity, participants vary in their exposure to, engagement in, and adherence to the intervention. Participants allocated to the intervention group may not attend the treatment sessions as planned; some leave prior to completion of a session and others are not present at all sessions. Therefore, they could miss information important for understanding and applying the treatment recommendations appropriately. In addition, participants may be selective in their engagement in the intervention activities (e.g., some do not feel comfortable and thus do not participate meaningfully in group discussion) and in carrying out the treatment recommendations (e.g., some do not follow a particular recommendation) at the optimal dose level. These variations yield differences in the extent to which participants adhere to the intervention and show improvement in the outcomes, resulting in loss of power to detect significant intervention effects.

Variations in participants' engagement are related to the following factors:

1. Participants' misunderstanding of the treatment recommendations and the dose at which they are to be applied. This happens when the treatment is complex, involving many complicated recommendations, or when the information about these recommendations is not conveyed clearly and in a way that is meaningful to them.
2. Limited acquisition and sustainability of the cognitive and practical skills required to carry out the treatment recommendations correctly. This is likely when the skills are demanding and not well explained, and when participants are not given adequate opportunity to apply and to receive feedback on the performance of the skills.
3. Unfavorable perception of the intervention. Participants who view the intervention activities or treatment recommendations as inconsistent with their beliefs and values, unsuitable to their lifestyle, and unacceptable to them, do not engage in the intervention or carry out the recommendations that do not fit with their views.
4. Unavailability of resources needed to implement the treatment recommendations. The resources may be material (e.g., low income preventing purchase of fruit and vegetables), physical (e.g., unsafe neighborhood preventing engagement in walking), or psychosocial (e.g., level of personal motivation or provision of support by significant others). In addition, uncontrollable life events interfere with full exposure, engagement, and adherence to treatment.

In summary, deviations in the implementation of the intervention introduce 1) treatment elements that do not reflect the intended intervention and that overlap with the comparison treatment, thereby presenting a threat to construct validity; 2) confounding factors (e.g., therapeutic alliance), other than the intervention's active ingredients, that contribute to improvement in outcomes and weaken internal validity; and 3) variability in the components, activities, mode of delivery, and dose to which participants are exposed, which dilutes the effects of the intervention and negatively affects statistical conclusion validity. These deviations and their consequences increase the likelihood of committing type III error, that is, reaching erroneous conclusions about the effects of an intervention that has not been implemented appropriately and consistently (Brandt et al., 2004; Carroll et al., 2007). Inappropriate and inconsistent implementation makes it difficult to replicate the intervention and its effects in different contexts, thereby limiting external validity (Dumas et al., 2001). Monitoring the fidelity of intervention implementation is an important strategy to minimize these potential threats to validity.

IMPLEMENTATION FIDELITY

The frequency with which variations in intervention delivery are encountered and the unfavorable consequences of these deviations on the validity of inferences prompted researchers to devise strategies aimed at improving and monitoring the implementation of the intervention. The ultimate goal is to maintain fidelity of implementation and to generate respective data that assist in clarifying what intervention elements are carried out and how, and to which extent they contribute to outcome achievement. This information facilitates interpretation of intervention evaluation findings, and translation of the intervention in different contexts (Melde et al., 2006). In general, fidelity of implementation refers to the degree to which the intervention is delivered as intended or planned (Gearing et al., 2011; Hasson, 2010). There are two levels of fidelity, theoretical and operational.

Theoretical Fidelity

Theoretical fidelity has to do with the design of the intervention. It refers to the congruence between the active ingredients that characterize the intervention, and the components and activities of which it is comprised (Bellg et al., 2004; Borrelli et al., 2005; Keller et al., 2009; Pearson et al., 2005). Theoretical fidelity is achieved through a systematic process of designing the health intervention. This process involves: 1) specification of the active ingredients that are hypothesized to induce the improvement in the outcomes; 2) derivation of the intervention components and activities that are in alignment with the active ingredients; 3) identification of the non-specific elements needed to facilitate the implementation of the intervention's active ingredients; 4) translation of the components and activities into a list of topics to be covered, series of actions to be performed by the interventionists, and treatment recommendations to be followed by participants; and 5) selection of the most appropriate mode for delivering the intervention components and activities.

The application of this process is facilitated by the generation of a matrix, the content of which shows the correspondence between each active ingredient and its respective component, activities, actions, topics, and recommendations, as well as the activities and actions linked to the non-specific elements of the intervention. The matrix is a useful tool to ensure alignment of the conceptualization (i.e., active ingredients and non-specific elements) and operationalization (i.e., components, activities, mode of delivery) of the intervention, thereby promoting theoretical fidelity. The matrix also guides the development of the intervention manual and content validation, which is a strategy for assessing theoretical fidelity. Content validation consists of requesting a group of experts to carefully review the matrix, to judge the extent of correspondence among the intervention's active ingredients, components, activities, actions, topics, and treatment recommendations. For details on and illustration of the matrix generation, and its use for content validation, refer to Sidani and Braden (2011).

Operational Fidelity

Operational fidelity has to do with the implementation of the intervention. It refers to the extent to which the intervention is applied as planned (Bellg et al., 2004); that is, the interventionists covered all topics and carried out the specific and non-specific actions as delineated in the manual, and the participants engaged in the treatment recommendations in the appropriate manner and dose. Maintenance of operational fidelity by both the interventionists and the participants is essential to trigger the mechanisms responsible for the health intervention's effects on the ultimate outcomes.

For interventionists, operational fidelity is reflected in the quality with which they implement the intervention. Quality is indicated in the interventionists' levels of adherence to the intervention protocol and competence in delivering the intervention. Adherence is the extent to which the interventionists provide the treatment components and activities in conformity with those delineated in the protocol, and consistently across participants allocated to the intervention group. Adherent interventionists perform the prescribed intervention activities in the way, frequency, and sequence described in the protocol, and refrain from applying proscribed activities used in alternative treatments for managing the same health problem; they should adhere to the intervention with all participants in the intervention group (Breitenstein et al., 2010; Forgatch et al., 2005; Hasson, 2010; Stein et al., 2007). Interventionists' adherence is enhanced by developing an intervention manual, which they are required to follow; by training them and assessing their cognitive and practical skills required for implementing the intervention; and by monitoring the implementation of the intervention on a regular basis (Gearing et al., 2011).

Competence relates to the interventionists' skillfulness in delivering the intervention. It entails the interpersonal process or the interactions between the interventionist and the participants through which treatment information is relayed, treatment recommendations are clarified, and strategies for applying them are discussed (Breitenstein et al., 2010; Stein et al., 2007). Competent interventionists are those capable of initiating and maintaining a therapeutic or working alliance with participants, and of actively engaging participants in understanding, valuing, and enacting treatment recommendations. Therapeutic alliance is a collaborative relationship between the interventionists and participants that involves agreement on the goals of treatment and shared understanding of the rationale for specific actions undertaken to facilitate goal achievement (Baldwin et al., 2007; Burns and Evon, 2007). Interventionists' competence is enhanced through careful selection and monitoring their performance throughout intervention implementation. It is considered important for motivating and promoting participants' application of treatment recommendations.

For participants, operational fidelity is reflected in their exposure, engagement, and adherence to the intervention. Exposure to the intervention refers to the extent of contact with its content, which is estimated with the dose actually received, as illustrated by the number of treatment sessions attended, and the amount of written material (e.g., booklet) read. Engagement in treatment represents the participants' active involvement in the intervention activities, such as participation in discussion, setting treatment goals, and development of an action plan. Adherence is the enactment or actual application of the treatment recommendations in everyday life during and following attendance at the intervention sessions (Borrelli et al., 2005; Carroll et al., 2007; Hart, 2009).

Strategies to Enhance Operational Fidelity

Three general strategies are often used to enhance operational fidelity: 1) development of an intervention manual to guide the interventionists' implementation of the treatment; 2) careful selection and training of interventionists; and 3) close monitoring of treatment implementation by interventionists and participants. The first two strategies are preparatory, done to equip interventionists with the skills needed for the actual delivery of the intervention. Monitoring of intervention implementation and collecting pertinent data provide empirical evidence of the extent to which the intervention components and activities are delivered successfully, in the appropriate mode and at the optimal dose. Such evidence indicates the feasibility of the intervention; the components implemented with fidelity, those requiring modification, those omitted, and other components added; and the contribution of the intervention components (reflecting its active ingredients) and non-specific elements (e.g., therapeutic alliance) to outcome achievement. This evidence is essential for the interpretation of findings, confirming the causal effects of the intervention or offering valid explanations of non-significant association between the intervention and outcomes (Melde et al., 2006; Saunders et al., 2005; Spillane et al., 2007).

Development of an intervention manual

The intervention manual is a document that describes the intervention protocol. It clarifies the logistics for implementing the intervention and details what is exactly done, how, and when. The manual serves as a reference for training interventionists, for guiding interventionists' delivery of the intervention with fidelity, and for developing tools to monitor and measures to document treatment implementation.

The development of the intervention manual is based on the information available in the matrix generated through the process for achieving theoretical fidelity. The matrix guides the specification of the list of actions, topics, and treatment recommendations operationalizing the intervention. Analysis of their nature and logic determines the sequence with which the actions, topics, and recommendations are to be presented and the dose of the intervention. The results of this analysis should identify: 1) the content for each session, that is, the topics to be covered, the type and sequence of activities to be performed by the interventionist and the participants, and the treatment recommendations to be applied by participants in daily life within the time interval between sessions; 2) the length of each session that is needed to adequately cover the content; and 3) the total number and frequency with which the sessions are to be offered.

The intervention manual has three main sections that assist interventionists in understanding the intervention and in preparing for and in implementing the intervention sessions: an overview of the intervention, the resources required for providing the intervention, and the procedure for carrying out the intervention.

Overview of intervention: The first section of the manual gives an overview of the intervention. The following points are covered: 1) explanation of the health problem as experienced by the target population, and the aspect of the problem addressed by the intervention; 2) the goals set for the intervention; 3) the active ingredients that characterize the intervention and hence should be implemented under any circumstances, and the non-specific elements that facilitate the delivery of the intervention's active ingredients; 4) the components, activities, mode of delivery, and dose for implementation of the intervention; and 5) modifications that are allowed in the delivery of the intervention to attend to participants' individual needs and circumstances, without jeopardizing fidelity of treatment implementation.

Resources: The second section of the manual presents a list of the general human and material resources required for the provision of the intervention, as well as those needed for carrying out the activities planned for each session. The list of resources serves as a reminder to ensure their availability, in the right amount for a proper and uneventful facilitation of the intervention sessions.

Procedure: The third section of the manual contains a description of the procedure to be followed in carrying out the activities planned for each session. The procedure details the sequence and the steps to be undertaken to cover the content and enact the specific actions identified for a particular session. The actions are often categorized into: 1) introduction, such as providing an overview of the intervention goals and components, and of the interventionists' and participants' responsibilities in carrying it out in the first session, and inquiring about participants' performance of the assigned treatment recommendations at the beginning of subsequent sessions; 2) main intervention activities, such as explaining each treatment recommendation and discussing potential challenges in enacting them; and 3) conclusion, such as recapping the main points covered during the session, emphasizing the importance of applying the assigned treatment recommendation, and reminding participants of the logistics of the next session. Each action to be performed is delineated in terms of who (interventionist or participant) is to do what (specific action) in what way. The description of each step is followed by a script stating the information to be relayed to participants to explain the content to be covered and the action to be enacted. The scripted information is prepared in simple, non-technical language, using simple sentence structure that is easy for participants with different educational levels to understand. In addition, this section of the manual should identify conditions under which some intervention actions can be modified and how, so their altered enactment maintains congruence with the active ingredients.

Although the preparation of the manual is time consuming and demands attention to detail and clear expression of the specific content and actions to be enacted, the resulting description reduces the potential for variability in interventionists' interpretation and implementation of the intervention. Flexibility in intervention delivery is allowed in effectiveness research; any alterations in implementation should be recorded, along with the reasons for doing so. This information helps to further delineate modifications to be made when providing the intervention in day-to-day practice, without influencing the potency of the intervention.

Selection and training of interventionists

The interactions between the interventionist and the participants are the means through which information related to the treatment recommendations are relayed and the application of these recommendations is fostered. These interactions represent the non-specific elements of the intervention; they are expected to be inert, playing no significant role in outcome achievement. Consequently, interventionists are assumed to be comparable, even inter-substitutable, requiring no particular attention at the stages of data analysis and interpretation of findings. Clinical observation and emerging empirical evidence, however, indicate that interventionists differ in their personal and professional qualifications. These differences translate into inter-interventionist variations in knowledge, beliefs, and values that inform their approach for implementing the intervention and their style of interactions with participants. These interactions actually contribute to participants' engagement in the intervention activities, motivation to enact the treatment recommendations, satisfaction with treatment, and consequently improvement in outcomes (Fuertes et al., 2007; Travaodo et al., 2005).

Careful selection and training of interventionists minimize the potential influence of interventionists on the implementation of the intervention and mitigate the possible impact of their interactions with participants, which confound the intervention effects on outcomes. Careful selection aims to choose interventionists who have the personal and professional qualities that facilitate the delivery of the intervention and promote meaningful and motivating interactions with participants. Personal characteristics to consider include: 1) socio-demographic characteristics such as sex and ethnicity, which may have to be comparable with those of the target population to enhance the perception of trust, understanding, and comfort when addressing sensitive topics; 2) professional competence indicated by formal training, licensing, and experience, which are required by professional regulatory bodies to provide some types of intervention; 3) an interactional style related to the use of support, warmth, empathy, respect for participants' autonomy, and willingness to collaborate with others, which influence the interventionist–participant interactions and participants' motivation to engage and enact the treatment recommendations (Najavits and Weiss, 1994); and 4) understanding and appreciation of the treatments under evaluation, which maintain the interventionists' enthusiasm and, hence, adequate performance of the intervention activities (Dumas et al., 2001).

Ascertainment of the interventionists' qualities is done informally and formally during the initial job interview with the candidates, training, and throughout the intervention implementation period. Informal ascertainment strategies consist of asking open-ended questions during the initial job interview and observing the style of interactions during training. Formal strategies focus on the assessment of interventionists' understanding of the intervention, scheduled following the training; and their interactional style, which involves use of validated measures to be completed by the interventionist prior to assuming their responsibilities, by researchers observing the interventionists to monitor their performance, and by participants. The latter measures are illustrated with the short instrument of therapeutic alliance developed by Joyce et al. (2003).

Adequate training is essential for the preparation and reinforcement of interventionists' competencies required for implementing the intervention with fidelity. Initial training is intensive, to enable interventionists to acquire the cognitive and practical skills needed to perform the intervention activities. It involves a didactic and an experiential component. The didactic component covers the conceptualization of the intervention, aimed at clarifying the health problem addressed by the intervention, with particular attention to its aspects directly targeted. Knowledge about the problem is critical for appreciating the utility of the intervention in preventing or managing it, understanding the participants' contexts, perception of the problem, and concerns, and anticipating and responding appropriately to participants' reactions to the intervention. The didactic component of training also includes the intervention's goals, active ingredients, and non-specific elements. Learning about what the intervention is set to achieve, how it addresses the problem, and what is absolutely necessary to implement in order to achieve the goals promotes an understanding of the rationale and appreciation of the significance of the intervention. Equipped with this knowledge, interventionists are able to convince participants of the intervention's value in addressing the problem, which in turn enhances participants' engagement in and adherence to the treatment recommendations. The third element of didactic training covers the intervention components, activities, mode of delivery, and dose. Explaining the nature of these intervention elements and pointing to their congruence with its goals, active ingredients, and non-specific elements help interventionists recognize the components and activities that are necessary to implement and the treatment recommendations that participants must enact to benefit from the intervention. Finally, interventionists receive instruction on the expected outcomes. Discussion of the immediate and ultimate outcomes, the mechanisms underlying the intervention effects, and the time points at which changes in the outcomes are to take pace, contributes to the interventionists' understanding of the intervention effects and ability to relay realistic expectations regarding improvement in outcomes to participants (Sidani and Braden, 2011). The didactic component also involves a review of the intervention manual.

The experiential component of the initial training focuses on skill performance and provides interventionists opportunities to apply the competencies. This is achieved with the use of various training strategies such as: 1) role play or modeling during which trainees practice some skills (e.g., handling a concern or unfavorable reaction); 2) review of archived audio or video recordings of intervention sessions followed with a discussion of the interventionists' performance; 3) case studies or vignettes presenting hypothetical or actual participants' condition and requesting trainees to delineate the course of action; and 4) actual delivery of the intervention to participants, which is done under close supervision, as part of what is considered a 'pilot run' of the intervention designed to ensure feasibility of and competence in implementation of the intervention in an efficacy or effectiveness trial. Assessment of interventionists' competence is highly recommended prior to assuming responsibility of intervention delivery (Bellg et al., 2004). This can be accomplished by administering a test containing questions related to the conceptualization of the intervention, and short vignettes followed by items evaluating application of skills in providing aspects of the intervention or handling issues that may arise. Interventionists' responses indicate the need for additional training.

Ongoing training is provided to maintain and reinforce the interventionists' competencies throughout the study period. It takes the form of 'booster' sessions (Bellg et al., 2004), designed to address concerns raised by interventionists, factors related to participants and context identified as interfering with the appropriate implementation of the intervention; and to discuss the cases of individual or subgroups of participants who may present with specific needs and the strategies to address those while ensuring fidelity in enacting the intervention's active ingredients. Adequate initial and ongoing training alone may not guarantee fidelity of implementation; it should be supplemented with monitoring of intervention implementation.

Monitoring of intervention implementation

Monitoring implementation of the intervention is important for identifying drifts in interventionists' performance and in participants' deviations in exposure, engagement, and adherence to treatment. Awareness of such variations in implementation assists in applying relevant remedial strategies to prevent further variations. Documentation of the variations provides data on the intervention components and activities frequently delivered with fidelity and those requiring modification, the dose tolerated by participants, and the components and activities contributing most significantly to and the minimal and optimal doses associated with the achievement of beneficial outcomes. This information guides refinement of the intervention and its translation in a way that fits with the features of the local context while maintaining congruence with its active ingredients.

Monitoring interventionists' performance

Interventionists' performance is evaluated for fidelity in carrying out the intervention components and activities, and for style in interacting with participants. Performance data are gathered through observation and participants' report. The observation covers the two aspects of performance and is done in a structured and unstructured format. The structured format consists of using a checklist to guide evaluation and documentation of the activities performed, and an instrument to assess interactional style. The unstructured format is complementary, providing a means for noting the nature and context of deviations.

The checklist is generated following the procedure suggested by Oxman et al. (2006) and Stein et al. (2007). The first step is concerned with the identification of the intervention's active ingredients and non-specific elements, and the respective activities as specified in the matrix. The second step involves the description of the activities in observable actions or behaviors exhibited by the interventionists when providing the intervention, available in the intervention manual. The third step entails the development of items that depict the actions or behaviors to be observed. The items should clearly describe what is to be done and how, and offer examples as necessary to illustrate the actions. The items can be arranged by intervention component or in the sequence of their performance during each intervention session; the latter arrangement is easier to follow. The fourth step consists of selecting a scale to rate the interventionists' performance. The most commonly used scale reflects the occurrence of the actions or behaviors (i.e., performed or not performed) (Melde et al., 2006; Oxman et al., 2006). Additional scales have been proposed to quantify the frequency (e.g., none to all of the time) with which the actions or behaviors are performed, or the quality (e.g., poor to excellent) of performance. A manual is prepared to explain how observers can use the checklist and how to record their observations (Hart, 2009). The checklist is subjected to psychometric testing (at least content validity and inter-rater reliability) before its use in a trial.

The structured observation also involves rating of the interventionists' style of interactions with participants. Validated instruments measuring therapeutic alliance, interpersonal skills, or communication skills can be completed by observers to rate the interventionists' interactional style. These instruments are also administered to participants during or immediately after the intervention delivery, to avoid recall bias. The unstructured observation allows observers to note and record any deviations in performance, and the context in which they occur; factors that interfere with the delivery of some aspects of the intervention; components or activities reflecting other treatments that are added; the reasons for doing so; and strategies applied by interventionists to deal with participants' concerns or reactions to the intervention or other issues encountered in the implementation of the intervention.

Structured and unstructured observations are done by well-trained observers. The observers attend the intervention sessions or review records of the sessions. Ideally, observations are conducted for interventionists providing all sessions to all participants to provide a comprehensive assessment of implementation fidelity. When this is not feasible, monitoring is done of each interventionist for 10–20 per cent of the sessions, randomly selected. Strategies for quantifying the level of implementation fidelity and accounting for its contribution to outcomes are presented in Sidani and Braden (2011).

Monitoring participants' exposure, engagement, and adherence

Participants' exposure to and engagement in the intervention activities are prerequisite for correctly understanding, enacting, and adhering to the treatment recommendations, which in turn produces the anticipated improvement in outcomes. Data on exposure are obtained from the interventionist and the participants, depending on the mode selected for intervention delivery. For health interventions involving direct contact between the interventionist and participants, exposure is represented by the number of sessions attended. The interventionist completes a session attendance log to document attendance of each participant at each session, whether the participant was present for the duration of the session and if feasible, the time at which the participant left the session; the latter information is useful in determining if participants missed content or activities related to a particular treatment recommendation and in accurately estimating the intervention dose to which participants are exposed. For health interventions involving review of material, given in written (e.g., booklet) or animated (e.g., video recording of how to perform treatment recommendations), passive or interactive format using hard or electronic copies, exposure is represented by the amount and frequency with which participants reviewed the material. Participants are requested to report whether or not they read the material, how much of the material is read (e.g., few, some or all sections of a booklet), and how many times the material was reviewed. A built-in system is devised to track participants' access to the different sections of computer-based material.

Participants' engagement in the intervention activities takes different forms, based on the nature of the planned activities. Accordingly, the type, source, and method for monitoring and gathering data on engagement vary. The following illustrate ways to operationalize engagement in health interventions: 1) participants' involvement in discussion of the treatment recommendations is best captured through video recording of the intervention session; research assistants review the recordings to document whether or not participants contribute to the discussion, and frequency of doing so; 2) participants' performance of a skill such as progressive muscle relaxation is monitored through direct or indirect observation; participants are requested to demonstrate the skill in-session and the interventionist determines the adequacy of the skill performance, guided by a checklist; 3) participants' engagement in setting individual goals, preparing an action plan and executing the plan is monitored by reviewing respective forms that participants keep to document pertinent information. Bruckenthal and Broderick (2007) proposed the use of qualitative interviews or quantitative checklists as general strategies for collecting data on participants' engagement in intervention activities.

Adherence to treatment recommendations has been extensively addressed in intervention research and numerous strategies have been used to assess adherence to pharmacological and behavioral treatments. The strategies can be categorized into three general approaches. The first approach consists of identifying objective indicators of adherence, where possible, and using appropriate devices to monitor and record adherence to treatment recommendations. An illustration of this approach is tracking the number of refilled prescriptions or using pedometers to monitor engagement in physical activity. The second approach involves participants' self-report on enactment of the treatment recommendations in their daily life. A checklist of the recommendations is developed to facilitate reporting. The checklist is either completed prospectively, in that participants are requested to indicate whether or not they carry out the treatment recommendation on a daily basis, during the intervention implementation period (which is useful for the interventionist to monitor adherence and provide feedback) and at each occasion of data collection following intervention delivery (which is useful to examine sustained implementation of the intervention); or it can be completed retrospectively, in that participants are asked to report on the actual performance and the frequency with which each treatment recommendation was carried out over a particular time period, such as the past week. The prospective completion of the checklist has the advantage of minimizing recall bias and improving the accuracy of adherence data, whereas the retrospective completion of the checklist has the advantage of reducing the burden of responding to the checklist on a daily basis. The checklist can be expanded to inquire about factors that influenced, favorably or unfavorably, enactment of the treatment recommendations, strategies applied to manage these factors, and alterations made in carrying out the recommendations and the reasons for these alterations (Bellg et al., 2004). The third approach entails report on adherence by the participants' significant others. Significant others (e.g., spouse, family member, friend) are in a position to observe participants' enactment of the treatment recommendations in daily life. They represent an alternative source of data to confirm participants' self-report (Hart, 2009). They are asked to indicate whether or not – or the frequency with which – participants adhere to the treatment recommendations. Convergence of the data obtained from participants and significant others enhances construct validity of adherence data. However, the information on adherence provided by significant others is limited by the nature and extent of their interactions with participants.

It is always recommended to use more than one approach to enhance the validity of adherence data. Incorporating adherence in data analysis is important for determining the extent to which enactment of each and all treatment recommendations is causally related to improvement in outcomes.

EMPIRICAL EVIDENCE

Emerging empirical evidence supports the importance of closely monitoring and accounting for intervention implementation in outcome analysis. The available evidence relates to the influence of the interventionist, of overall fidelity, and of participant adherence to treatment recommendations. Reviewing the evidence on adherence is beyond the scope of this book.

Evidence on Interventionist Influence

Evidence, primarily from the field of psychotherapy, indicates that participants receiving treatment from different interventionists vary in treatment attrition and outcome achievement. Two studies reported on differences in treatment attrition across interventionists. The results were inconsistent. Whereas Elkin et al. (2006) found differences in attrition for participants with major depression assigned to different therapists, Kleinman et al. (1990) did not find such differences among participants with substance abuse. The inconsistent results are due to variability in the type of therapies, the target population, and statistical tests used in the data analysis (i.e., whether or not the nesting of participants within therapist was accounted for).

The association between interventionist assignment and outcomes was examined in several efficacy and effectiveness trials. The efficacy studies included two or more interventions for the management of the same health problem (such as cognitive and interpersonal therapy for depression), delivered by well-trained therapists ranging in number between 5 and 54 and requested to follow the intervention protocol. The findings were comparable, showing that assignment to interventionists accounted for up to 13.5 per cent of the variance in the post-test outcomes (Elkin et al., 2006; Huppert et al., 2001; Kim et al., 2006; Luborsky et al., 1997; Project MATCH Research Group, 1998). These findings are also consistent with those of a systematic review conducted by Crits-Christoph et al. (1991). Wampold and Brown (2005) reported that the amount of variance in post-test outcomes related to interventionists (up to 13.5 per cent) was larger than that associated with treatment (up to 2 per cent).

Four effectiveness trials evaluated the influence of interventionists on outcomes. The studies included patients presenting with various psychological problems (e.g., depression, anxiety, adjustment disorders) and assigned to therapists ($N > 50$ per study) based on availability. As anticipated under real world conditions, the therapists' caseload differed, with some having a large number of clients or clients with higher levels of problem severity than others. The findings consistently showed differences in outcomes for clients assigned to different therapists (Dinger et al., 2008; Lutz et al., 2007; Okiishi et al., 2003; Wampold and Brown, 2005). Therapist assignment explained 8 per cent of the variance in patient outcomes, which was reduced to 5.5 per cent after controlling for severity of the presenting problem. Kim et al. (2006) estimated the therapist effect to be of a small-to-moderate magnitude.

Additional research was conducted to understand the interventionists' influence on outcomes. Two categories of interventionists' characteristics were explored. The first category consisted of interventionists' personal and professional qualities. Results of individual studies and a systematic review indicated non-significant associations between interventionists' qualities, except for years of experience, and improvement in client outcomes (Crits-Christoph and Mintz, 1991; Dinger et al., 2008; Okiishi et al., 2003; Wampold and Brown, 2005). Less experienced therapists were reported to have larger variability in outcome achievement by clients assigned to their care. The second category focused on the working alliance that develops between the interventionist and client. The findings of several studies showed the following pattern: 1) clients' perception of the working alliance differed across therapists; 2) the magnitude of the association between the clients' perceived working alliance and post-test outcomes was larger than the magnitude of the association between therapist assignment and post-test outcomes (Dinger et al., 2008); 3) clients' perceived working alliance was positively related to high levels of satisfaction and adherence to the intervention (Fuertes et al., 2007); and 4) clients who perceived a positive working alliance reported improvement in outcomes (Burns and Evon, 2007; Dinger et al., 2008; Joyce et al., 2003). The relationship between alliance and outcomes was estimated of a low-to-moderate magnitude, ranging from .26 (Messer and Wampold, 2002) to .45 (Martin et al., 2000). It poses a potential threat to internal validity, and should be examined in intervention evaluation studies.

Evidence on Impact of Fidelity of Implementation

Fidelity of treatment implementation has been examined in several studies. Despite variability in the type of interventions, target population, and settings, the findings converged in supporting a positive relationship between high fidelity in intervention implementation and improvement in client outcomes. For instance, Oxman et al. (2006) assessed the fidelity of a three component model for the management of depression with a log. The log captured the activity that reflected the model's active ingredient, i.e., case management. The researchers found that clients who received no case management achieved the lowest response and remission rates, comparable to those achieved by clients allocated to the control group, and clients exposed to case management, delivered with fidelity, attained the best outcomes. Pearson et al. (2005) monitored the implementation of the Chronic Care Model aimed to improve the processes and outcomes of care for clients with chronic illnesses. They quantified treatment implementation as the percentage of the planned model activities actually performed and rated the depth of the change made in care activities. They reported a positive, moderate (r = .44) relationship between implementation depth and pre-to-post change in outcomes. Forgatch et al. (2005) developed a multidimensional measure of treatment fidelity covering interventionists' knowledge of the intervention, skills (e.g., teaching), clinical process (i.e., support), and overall quality of performance. Latent factor (i.e., combination of all dimensions) scores were generated to quantify implementation fidelity, which were found to be associated with the amount of change in client outcomes; after controlling for baseline client characteristics, fidelity accounted for 30 per cent of the variance in outcomes. Similarly, Keith et al. (2010) reported a significant relationship between fidelity of implementing a case management program by nurse practitioners and cardiac clients' achievement of beneficial outcomes (i.e., decreased use of services and mortality rate). In a meta-analysis, Durlack and DuPre (2008) reviewed studies that monitored fidelity of treatment implementation. The types of treatment investigated varied and included mentoring, anti-bullying, and drug prevention programs. The results indicated: 1) the effect sizes estimated for programs that monitored implementation were larger than effect sizes for programs that did not; 2) the relationship between program implementation and outcome achievement was positive, implying that high levels of implementation fidelity yield high improvement in outcomes; and 3) implementation fidelity was the second most important variable in predicting outcome, and the most important program feature that affected outcomes.

The evidence clearly demonstrates the importance of monitoring the fidelity of the intervention implementation and of examining its impact on the outcomes, in order to make valid inferences on its causal effects, in efficacy and effectiveness trials. However, it is equally useful to carefully select, implement, and monitor the delivery of the comparison treatment.

COMPARISON TREATMENT

The type of comparison treatment to select for a particular study differs with the phase and aim of the intervention evaluation trial. The comparison treatment should not incorporate components and activities that represent the active ingredients characterizing the intervention under evaluation. In some instances (e.g., placebo), the non-specific elements of the intervention are replicated in the design of the comparison treatment in order to identify the unique impact of the intervention's active ingredients. However, any overlap in the specific and non-specific elements and activities of the intervention and comparison treatment has the potential to reduce the difference in the levels of post-test outcomes achieved by participants in the two groups. This, in turn, decreases the power to detect significant intervention effects and thus increase the likelihood of type II error in efficacy trials. In contrast, finding no differences in outcomes indicates comparability in the impact of the treatment options under investigation in effectiveness trials. Consequently, it is important to monitor the implementation of the selected comparison treatment, using the same strategies discussed in this chapter, to determine the extent of overlap between the two treatments and the treatment component and activities that most significantly contribute to outcome achievement.

No-treatment Control Condition

Participants assigned to this condition receive no treatment, and those who are under treatment for the target health problem may be requested to withhold it for the duration of the trial. The no-treatment control condition is most suitable for a pilot and efficacy study aimed to evaluate the causal effects of a newly designed intervention; this condition creates the counterfactual condition and meets the covariation criterion needed to demonstrate that participants exposed to the intervention exhibit the hypothesized improvement in the outcomes and those receiving no treatment at all experience no change in the outcomes (Borkovec, 1993). Despite its advantage in demonstrating the causal effects of the intervention, the no-treatment control condition is difficult to execute and introduces some bias. Denying or requesting participants to stop treatment raises ethical issues. Participants randomized to the no-treatment control condition demand an explanation for withholding treatment to which they are entitled; they might lose interest in the study and withdraw from the trial; experience demoralization and worsening of the health problem; and seek treatment outside the trial (Barkauskas et al., 2005; De Maat et al., 2007). Differential attrition presents major threats to statistical conclusions and internal validity. Participants who seek treatment may be exposed to some or all components characterizing the intervention under investigation, and therefore report improvement in post-test outcomes, which reduces the extent of the between-group differences and the power to detect significant intervention effects.

Waiting-list Control Condition

This condition is incorporated in a waiting-list control group or modified cross-over design in which participants are randomized to the immediate or delayed treatment group. Participants in the delayed treatment group are given no treatment initially, which creates the counterfactual condition and covariation criterion required to demonstrate the causal effects of the intervention (D'Agostino, 2009). The advantages of this condition include: 1) addressing ethical dilemmas encountered in the no-treatment control condition as all participants eventually receive the intervention; 2) reflecting the reality of day-to-day practice as some participants have to 'wait' to get treatment; and 3) replicating the effects of the intervention in the delayed group as these participants are exposed to it and may experience improvement in the outcomes (Borkovec, 1993). Accordingly, the waiting-list control condition is appropriate for pilot, efficacy, and effectiveness trials, in particular when no standard or alternative treatment is available to manage the target health problem. However, participants assigned to the delayed treatment group may 1) withdraw from the study if they believe that they need or are entitled to immediate assistance; 2) seek treatment outside the trial if they experience the problem at high levels of severity or are prone to rapid deterioration; or 3) develop motivation and expectations related to their awareness of delayed treatment, which result in some changes in the outcomes prior to the intervention (Barkauskas et al., 2005; De Maat et al., 2007). These changes affect the magnitude of the between-group differences in post-test outcomes and consequently the inferences about intervention effects.

Usual Care or Treatment-as-usual

Participants assigned to this condition continue to receive the treatment prescribed by their healthcare provider to manage the target problem. Usual care or treatment-as-usual is used in comparison to either 1) the intervention only, that is, participants allocated to the intervention group are exposed to the intervention but are not offered usual care; in this case, differences in post-test outcomes between the intervention and usual care groups capture the unique effects of the intervention; or 2) the intervention given above and beyond usual care; in this case, differences in post-test outcomes reflect the contribution of the intervention combined with usual care (Barkauskas et al., 2005). The combined implementation has the potential to induce interactions between the intervention and usual care, which may either strengthen or weaken the effects of the intervention on the outcomes, leading to invalid inferences about the intervention itself. Usual care or treatment-as-usual is an appropriate comparison treatment in efficacy trials in situations when it is unethical to discontinue it, and in effectiveness trials. The use of usual care in any intervention evaluation study generates methodological challenges related to the variability in its definition and implementation within and across participants and sites. The specific treatments given under the umbrella of usual care may differ for the same participant over time, in response to changes in condition or reaction to treatment, and for different participants assigned to the intervention and comparison groups. The treatment-as-usual may contain specific and non-specific elements that overlap with the intervention under evaluation. Similarly, the dose at which treatments-as-usual are given varies across participants. This heterogeneity in the type, implementation, and dose of treatment-as-usual results in variability in the levels of post-test outcomes observed for participants within and across study groups. This variability obscures the intervention effects (Barkauskas et al., 2005; De Maat et al., 2007) due to the high within-group variance and low between-group variance, which reduces the power to detect significant intervention effects. Accordingly, it is critical to monitor the implementation of usual care and document the specific treatments received by all participants. Alternatively, Barkauskas et al. (2005) suggested the use of 'devised' usual care, that is, the treatment for the health problem is derived from available best practice guidelines and is delivered in a standardized, consistent, and constant manner by the interventionists hired for the trial.

Placebo Condition

Placebo is an inert, innocuous treatment that is believed to have no inherent power to produce any effect. Placebo treatments are comparable to the experimental intervention in that they have the same non-specific elements (or common factors) but they lack the specific elements (or active ingredients) which distinguish the intervention under evaluation (Stewart-Williams and Podd, 2004). In medicine, placebo treatments consist of preparation, pills, or procedures (i.e., surgery or physical intervention) that have the same appearance or process of implementation as the intervention; however, they do not contain the active ingredients that characterize the intervention. In behavioral and social sciences, placebo treatments are designed to be structurally equivalent to the intervention. Placebo treatments incorporate the same non-specific elements as those used in the implementation of the intervention, but not the active ingredients. They are delivered by trained interventionists, in the same mode or format, at the same dose, in the same setting. Participants are given a rationale for the treatment, which is necessary to maintain the credibility of the placebo treatment and to reduce disappointment associated with receipt of a less desirable treatment. Participants are exposed to non-specific activities such as discussion of the health problem or engagement in problem solving (Baskin et al., 2000; Kazdin, 2003), which facilitates the development of a working alliance between the interventionist and participants assigned to the placebo treatment group. Well-designed placebo treatments are usually selected for comparison in efficacy trials, particularly when there is no other effective treatment (Margo, 1999), with the assumption that participants in the intervention and the placebo groups are exposed to the same non-specific elements. Therefore, differences in post-test outcomes are attributed solely to the intervention's active ingredients (reflected in the respective specific activities) thereby enhancing the validity of causal inferences (Van Die et al., 2009).

Empirical evidence indicates that placebo treatments induce what is called placebo effects manifested in favorable (i.e., improvement) or unfavorable (i.e., development of side effects) responses. Results of several meta-analyses demonstrate the occurrence of placebo effects; however, the observed magnitude of these effects is not consistently estimated due to variability in the design of the placebo treatment (i.e., whether or not it is structurally equivalent to the intervention), the type of treatment condition to which it is compared (active or control), the nature of the target health problem, the target population, and the outcomes (objectively or subjectively measured) investigated across studies. Bowers and Clum (1998) computed the effect sizes for active and placebo treatment (mean effect size = .55) and for active treatment and no treatment (mean effect size = .76). They concluded that placebo treatments exert much less of an effect than previously believed. A similar conclusion was reached by a number of other studies. Stewart-Williams and Podd (2004) state that placebo effects are less widespread and weaker than formerly thought; Finnis et al. (2010) found a small placebo effect; and Kaptchuk et al. (2010) reported no evidence of clinically meaningful placebo effects. This conclusion is in contrast to other reports, which have shown 1) a rather high prevalence of the placebo response, as was found in 61 per cent of studies that compared active to placebo treatments for Parkinson disease (Shetty et al., 1999); 2) a large percentage of participants demonstrating a placebo response, where up to 80 per cent of the response to anti-depressants was exhibited by participants receiving a placebo drug (Hamunen and Kalso, 2005;

Quitkin, 1999; Van Die et al., 2009); and 3) a large magnitude of the placebo effects, estimated at about one-fifth of the active drug (Autret et al., 2012). Placebo effects have been found to be larger for subjective outcomes (Finnis et al., 2010; Stewart-Williams and Podd, 2004); for placebo treatments that are structurally non-equivalent (mean effect size = .46) as compared to those that are structurally equivalent (mean effect size = .14) to the experimental intervention (Baskin et al., 2000); for interventionists showing no enthusiasm, empathy, and support (Kaptchuk et al., 2010); and for treatment conditions involving frequent encounters between interventionists and participants (Ilnyckyj et al., 1997).

Several mechanisms have been proposed to explain the placebo effects, including: 1) natural resolution of the health problem over the study period or fluctuation in the level of severity at which the problem is experienced (Finnis et al., 2010; Hamunen and Kalso, 2005); 2) motivation to apply the treatment recommendations generated from the perception of a positive working alliance with the interventionist (Bootzin and Bailey, 2005; Finnis et al., 2010); 3) expectancy, that is, anticipation that the treatment is effective in improving the health problem (Autret et al., 2012; Margo, 1999); 4) classical conditioning, that is, experience of improvement in the problem is related to the mere fact of receiving a treatment (Finnis et al., 2010; Stewart-Williams and Podd, 2004); and 5) neurobiological changes in response to placebo treatment reflected in endogenous opoids (Finnis et al., 2010; Van Die et al., 2009). Although placebo treatments are beneficial in isolating the unique effects of the intervention's active ingredients, they are challenging to design in a way that is structurally equivalent to health interventions; this, in turn, may influence participants' perception of the placebo treatment's credibility and therefore, participants' willingness to be randomized to the less desirable treatment. Further, participants allocated to the placebo treatment may not experience improvement and withdraw from the study yielding differential attrition; or attempt to please the researcher, resulting in response bias (social desirability) and potential overestimation of the placebo effects (Barkauskas et al., 2005).

Active Treatment

Different types of active treatment are usually used in effectiveness trials. These can include individual components of a complex intervention, whose effectiveness in improving the outcomes is compared to that of the intervention in order to determine the relative contribution of the components and to identify those with and without beneficial effects. This information is used to streamline the intervention design and hence increase its efficiency. Second, the active intervention is given at a low dose level (Barkauskas et al., 2005), which is viewed as credible and acceptable to participants thereby overcoming issues of recruitment, willingness to be randomized, and attrition; however, it may yield outcomes that are comparable to those produced by the intervention. Some effectiveness trials may incorporate different levels of the active intervention to examine the dose–response relationship and identify the minimal and optimal dose required to achieve the outcomes. Third, an alternative treatment with an assumed but not proven efficacy or with known minimal effects is given; or the alternative treatment is one with established efficacy (De Maat et al., 2007). Alternative treatments have active ingredients that differ from those characterizing the intervention under evaluation. They are used in comparative effectiveness research to demonstrate that the intervention under evaluation has comparable effects on the outcomes (i.e., non-inferiority trial) or more beneficial outcomes (i.e., superiority trial). The implementation of alternative active treatments may enhance recruitment and retention of participants and assist in determining which treatment is most beneficial in achieving the intended outcomes.

Summary

- Deviations in the implementation of the intervention introduce: treatment elements that do not reflect the intended intervention (issue of construct validity); potentially confounding factors (issue of internal validity); and variability in exposure to the intervention (issue of statistical conclusion validity). Inappropriate and inconsistent delivery makes it difficult to replicate the intervention and its effects (issue of external validity)
- Strategies to maintain fidelity include: having experts validate the adequacy of the intervention operationalization relative to its conceptualization; development of an intervention manual; careful selection and training of interventionists; close monitoring of intervention implementation by interventionists and participants
- Monitoring interventionists' performance is done through observation using structured (checklist of activities) or unstructured (open-ended questions) formats, and participants' report on interventionists' interactional style
- Monitoring of participants' enactment and adherence to treatment recommendations is done with attendance log and diary of the treatment recommendations carried out
- Monitoring is also done of the comparison treatment, to determine potential for overlap

12

PRINCIPLES OF OUTCOME MEASUREMENT AND ANALYSIS

Outcomes are considered the yardstick or criteria for determining the efficacy and effectiveness of health interventions, and for comparing the effects of different interventions targeting the same health problem. They form the basis for claiming the intervention as beneficial. Therefore, outcomes should be carefully selected, assessed with appropriate measures and at opportune times to capture changes that accurately reflect the intervention effects. Outcome data must be properly analyzed, using relevant statistical tests, to detect significant intervention effects. It is beyond the scope of this chapter to discuss all aspects of measurement and data analysis; however, principles and points most relevant to outcome measurement and analysis in intervention evaluation studies are reviewed.

OUTCOME SELECTION

A wide range of outcomes have been of interest in the evaluation of health interventions. Different classification schemes have been used to identify health outcomes. The first categorizes the outcomes substantively into: 1) clinical end-points, covering objective indicators of general health and of the health problem addressed by the intervention; these include signs and symptoms of illness, laboratory or test values, development of complications, and mortality; 2) functional outcomes related to performance of activities of daily living (e.g., bathing and dressing), and engagement in physical (e.g., walking) and social (e.g., visitation with friends) functions and in healthy behaviors (e.g., exercise); 3) perceptual outcomes encompassing a sense of general and psychological well-being, overall health, and satisfaction with life; and 4) financial outcomes associated with use of resources and cost of care incurred by clients and the healthcare system. This classification provides for a listing of types of outcome to consider in the evaluation of interventions. For example, diabetes self-management programs are often evaluated for their effects on the clinical end-points of HbA1c and fasting blood glucose, the functional outcomes of engaging in healthy eating and physical activity, the perceptual outcomes of health-related quality of life, and the cost associated with the number of hospital readmissions for the management of complications such as foot ulcers.

The second classification divides outcomes on the basis of their specificity in relation to the intervention under evaluation. Specific outcomes are those expected of the intervention, whereas generic outcomes represent indicators of general health. This classification has guided much work to develop measures of health-related quality of life that are specific to some diseases (e.g., cancer) and to some forms of the disease (e.g., breast and prostate cancer). Generic outcomes reflect clients' response to care in general and are posited as criteria for evaluating the effectiveness of a variety, if not all, health interventions. A recent classification focuses on outcomes of relevance to patients. This is illustrated by the list of patient-centred or patient-oriented outcomes generated by the Patient-Centered Outcomes Research Institute (PCORI) in the US. The list consists of functional outcomes and physical (e.g., pain and fatigue) and psychological (e.g., anxiety and depression) symptoms commonly experienced by different client populations.

The combination of classifications offers a comprehensive listing of types of outcomes to choose for an intervention evaluation study. Selecting outcomes to reflect all categories is potentially useful in determining the impact of the intervention on various domains of health that are of interest to different stakeholder groups (clients, healthcare professionals, and policy makers) and in comparing the effectiveness of different interventions relative to the same set of criteria. Further, this practice assists in identifying intended and unintended outcomes. The intended outcomes are the hypothesized, desired or beneficial effects that the intervention strives to achieve. Unintended outcomes are changes in domains of health that occur as a result of the intervention but were not anticipated (Sidani and Braden, 1998). They can be either beneficial (e.g., blood thinning effects of aspirin) or unfavorable (e.g., maintenance of same weight, due to increased muscle mass, with rigorous, intensive exercise). The disadvantages of including a large number of outcomes are as follows:

1. The high possibility of selecting the wrong outcomes which are not sensitive to the intervention under evaluation. No significant improvement is observed in these outcomes, leading to the conclusion that the intervention is not effective.
2. Increased participant burden. Participants are requested to provide data on a large number of outcomes, which may be time consuming and tiring. Participant burden affects the quality of outcome data, which has negative consequences on construct validity. Respondents may skip some items, particularly those with unclear and irrelevant content, resulting in the problem of missing data (also called 'missingness'). This problem

reduces the number of cases included in the outcome analysis, with the potential of loss of statistical power to detect significant intervention effects (McKnight et al., 2007). Alternatively, participants when tired may not be careful in choosing responses to items. This may take the form of satisficing or acquiescence. Satisficing refers to participants' tendency to give a response that satisfies the minimal requirement of simply providing a response. They select any response option, regardless of its content and of its correspondence with their actual status. Acquiescence or yea-saying is illustrated by the selection of response options that reflect agreement with every item, regardless of its content (Streiner and Norman, 2008). Satisficing and acquiescence introduce bias in outcome measurement and weaken the accuracy of the measures' scores in quantifying participants' status on the respective outcome.

3. The problem of multiplicity. This problem arises with examining the impact of the intervention on several outcomes. With repeated testing, the probability of committing type I error is increased. The results of some tests demonstrate significant intervention effects, which may be chance occurrences.

Although potentially useful in guiding outcome selection, these classifications should not be relied on as the sole basis for the specification of outcomes expected of a particular intervention. Rather, outcome selection is more meaningfully guided by an understanding of the mechanism responsible for producing the intervention effects (as explained in Chapter 1). Outcomes are consequences of interventions and conceptualized as immediate and ultimate. The immediate outcomes are expected to take place shortly after the implementation of the intervention. They are sensitive to the intervention and are anticipated to show large improvement. Immediate outcomes also contribute to the achievement of the ultimate outcomes.

The systematic, programmatic approach (see Chapter 3) followed to evaluate the impact of the intervention provides for a sequential examination of the intervention's effects on immediate and ultimate outcomes. Phase 2 trials focus on exploring the extent to which the intervention actually induces the hypothesized changes in the immediate outcomes. At this stage, it is important to show that the intervention is successful in achieving the immediate outcomes, which are responsible for producing the ultimate outcomes. Phase 2 trials also provide an opportunity to examine the appropriateness (i.e., comprehension, relevance of content, and ease of completion) of the selected outcome measures for the target population, as well as the measures' ability to detect change in the outcome levels from pre-test to post-test. The results of Phase 2 trials confirm the sensitivity of the outcome variables and the respective measures in capturing the anticipated immediate effects. Those found sensitive are retained and those reported to show no changes over time are either excluded from or modified as needed prior to further intervention evaluation studies. Phase 3 trials are concerned with determining the efficacy of the intervention. They are designed to validate the effects of the intervention on the immediate outcomes, and to examine its impact on select ultimate outcomes. These are outcomes that can be reasonably achieved (i.e., for which significant changes can be captured) with the accrued sample size and the follow-up time points that are feasible within the constraints of the study time frame and resources. For instance, it may not be practical to assess outcomes that occur too rarely or too far in the future (e.g., death, tumor recurrence, prevention of heart disease) for all persons participating in a time-limited trial. Phase 4 and Phase 5 trials offer excellent opportunities for examining the direct and indirect impact of the intervention on immediate and ultimate outcomes, respectively. This is feasible because of the large sample size and long follow-up period included in available databases, which are used as the main or complementary source of outcome data in this type of trials.

A thorough understanding of the mechanism underlying the intervention effects is critical in directing outcome measurement and analysis. In particular, knowledge of:

1. What the outcomes are about guides the selection of measures and the method for gathering data on immediate and ultimate outcomes.
2. When changes in the outcomes are expected to occur assists in the specification of the time points for the assessment of outcomes.
3. What is the hypothesized pattern of change directs the identification of the mathematical function for quantifying change over time to be used in outcome analysis (using hierarchical linear or mixed models) and the interpretation of findings (e.g., non-significant between-group differences in, or small effect sizes for, the ultimate outcomes are anticipated immediately following treatment).
4. How the outcomes relate to each other is useful in planning data analysis to examine the direct impact of the intervention on immediate outcomes (e.g., traditional analysis of variance) and the indirect effects of the intervention on ultimate outcomes, mediated through changes in the immediate outcomes (e.g., path analysis or structural equation models).

OUTCOME MEASUREMENT

Once identified, the immediate and ultimate outcomes are to be assessed with valid and reliable measures, at the right time, so that they capture true changes following implementation of the intervention. Validity and reliability of measures are essential for maintaining construct and statistical conclusion validity in an intervention evaluation study.

Validity of Outcome Measures

A valid instrument measures the outcome concept that it is designed to measure. It generates unbiased scores that accurately reflect the participants' standing or level on the outcome. Therefore, valid measures enhance the confidence in making correct inferences about the intervention effects (Streiner and Norman, 2008). Valid measures capture the outcomes expected of the intervention and the anticipated changes in the outcomes for participants who receive the experimental intervention and show no changes in the outcomes for participants who do not receive the intervention, which is the evidence required to conclude that the intervention is effective. Accordingly, valid outcome measures should adequately operationalize the outcome and be minimally responsive to other conceptual or methodological factors that may influence participants' responses (Messick, 1995). Further, the measures should detect changes in the outcomes when they occur. Last, the measures have to be relevant to the target population. Therefore, outcome measures are carefully selected, following a systematic process.

The process begins once the immediate and ultimate outcomes are identified, by defining each outcome at the conceptual and operational levels. The conceptual definition delimits the domains and the attributes that characterize the outcome and distinguish it from other relevant ones. The operational definition specifies the indicators that reflect the attributes of the outcome and that can be directly measured; it also specifies the dimension (e.g., severity, frequency) to be assessed. For example, the subjective symptom of fatigue is defined as a feeling of tiredness, experienced physically and mentally. The physical indicators include muscle weakness and lack of energy, whereas the mental manifestations consist of difficulty remembering and difficulty concentrating. The severity with which fatigue is experienced is an outcome of interest in evaluating an intervention to promote engagement in physical activity to relieve fatigue. The conceptual and operational definitions guide the selection of measures. The measure to be selected for assessing a particular outcome should demonstrate content and construct validity.

Content validity refers to the congruence between the content areas covered by the measure and the conceptual and operational definitions of the outcome. Evaluating content validity consists of judging the correspondence between the content of the measure and the indicators of the outcome specified in the definition. A measure is considered content valid if it captures all indicators that reflect the domains and attributes identifying the outcome. It is important to determine if any content reflects indicators of other related outcomes. For instance, some self-report measures of depression and insomnia have overlapping content, which may explain the often reported positive, moderate correlation between these two conditions. Overlapping content is excluded to minimize the potential for confounding the intervention effects on the outcome. In addition, the content of the outcome measure must be relevant to the target population. The indicators included in the measure should be consistent with how members of the population experience the outcome. This is particularly applicable to persons of diverse cultural backgrounds. For instance, individuals of an Asian background express depression somatically; using a measure that excludes somatic indicators of depression, such as the Hospital Anxiety and Depression Scale, may not accurately reflect their experience. Content validity is not only applicable to single or multi-item, self-report or observational measures but it should also be considered for objective measures. Standard procedures are used for assessing accurately objective outcomes such as blood pressure, blood cholesterol level, and drug level. However, the extent to which these objective measures, which are highly valued and recommended to include in the evaluation of health interventions, represent specific indicators of the respective outcome has to be carefully examined when selecting them. For instance, high blood pressure, pulse rate, and respiratory rate are often posited as physiological indicators of state anxiety; however, they are also associated with the experience of pain; so, in trials of interventions targeting both symptoms, which may co-occur in patients presenting with an acute illness, it may be difficult to tease out whether these objective indicators represent anxiety or pain.

In situations where the content of available instruments is not congruent with the conceptual and operational definitions of an outcome, new measures are developed and pilot tested. This is often the case for outcomes representing health-related knowledge and behavior that are specifically targeted by educational and behavioral interventions. In these instances, some researchers advocate the development of instruments whose content captures only the specific attributes of the outcome that are hypothesized to improve with the implementation of the intervention. This type of outcome measure is called edumetric (Carver, 1974). Edumetric measures are generated 'by sampling some defined concept domain which represents the new responses subjects are expected to acquire as a result of the treatment' (Lipsey, 1990: 103). Edumetric measures draw upon salient attributes or indicators of the outcome that are likely to undergo significant changes. Consequently, participants are expected to have low scores on these measures at baseline, reflecting the fact that they do not experience the outcome (e.g., they do not have the knowledge or do not perform the behavior), and high scores after treatment indicating the hypothesized improvement in the outcome. The advantage of edumetric measures is that they are maximally responsive to the intervention effects and not to other factors with a direct, confounding influence on the expected changes in outcomes. Goal attainment scales are other examples of edumetric measures. The scales are used when the outcome is both the indicator for and the outcome of an intervention, and when the intervention and the outcome are tailored to the individual needs of participants. They consist of specifying the outcome that is directly linked to the overall health problem addressed by the intervention or to its attributes that participants want to achieve, and assessing participants' improvement toward achieving the outcomes, or its attributes post-treatment, using a common metric (Zatzick et al., 2001). Despite their potential utility, goal attainment scales have not been extensively used in health intervention evaluation research.

The content validity of newly developed outcome measures and of outcome measures to be used for the first time in a new patient population should be examined. This can be accomplished in two ways. The first involves having experts, including researchers (who have theoretical knowledge), healthcare professionals (who have clinical expertise), and patients representative of the target population (who have the experiential knowledge), review the content of the measure and rate the extent to which its items are relevant in capturing the domains and attributes of the outcome. A measure is claimed to be content valid if at least

80 per cent of its items are judged relevant or very relevant by at least 78 per cent of the experts (Armstrong et al., 2005; Polit et al., 2007). The second approach for examining content validity is a modified cognitive interviewing technique, done in an individual or group format. Originally, the cognitive interviewing technique was proposed to assess the comprehension of newly developed (e.g., Jobe, 2003) or translated (e.g., Eremenco et al., 2005) measures. The technique follows a process in which participants read each item in a measure, restate the meaning conveyed by the item as they understand it, read the response options, and think aloud when selecting the most appropriate response (see Chapter 3). The modified technique extends this process by adding questions related to the participants' perception of the relevance of the item content in reflecting their experience of the outcome and of the items that capture the outcome indicator of importance to the target population (Sidani et al., 2010).

The outcome measures should also demonstrate *construct validity*. Recent standards of measurement view construct validity as a unitary concept rather than divided into traditionally distinct types such as criterion, concurrent, and discriminant validity. Validity refers to the accuracy with which an instrument measures what it purports to measure (DeVellis, 2003). The focus is on the methods used to generate the evidence that supports construct validity. The evidence of relevance in the validation of outcome measures should indicate that the measures are capable of distinguishing different levels of the outcome (i.e., as reported by participants exposed and not exposed to the intervention) and of detecting changes in the outcome levels (i.e., as reported by participants receiving the intervention, over time). The observed changes should reflect those expected for the outcome being measured and not random fluctuations attributable to situational variability. Assessment of the measures' ability to distinguish different levels of the outcome is done with the contrasted group approach. Persons belonging to naturally occurring or experimentally induced groups, known on theoretical or clinical grounds to differ in the outcome variable, are requested to complete the measure. Results of comparisons showing significant between-group differences in the measured outcome provide evidence of the measure's validity. A word of caution: the naturally-occurring groups need not be based on a participant characteristic (such as age or sex) that is known to be associated with the outcome, to avoid the potential of confounding. In the latter case, the presence or absence of differences in the outcome observed between the experimental and comparison groups at post-test may be attributable to either the participant characteristic or the treatment group.

Assessment of the measure's ability to detect true changes is accomplished with any of the following approaches: 1) judging the congruence between the hypothesized and the empirically derived magnitude of change in the outcomes (Carver, 1974); 2) examining changes in the outcome scores following an intervention of known efficacy (Deyo and Centor, 1986); 3) comparing the change scores on the outcome measures with scores on a criterion measure indexing change; the criterion measure can be another subjective measure completed by the participants, their healthcare providers, or the interventionist (e.g., goal attainment or transition scale – discussed later) or an objective index indicating the extent of improvement in participants' status on the outcome; and 4) applying an appropriate formula for estimating true change (e.g., Liang, 2000).

Measures believed to have the ability to register changes have fine scaling of the response options. Measures using a graduated scale are more sensitive than those using categorical scaling in detecting change. Instruments that have demonstrated floor or ceiling effects are not useful for measuring outcomes; with such instruments, participants have low or high scores, respectively, at pre-test, which limit upward or downward change in the outcome over time (Lipsey, 1990).

Transition scales are suggested as a means to capture changes in outcomes, as perceived by participants (Liang, 2000). They consist of items that ask participants to indicate the extent to which their status on the outcome at post-test has changed in comparison to their status on the same outcome experienced at pre-test. The response scale represents levels of change, varying along the continuum of: much better, better, no change, worse, and much worse. They are often used to examine change in the overall outcome (e.g., general health, insomnia) rather than the attributes characterizing the outcome. Transition scales are advantageous as they provide a direct, easy, effective, and efficient quantification of change in outcomes. They offer a means for capturing participants' perception on the extent and direction of change between two points in time, thereby eliminating the need for prospective measurement. Further, the scales are short and simple to administer, which reduces response burden (Epstein, 2000). They are often used in day-to-day practice by healthcare professionals who inquire about the clients' change in status. Transition scales have been validated and have shown ability to detect clinically important changes in different patient populations exposed to different treatments (e.g., Aseltine et al., 1995; Fischer et al., 1999; Fitzpatrick et al., 1993). The disadvantages of transition scales relate to their focus on global rating of the outcome (excluding assessment of its attributes) which may limit their content validity, and on subjective judgement of change, which can be affected by the participants' state (e.g., psychological mood, ability to recall the status at pre-test) at the time of completing the scales. Participants' state could bias their responses.

Reliability of Outcome Measures

A reliable measure assesses the outcome with consistency or precision and minimal error. Error represents fluctuations in the measure's scores; however, these fluctuations are not related to the outcome being measured; they can be random or systematic.

Random error is due to chance factors that are introduced by the properties of the measure (e.g., lack of clarity or specificity of the instructions to complete the measure, typing or grammatical mistakes that may change the meaning of the items), the application of the measure (e.g., poorly functioning equipment, participants' guessing), or the context under which the measure is administered (e.g., level of participants' fatigue, heat and lighting in the room, method for storing specimens and time to sending them for analysis). Systematic error is associated with factors such as the participants' ability to understand the instructions, to comprehend the content of the items, test-taking skills, or social desirability.

Whether random or systematic, error of measurement generates variability in the distribution of the scores on the outcomes observed for participants in the intervention and comparison groups, at post-test. However, this variability is undesirable because it is not associated with true differences in the outcome and with the effects expected of the intervention. In other words, this variability is unexplained and contributes to within-group or error variance in tests of statistical significance. Increased error variance reduces the statistical power to find significant intervention effects. Therefore, reliability of outcome measures enhances statistical conclusion validity in intervention evaluation studies.

The strategies for reducing measurement error, in addition to selecting outcome measures that demonstrate reliability in previous research, involve: maintaining consistency in the method and context for administering the measure to all participants across the selected time points; standardizing the procedure for obtaining specimens and storing them, and the time interval to send them for analysis; carefully reviewing the measure for clarity of content and typing or grammatical mistakes before administering it, or calibrating the equipment periodically throughout the study period; measuring social desirability and accounting for or partialing out its influence on participants' scores prior to conducting the comparative outcome analysis; and using multiple indicators of the same outcome (e.g., multiple items or multiple measures) and aggregating their scores to quantify the participants' level on the outcomes. The latter practice is believed to counterbalance the error inherent in each item or measure, so that the aggregate score is highly reliable. Because measurement error is situational and associated with the characteristics of the participants and the context of measurement, it is highly recommended to examine the reliability of the outcome measures used in each intervention evaluation trial.

The type of reliability to assess varies with the type of measure used. For bio-physiological and physical measures, the precision of the tests done and the equipment used is reviewed from data available from the laboratory that conducts the tests and the manufacturer of equipment. For behavioral measures, inter-rater reliability is evaluated by having observers (at least two) independently rate the participants relative to the presence, frequency, or severity (or other relevant dimension) of the outcome. The level of agreement among raters is estimated with the intra-class correlation coefficient. For self-report measures containing multiple items, the internal consistency reliability is assessed by examining the inter-item correlation in the responses of the items. It is quantified with Cronbach's alpha coefficient. The values of these reliability coefficients should be ≥ .70 for newly developed and ≥ .80 for established measures to indicate high reliability. However, in intervention evaluation research, a low internal consistency reliability coefficient may be observed at pre-test and a high coefficient value at post-test. This is anticipated with homogeneous samples responding to edumetric measures in that participants show minimal variability in their responses before implementation of the intervention (since they are expected to have low scores on the outcomes) and high variability in the responses after treatment (since participants in the intervention group report improvement in the outcomes and those in the comparison group do not). Selecting measures that demonstrate high test-retest reliability (i.e., consistency in the scores provided by the same participants at two points in time) may not be appropriate for assessing outcomes. Measures with high test-retest reliability may not capture change in the outcomes expected of the intervention. For self-report measures consisting of single items, inter-rater reliability can be assessed if the outcome is observable by a rater and reported by the participant; or test-retest reliability can be examined within a very short time interval (e.g., minutes) during which no change in outcomes is expected, as has been done for the one-item, numeric rating scales measuring symptoms globally (e.g., pain, dyspnea). For more details on measurement, refer to Nunnally and Bernstein (1994) and Norman and Streiner (2008).

Issues with Different Methods of Data Collection

The method for collecting outcome data is mandated by the operationalization of the outcome concept and the selected measure. Each method has its advantages and limitations. The use of multiple measures to obtain data from different sources (e.g., participants, healthcare professionals, significant others, existing databases), using different methods, is the ideal to counterbalance the bias or error inherent in each and, hence, to improve the validity of inferences. There are issues with the application of the different methods that should be considered when making the decision to select them for intervention evaluation studies. The key issues are highlighted.

Bio-physiological markers

- The range or normative values may be narrow for many of the markers. Changes in these measures tend to be of a small magnitude. Large sample sizes, often exceeding the available sampling pool, are needed to demonstrate meaningful change.
- Assessment of bio-physiological markers may involve intrusive, demanding, discomforting, even painful procedures; these may not be well received by participants who undergo the same procedures as part of their usual care. Results of these tests reported in the patient's health records could be extracted as a substitute to actually performing the procedures, if the tests are done by a credible laboratory and within a time interval that is within the time points set for the trial.
- The accuracy of the data may be questionable and could mask the intervention effects. Patients may take necessary precautions prior to providing the specimen (e.g., decrease their carbohydrate intake a few days before the scheduled test).

Behavioral measures

- The use of these measures is confined to outcomes that can be noticed by observers, at the time points selected for outcome measurement.
- Participants may find the observation (whether done in vivo or recorded) intrusive and may not consent to this outcome assessment, leading to missing data. Alternatively, participants may behave in a socially acceptable manner thereby introducing bias.
- Observations are demanding; they require the appropriate human and material resources to conduct at a time that is convenient to participants or the most opportune time that may not be convenient; observations may require continuous attention of the raters, which leads to fatigue and the potential for missing information. This problem can be mitigated with time or event sampling of the behavior to be observed and recorded.
- Raters should be intensively trained to achieve acceptable levels of inter-rater reliability. Raters' performance should also be monitored periodically, on randomly selected occasions, throughout the study period.

Self-report measures

- Most participants are familiar with self-report measures.
- When administered by research staff in face-to-face or telephone interview format, the context and procedure for completing the measures are standardized. Content or words are clarified as needed, thereby reducing misunderstanding that contributes to random error. All items are read, which reduces the potential for missingness. When self-completed at participants' convenience, standardization of the administration procedure and context is not feasible; items lacking clarity are skipped, which increases the possibility of missingness. Assistance of significant others may be sought in completing the measure; thus there is increased possibility of measurement error across participants within and across time points.

Existing databases

- Different databases exist, such as administrative and clinical records, and health surveys maintained by healthcare institutions, state or provincial and federal health departments.
- The advantages of existing databases are:

  o Cost and convenience. Because the data already exist, the researcher does not have to set up elaborate systems to gather, enter, and store them. Some organizations may impose charges for using the data.

  o Reduced burden placed on the participants. They do not have to spend time filling out measures.

- o Reduced recall bias when data are collected routinely about people (e.g., people don't have to try to remember all comorbid conditions they have and treatments they are receiving).
- o Data are available for large samples, making it possible to do studies on rare conditions and outcomes. Data are often longitudinal in nature; they are useful to examine change or trends over time.
- o Data exist in computerized form. This means that researchers do not have to abstract the information, code it, and enter it into a computer, resulting in a great saving of time and effort.

- The disadvantages of existing databases are:

  - o Nature of the data, which are rarely set up for research purposes. The databases do not include variables that are important to researchers, such as illness severity, or of relevance to the intervention evaluation study, such as satisfaction with the experimental intervention.
  - o Need to be aware of the definitions used for the variables, because they may not correspond to the conceptual and operational definitions specified for the intervention evaluation study (e.g., rate of infection is computed with formulae using different denominators such as number of patients or patient days). Also, the definitions may change over time, and this is poorly documented and has the potential to confound the intervention effects.
  - o Databases are not representative of the general population because who is included or excluded is determined by the purpose of the database.
  - o Accuracy of the data is of major concern. For example Peabody et al. (2004) compared the diagnoses in the charts of 348 patients with what was recorded in the computerized administrative database. The primary diagnosis was correct only 57 per cent of the time; 13 per cent of the errors were due to the physician, 8 per cent to missing encounter forms, and 22 per cent to incorrectly entered data.
  - o 'Upcoding', which is often encountered where clinicians, hospitals, or nursing homes are paid on a fee-for-service basis. This means assigning a code for a more serious disorder than what the patient actually has, in order to receive a higher reimbursement. For example Silverman and Skinner (2004) found that between 1989 and 1996, the incidence of the most expensive procedure for respiratory disorders increased by 10 percentage points in not-for-profit hospitals, by 23 percentage points in for-profit ones, and by 37 percentage points in hospitals that switched from non-profit to for-profit status. Simply looking at the increase in incidence without being aware of the factors that may influence it would likely lead to the erroneous conclusion that the disorder is occurring more frequently.
  - o Timeliness of the data, that is, databases are usually not up-to-date.

OUTCOME ANALYSIS

The analysis of data in intervention evaluation research aims at determining the extent to which the experimental intervention is effective in producing the hypothesized outcomes. This is accomplished by comparing the outcomes reported by participants who receive the intervention and the outcomes of participants who do not receive the intervention. The comparisons are done between and within groups, using a variety of multivariable statistical tests.

The traditional test such as repeated measure analysis of variance examines differences in the mean scores on the outcomes observed for the intervention and the comparison groups across time points (e.g., pre-test, post-test, follow-up). Variables showing between-group differences at baseline and correlation with the post-test outcomes are controlled for statistically, using analysis of covariance. In this analysis the variables with baseline differences are identified as covariates, whose influence on the post-test outcomes is residualized prior to comparing the mean scores on the post-test outcomes between the intervention and comparison groups.

Subgroup analyses are done to determine the effects of the intervention on the outcomes in different segments of the sample defined by a particular characteristic (e.g., sex, concurrent treatment) known to affect the outcomes. The characteristic is considered a between-subject factor in a factorial analysis of variance of which the independent (i.e., main) and interactive (i.e., characteristic × treatment group) effects on the outcome are examined. The participants' scores on the characteristic have to be dichotomized or categorized to generate the between-subject factor. This practice yields loss of information and statistical power.

Traditional statistical tests have some limitations: 1) the focus is on the mean outcome scores exhibited by the groups at the different time points; inter-individual variability in outcome achievement is ignored and posited as error variance; 2) the number of variables to include in an analysis as covariate or additional between-subject factor is small; 3) the clustering of participants within sites and treatment groups cannot be accounted for; 4) outcome data that are missing for some participants at some time points must be handled prior to conducting the analysis; 5) significant main (treatment group, time) and interaction (treatment group × time) effects are followed by post-hoc comparisons to determine where the differences in outcomes occur (i.e., between which groups and at what time points); post-hoc comparisons generate the problem of multiplicity and associated inflated rate of type I error; 6) the tests examine the direct effects on all outcomes and are of limited utility in determining the mechanism mediating the intervention effects on the ultimate outcomes.

Recent statistical techniques, including hierarchical linear or mixed models and structural equation modeling, overcome some of the limitations. Specifically, hierarchical linear models allow examination of the pattern of change in the outcomes for individual participants, and the association of the pattern of change with relevant variables (e.g., personal characteristics, treatment group, reaction and adherence to treatment) while accounting for the clustering effects. The pattern of change is estimated on the basis of outcome data available for each participant, thereby addressing the problem of missingness; however, the precision of the estimate may be affected (i.e., estimates based on complete data are more precise). Structural equation modeling is useful in examining, simultaneously, the direct effects of the intervention on the immediate outcomes and its indirect effects on the ultimate outcomes, mediated by the participants' reactions to treatment and immediate outcomes. The influence of additional variables (e.g., baseline characteristics, treatment dose) on the direct and indirect effects of the intervention can also be tested.

Two issues have been of concern in outcome analysis: protocol violation and missing data. To address the first, per protocol and intention-to-treat analyses are done. Different techniques can be used to handle missing data.

Per Protocol Analysis

Per protocol means that only those who complete the trial according to the study's protocol are counted in the outcome data analysis. Participants who withdraw before, during, or after exposure to the allocated treatment are eliminated from the analysis. Also, participants allocated to the intervention group who do not engage in the intervention at all are analyzed as if they were in the comparison arm, whereas participants assigned to the comparison group who are exposed to any component of the intervention are analyzed as if they were in the intervention arm. The rationale is that the effects of the intervention cannot be validly and accurately assessed in participants who do not receive it.

Intention-to-treat Analysis

The intention-to-treat (ITT) principle means that people are analyzed in the group to which they were randomized, whether or not they actually receive the intervention (Wertz, 1995). The rationale behind this approach is that it more closely mirrors the effectiveness of the treatment in the real world and it preserves the randomization scheme. Deviation from this scheme introduces bias, in that only compliant patients are assessed. ITT analyses require complete data from all participants. Missing data are managed prior to the ITT analysis.

Evidence

ITT analysis yields smaller estimates of the intervention's effects than per protocol analysis, because those who are included in the ITT analysis consist of participants who had the full course of treatment, those who had only partial courses, and those who received no treatment at all. Empirical evidence supports this expectation. Hollis and Campbell (1999) showed that in one study comparing surgical vs. medical treatment of angina pectoris, the difference in two-year mortality rates was 2.4 percentage points higher in the medical arm using ITT analysis, and this was not statistically significant. However, the difference was 4.3 percentage points using per protocol analysis and 5.4 percentage points if the analysis was done according to what the patients actually received, and both of these differences were significant.

Handling Missing Data

Two general approaches are available to address missingness (Little and Rubin, 2002; McKnight et al., 2007). The first consists of analyzing available data. This means running the analysis only with participants who have complete outcome data across time points. In most statistical packages, this technique is called listwise deletion or completer analysis. This technique reduces sample size; the results are biased if those with complete data form a select subgroup of the target population. The second involves imputation. This strategy involves replacing the data missing on outcome variables on some time points, with some values. The values may include: 1) the mean score for the outcome variable estimated for the total sample at the respective time point; 2) the mean score for the outcome variable estimated for the group to which participants with missing data are assigned, at the respective time point; 3) the mean score for the outcome variable estimated for participants with missing data at one point in time; for instance, if data are missing at post-test, then the mean is computed from the outcome scores observed at pre-test and follow-up; and 4) the last observation carried forward for participants who have provided data at one point in time (e.g., pre-test) and withdraw from the study thereafter; in this case, the score observed for the outcome at pre-test is imputed for participants across all remaining time points. The use of the last observation carried forward for missing data imputation assumes that participants who drop out did not benefit from treatment; yet experience indicates that this assumption is not always correct, as some participants showing improvement in the outcomes may withdraw for various reasons; therefore, imputing the last observation has the potential to underestimate the intervention effects (Shadish et al., 1998).

Summary

- Outcomes are criteria for determining the benefits of interventions
- Outcomes should be carefully selected, assessed with appropriate measures and at opportune times to accurately reflect the intervention effects
- Selection of outcomes is guided by an understanding of the mechanism underlying the intervention effects
- Outcome measures should be 1) valid to accurately reflect the outcome concept and detect the anticipated changes, and 2) reliable to minimize error variance and increase the power to detect significant intervention effects
- Data analysis involves comparisons on outcomes between the intervention and comparison groups, over time

REFERENCES

Abel, U. and Koch, A. (1999) The role of randomization in clinical studies: Myths and beliefs. *Journal of Clinical Epidemiology*, 52: 487–497.

Ablon, J.S. and Marci, C. (2004) Psychotherapy process: The missing link: Comment on Westen, Novotny, and Thompson-Brenner (2004). *Psychological Bulletin*, 130: 664–668.

Adamson, S.J., Sellman, J.D. and Dore, G.M. (2005) Therapy preference and treatment outcome in clients with mild to moderate alcohol dependence. *Drug and Alcohol Review*, 24: 209–216.

Agodini, R. and Dynarski, M. (2004) Are experiments the only option? A look at dropout prevention programs. *The Review of Economics and Statistics*, 86: 180–194.

Ahern, K. and Le Brocque, R. (2005) Methodological issues in the affects of attrition: Simple solutions for social scientists. *Field Methods*, 17: 53–69.

Aiken, L.S., West, S.G., Schwaim, D.E., Carroll, J.L. and Hsiung, S. (1998) Comparison of a randomized and two quasi-experimental designs in a single outcome evaluation: Efficacy of a university-level remedial writing program. *Evaluation Review*, 22 (2): 207–244.

Ajzen, I. (1991) The theory of planned behavior. *Organizational Behavior and Human Decision Processes*, 50 (2): 179–211.

Ames, S.C., Rock, E., Hurt, R.D., Patten, C.A., Craghan, J.T., Stoner, S.M., Decker, P.A., Offord, K.P. and Nelson, M. (2008) Development and feasibility of a parental support intervention for adolescent smokers. *Substance Use and Misuse*, 43: 497–511.

Amir, L.H., Lumley, J. and Garland, S.M. (2004) A failed RCT to determine if antibiotics prevent mastitis: Cracked nipples colonized with Staphylococcus aureus: A randomized treatment trial [ISRCTN65289389]. *BMC Pregnancy and Childbirth*, 4: 19.

Anderson, T.R., Hogg, J.A. and Magoon, T.M. (1987) Length of time on a waiting list and attrition after intake. *Journal of Counseling Psychology*, 34: 93–95.

Armstrong, T.S., Cohen, M.Z., Erikson, L. and Cleeland, C. (2005) Content validation of self-report measurement instruments: An illustration from the development of a brain tumor module of the M.D. Anderson Symptom Inventory. *Oncology Nursing Forum*, 3: 669–676.

Aseltine, R.H., Carlson, K.J., Fowler, F.J. and Barry, M.J. (1995) Comparing prospective and retrospective measures of treatment outcomes. *Medical Care*, 33 (Suppl): AS–67–76.

Autret, A., Valade, D. and Debiais, S. (2012) Placebo and other psychological interactions in headache treatment. *Journal of Headache and Pain*, 13: 191–198.

Awad, M.A., Shapiro, S.H., Lund, J.P. and Feine, J.S. (2000) Determinants of patients' treatment preferences in a clinical trial. *Community Dental Oral Epidemiology*, 28: 119–125.

Baekeland, F. and Lundwall, L. (1975) Dropping out of treatment: A critical review. *Psychological Bulletin*, 82: 738–783.

Baker, L., Lavender, T. and Tincello, D. (2005) Factors that influence women's decisions about whether to participate in research: An exploratory study. *Birth*, 32: 60–66.

Baldwin, S.A., Wampold, B.E. and Imel, Z.E. (2007) Untangling the alliance-outcome correlation: Exploring the relative importance of therapist and patient variability in the alliance. *Journal of Consulting and Clinical Psychology*, 75 (6): 842–852.

Balk, E.M., Bonis, P.A., Moskowitz, H., Schmid, C.H., Ioannidis, J.P., Wang, C. and Lau, J. (2002) Correlation of quality measures with estimates of treatment effect in meta-analyses of randomized controlled trials. *JAMA: The Journal of the American Medical Association*, 287: 2973–2982.

Bamberger, M. and White, H. (2007) Using strong evaluation designs in developing countries: Experience and challenges. *Journal of MultiDisciplinary Evaluation*, 4 (8): 58–73.

Barkauskas, V.H., Lusk, S.L. and Eakin, B.L. (2005) Intervention research: Selecting control interventions for clinical outcome studies. *Western Journal of Nursing Research*, 27(3): 346–363.

Barrett, R. (2002) A nurses' primer on recruiting participants for clinical trials. *Oncology Nursing Forum*, 29: 1091–1096.

Basch, C.E. and Gold, R.S. (1986) The dubious effects of type V errors in hypothesis testing on health education practice and theory. *Health Education Research*, 1 (4): 299–305.

Baskin, T.W., Tierney, S.C., Minami, T. and Wampold, B.E. (2000) Establishing specificity in psychotherapy: A meta-analysis of structural equivalence of placebo controls. *Journal of Consulting and Clinical Psychology*, 71 (6): 973–979.

Becker, B.J. (1990) Coaching for the Scholastic Aptitude Test: Further synthesis and appraisal. *Review of Educational Research*, 60: 373–417.

Becker, H.S. (2008) *Tricks of the Trade: How to Think about Your Research While You're Doing it*. Chicago: University of Chicago Press.

Becker, H., Roberts, G. and Voelmeck, W. (2003) Explanations for improvement in both experimental and control groups. *Western Journal of Nursing Research*, 25: 746–755.

Bedi, N., Chilvers, C., Churchill, R., Dewey, M., Duggan, C., Fielding, K., Gretton, V., Miller, P., Harrison, G., Lee, A. and Williams, I. (2000) Assessing effectiveness of treatment of depression in primary care: Partially randomized preference trial. *British Journal of Psychiatry*, 177: 312–318.

Bellg, A.J., Borrelli, B., Resnick, B., Hecht, J., Sharp-Minicucci, D., Ory, M. et al. (2004) Enhancing treatment fidelity in health behaviour change studies: Best practices and recommendations from the NIH behaviour change consortium. *Health Psychology*, 23 (5): 443–451.

Benson, K. and Hartz, A.J. (2000) A comparison of observational studies and randomized, controlled trials. *The New England Journal of Medicine*, 342 (25): 1878–1886.

Berwick, D.M. (2008) The science of improvement. *The Journal of the American Medical Association*, 299 (10): 1182–1184.

Bloom, H.S., Michalopoulos, C. and Hill, C.J. (2005) Using experiments to assess non-experimental comparison-group methods for measuring program effects. In H.S. Bloom (ed.), *Learning More from Social Experiments*. New York: Russell Sage Foundation, pp. 173–235.

Bluestein, D., Healy, A.C. and Rutledge, C.M. (2011) Acceptability of behavioral treatments for insomnia. *Journal of the American Board of Family Medicine*, 24: 272–280.

Bootzin, R.R. and Bailey, E.T. (2005) Understanding placebo, nocebo, and iatrogenic treatment effects. *Journal of Clinical Psychology*, 61 (7): 871–880.

Borglin, G. and Richards, D.A. (2010) Bias in experimental nursing research: Strategies to improve the quality and explanatory power of nursing science. *International Journal of Nursing Studies*, 47: 123–128.

Borkovec, T.D. (1993) Between-group therapy outcome research: Design and methodology. In L.S. Onken, J.D. Blaine and J.J. Oren (eds), *Behavioral Treatments for Drug Abuse and Dependence*. National Institute on Drug Abuse (NIDA) Research Monograph Series 137. Washington, DC: US Department of Health and Human Services, pp. 249–289.

Borradaile, K.E., Halpern, S.D., Wyatt, H.R., Klein, S., Hill, J.O., Bailer, B., Brill, C., Stein, R.I., Miller, B.V. and Foster, G.D. (2011) Relationship between treatment preference and weight loss in the context of a randomized controlled trial. *Obesity*, 20(6): 1218–1222.

Borrelli, B., Sepinwall, D., Ernst, D., Bellg, A.J., Czajkowski, S., Breger, R. et al. (2005) A new tool to assess treatment fidelity and evaluation of treatment fidelity across 10 years of health behaviour research. *Journal of Consulting and Clinical Psychology*, 73 (5): 852–860.

Bottomley, A. (1997) To randomize or not to randomize: Methodological pitfalls of the RCT design in psychosocial intervention studies. *European Journal of Cancer Care*, 6: 222–230.

Boutron, I., Estellat, C. and Ravaud, P. (2005) A review of blinding in randomized controlled trials found results inconsistent and questionable. *Journal of Clinical Epidemiology*, 58: 1220–1226.

Bowers, T.G. and Clum, G.A. (1998) Relative contribution of specific and nonspecific treatment effects: Meta-analysis of placebo-controlled behavior therapy research. *Psychological Bulletin*, 103 (3): 313–323.

Bowling, A. (2005) Mode of questionnaire administration can have serious effects on data quality. *Journal of Public Health*, 27 (3): 281–291.

Bowling, A. and Rowe, G. (2005) 'You decide doctor': What do patient preference arms in clinical trials really mean? *Journal of Epidemiology and Community Health*, 59: 914–915.

Boyd, N.F., Cousins, M. and Kriukov, V. (1992) A randomized controlled trial of dietary fat reduction: The retention of subjects and characteristics of drop outs. *Journal of Clinical Epidemiology*, 45 (1): 31–38.

Bradley, C. (1993) Designing medical and educational intervention studies. *Diabetes Care*, 16: 509–518.

Brandt, P.A., Davis Kirsch, S., Marcus Lewis, F. and Casey, S.M. (2004) Assessing the strength and integrity of an intervention. *Oncology Nursing Forum*, 31 (4): 833–837.

Breitenstein, S.M., Gross, D., Garvey, C.A., Hill, C., Fogg, L. and Resnick, B. (2010) Implementation fidelity in community-based interventions. *Research in Nursing and Health*, 33(2): 164–173.

Britton, A., McPherson, K., McKee, M., Sanderson, C., Black, N. and Bain, C. (1998) Choosing between randomised and non-randomised studies: A systematic review. *Health Technology Assessment*, 2 (13).

Brown, S.J. (2002) Nursing intervention studies: A descriptive analysis of issues important to clinicians. *Research in Nursing and Health*, 25: 317–327.

Bruckenthal, P. and Broderick, J.E. (2007) Assessing treatment fidelity in pilot studies to assist in designing clinical trials: An illustration from a nurse practitioner community-based intervention for pain. *Advances in Nursing Science*, 30 (1): E72–E84.

Buckwalter, K.C., Grey, M., Bowers, B., McCarthy, A.M., Gross, D., Funk, M. and Beck, C. (2009) Intervention research in highly unstable environments. *Research in Nursing and Health*, 32: 110–121.

Buddelmeyer, H. and Skoufias, E. (2003) *An Evaluation of the Performance of Regression Discontinuity Design on PROGRESA*. Bonn: IZA.

Burns, J.W. and Evon, D. (2007) Common and specific factors in cardiac rehabilitation: Independent and interactive effects of the working alliance and self-efficacy. *Health Psychology*, 26 (6): 684–692.

Butterfield, P.G., Yates, S.M., Rogers, B. and Healow, J.M. (2003) Overcoming subject recruitment challenges: Strategies for successful collaboration with novice research agencies. *Applied Nursing Research*, 16 (1): 46–52.

Califf, R.M., Zarin, D.A., Kramer, J.M., Sherman, R.E., Aberle, L.H. and Tasneem, A. (2012) Characteristics of clinical trials registered in ClinicalTrials.gov, 2007–2010. *Journal of the American Medical Association*, 307 (17): 1838–1847.

Campbell, J.P., Maxey, V. and Watson, W.A. (1995) Hawthorne effects: implications for prehospital research. *Annals of Emergency* Medicine, 26 (5): 590–594.

Campbell, M., Fitzpatrick, R., Haines, A., Kinmonth, A.L., Sandercock, P., Spiegelhalter, D. and Tyrer, P. (2000) Framework for design and evaluation of complex interventions to improved health. *British Medical Journal*, 321: 694–696.

Campbell, N.C., Murray, E., Darbyshire, J., Emery, J., Farmer, A., Griffiths, F. et al. (2007) Designing and evaluating complex interventions to improve health care. *British Medical Journal*, 334: 455–459.

Campbell, R., Peters, T., Grant, C., Quilty, B. and Dieppe, P. (2005) Adapting the randomized consent (Zelen) design for trials of behavioural interventions for chronic disease: Feasibility study. *Journal of Health Sciences Research and Policy*, 10 (4): 220–225.

Cappelleri, J.C., Darlington, R.B. and Trochim, W.M. (1994) Power analysis of cutoff-based randomized clinical trials. *Evaluation Review*, 18 (2): 141–152.

Carroll, C., Patterson, M., Wood, S., Booth, A., Rick, J. and Balain, S. (2007) A conceptual framework for implementation fidelity. *Implementation Science*, 2: 40–48.

Cartwright, N. (2007) Are RCT's the gold standard? *BioSocieties*, 2: 11–20.

Cartwright, N. and Munro, E. (2010) The limitations of randomized controlled trials in predicting effectiveness. *Journal of Evaluation in Clinical Practice*, 16: 260–266.

Carver, R.P. (1974) Two dimensions of tests: Psychometric and edumetric. *American Psychologist*, 29: 512–518.

Chalmers, T.C., Celano, P., Sacks, H.S. and Smith, H. (1983) Bias in treatment assignment in controlled clinical trials. *The New England Journal of Medicine*, 309: 1358–1361.

Charlson, M.E. and Horwitz, R.I. (1984) Applying results of randomised trials to clinical practice: Impact of losses before randomisation. *British Medical Journal (Clinical research ed.)*, 289 (6454): 1281.

Chatterji, M. (2007) Grades of evidence: Variability in quality of findings in effectiveness studies of complex field interventions. *American Journal of Evaluation*, 28 (3): 239–255.

Chung, L.K., Cimprich, B., Janz, N.K. and Mills-Wismeski, S.M. (2009) Breast cancer survivorship program: Testing for cross-cultural relevance. *Cancer Nursing*, 32 (3): 236–245.

Coday, M., Boutin-Foster, C., Goldman Sher, T., Tennant, J., Greaney, M.L., Saunders, S.D. and Somes, G.W. (2005) Strategies for retaining study participants in behavioural intervention trials: Retention experiences of the NIH behaviour change consortium. *The Society of Behavioural Medicine*, 29 (Suppl): 55–65.

Cohen, J. (1988) *Statistical Power Analysis for the Social Sciences* (2nd ed.). Hillsdale, NJ: Lawrence Erlbaum.

Colditz, G.A., Miller, J.N. and Mosteller, F. (1988) The effect of study design on gain in evaluation of new treatments in medicine and surgery. *Drug Information Journal*, 22 (3): 343–352.

Concato, J. and Horwitz, R.I. (2004) Commentary: Beyond randomised versus observational studies. *The Lancet*, 363 (9422): 1660–1661.

Concato, J., Shah, N. and Horwitz, R.I. (2000) Randomised, controlled trials, observational studies, and the hierarchy of research designs. *New England Journal of Medicine*, 342 (25): 1887–1892.

Connolly, N.B., Schneider, D. and Hill, A.M. (2004) Improving enrollment in cancer clinical trials. *Oncology Nursing Forum*, 31 (3): 610–614.

Cook, T.D. (1993) A quasi-sampling theory of the generalization of causal relationships. *New Directions for Program Evaluation*, 57: 39–81.

Cook, T.D. (2006) Describing what is special about the role of experiments in contemporary educational research: Putting the 'gold standard' rhetoric into perspective. *Journal of Multi-Disciplinary Evaluation*, 6: 1–7.

Cook, T.D. (2007) Randomized experiments in education: Assessing the objections to doing them. *Economics of Innovation and New Technology*, 16 (5): 331–355.

Cook, T.D. and Campbell, D.T. (1979) *Quasi-experimentation: Design and Analysis Issues for Field Settings*. Boston, MA: Houghton Mifflin.

Cook, T.D., Scriven, M., Coryn, C.L.S. and Evergreen, S.D.H. (2010) Contemporary thinking about causation in evaluation: A dialogue with Tom Cook and Michael Scriven. *American Journal of Evaluation*, 31 (1): 105–117.

Cook Gotay, C. (1991) Accrual to cancer clinical trials: Directions from the research literature. *Social Science and Medicine*, 33 (5): 569–577.

Cooley, M.E., Sarna, L., Brown, J.K., Williams, R.D., Chernecky, C., Padilla, G. and Danao, L.L. (2003) Challenges of recruitment and retention in multisite clinical research. *Cancer Nursing*, 26 (5): 376–386.

Cooper, L.A., Gonzales, J.J., Gallo, J.J., Rost, K.M., Meredith, L.S., Rubenstein, L.V. et al. (2003) The acceptability of treatment of depression among African-American, Hispanic and White primary care patients. *Medical Care*, 41(4): 479–489.

Copeland, A., Martin, P., Geiselman, P., Rash, C. and Kendzor, D. (2006) Predictors of pretreatment attrition from smoking cessation among pre- and postmenopausal, weight-concerned women. *Eating Behaviours*, 7: 243–251.

Coward, D.D. (2002) Partial randomization design in a support group intervention study. *Western Journal of Nursing Research*, 24: 406–421.

Craig, P., Dieppe, P., Macintyre, S., Michie, S., Nazareth, I. and Petticrew, M. (2008) Developing and evaluating complex interventions: The New Medical Research Council guidance. *British Medical Journal*, 337: a1655.

Crits-Christoph, P. and Mintz, J. (1991) Implications of therapist effects for the design and analysis of comparative studies of psychotherapies. *Journal of Counsulting and Clinical Psychology*, 59: 20–26.

Crits-Christoph, P., Baranackie, K., Kurcias, J., Beck, A., Carroll, K., Perry, K. et al. (1991) Meta-analysis of therapist effects in psychotherapy outcome studies. *Psychotherapy Research*, 1 (2): 81–91.

Curtin, L., Brown, R. and Sales, S. (2000) Determinants of attrition from cessation treatment in smokers with a history of major depressive disorder. *Psychology of Addictive Behaviours*, 14 (2): 134–142.

D'Agostino, R.B. (2009) The delayed-start study design. *New England Journal of Medicine*, 361: 1304–1306.

Damschroder, L.J., Aron, D.C., Keith, R.E., Kirsh, S.R., Alexander, J.A. and Lowery, J.C. (2009) Fostering implementation of health services research findings into practice: A consolidated framework for advancing implementation science. *Implementation Science*, 4: 50–64.

Daunt, D.J. (2003) Ethnicity and recruitment rates in clinical research studies. *Applied Nursing Research*, 16 (3): 189–195.

Davidson, E.J. (2006) The RCTs only doctrine: Brakes on the acquisition of knowledge? *Journal of MultiDisciplinary Evaluation*, 6: ii–v.

Deacon, B.J. and Abramowitz, J.S. (2005) Patients' perceptions of pharmacological and cognitive-behavioral treatments for anxiety disorders. *Behavior Therapy*, 36: 139–145.

De Maat, S., Dekker, J., Schoevers, R. and de Jonghe, F. (2007) The effectiveness of long term psychotherapy: Methodological research issues. *Psychotherapy Research*, 17 (1): 59–65.

Demissie, K., Mills, O.F. and Rhoads, G.G. (1998) Empirical comparison of the results of randomized controlled trials and case-control studies in evaluating the effectiveness of screening mammography. *Journal of Clinical Epidemiology*, 51 (2): 81–91.

DeVellis, R.F. (2003) *Scale Development: Theory and Applications* (2nd ed.). Thousand Oaks, CA: Sage.

Devine, D.A. and Ferrald, P.S. (1973) Outcome effects of receiving a preferred, randomly assigned, or nonpreferred therapy. *Journal of Consulting and Clinical Psychology*, 41: 104–107.

Deyo, R.A. and Centor, R.M. (1986) Assessing the responsiveness of functional scales to clinical change: An analogy to diagnostic test performance. *Journal of Chronic Disease*, 39 (11): 897–906.

DiMattio, M.J.K. (2001) Recruitment and retention of community-dwelling, aging women in nursing studies. *Nursing Research*, 50 (6): 369–373.

Dinger, U., Strack, M., Leichsenrig, F., Wilmers, F. and Schauenburg, H. (2008) Therapist effects on outcome and alliance in inpatient psychotherapy. *Journal of Clinical Psychology*, 64 (3): 344–354.

Donaldson, S.I. and Christie, C.A. (2004) Determining causality in program evaluation and applied research: Should experimental evidence be the gold standard? *Journal of MultiDisciplinary Evaluation*, 3: 60–77.

Donner, A. and Klar, N. (2000) *Design and Analysis of Cluster Randomization Trials in Health Research.* London: Arnold Publishers, pp. 81–82.

Donner, A. and Klar, N. (2004) Pitfalls of and controversies in cluster randomization trials. *American Journal of Public Health*, 94 (3): 416–422.

Donner, A., Taljaard, M. and Klar, N. (2007) The merits of breaking the matches: A cautionary tale. *Statistics in Medicine*, 26 (9): 2036–2051.

Douglas, H.R., Normand, C.E., Higginson, I.J. and Goodwin, D.M. (2005) A new approach to eliciting patients' preferences for palliative day care: The choice experiment method. *Journal of Pain and Symptom Management*, 29: 435–445.

Dumas, J.E., Lynch, A.M., Laughlin, J.E., Phillips Smith, E. and Prinz, R.J. (2001) Promoting intervention fidelity: Conceptual issues, methods, and preliminary results from the early alliance prevention trial. *American Journal of Preventative Medicine*, 20 (1S): 38–47.

Dumbrigue, H.B., Al-Bayat, M.I., Ng, C.C.H. and Wakefield, C. W. (2006) Assessment of bias in methodology for randomized controlled trials published on implant dentistry. *Journal of Prosthodontics*, 15 (4): 257–263.

Dumville, J.C., Torgerson, D.J. and Hewitt, C.E. (2006) Reporting attrition in randomized controlled trials. *British Medical Journal*, 332 (22): 969–971.

Durlack, J.A. and DuPre, E.P. (2008) Implementation matters: A review of research on the influence of implementation on program outcomes and the factors affecting implementation. *American Journal of Community Psychology*, 41: 327–350.

Dwight-Johnson, M., Unutzer, J., Sherbourne, C., Tang, L. and Wells, K.B. (2001) Can quality improvement programs for depression in primary care address patient preferences for treatment? *Medical Care*, 39 (9): 934–944.

Earle, C.C., Tsai, J.S., Gelber, R.D., Weinstein, M.C., Neumann, P.J. and Weeks, J.C. (2001) Effectiveness of chemotherapy for advanced lung cancer in the elderly: Instrumental variable and property analysis. *Journal of Clinical Oncology*, 19 (4): 1064–1070.

Eccles, M., Grimshaw, J., Walker, A., Johnston, M. and Pitts, N. (2005) Changing the behavior of healthcare professionals: The use of theory in promoting the uptake of research findings. *Journal of Clinical Epidemiology*, 58: 107–112.

Eckert, T.L. and Hintze, J.M. (2000) Behavioral conceptions and applications of acceptability: Issues related to service delivery and research methodology. *School Psychology Quarterly*, 15 (2): 123–149.

Edinger, J.D., Wohlgemuth, W.K., Radtke, R.A., Coffman, C.J. and Carney, C.E. (2007) Dose-response effects of cognitive-behavioral insomnia therapy: A randomized clinical trial. *Sleep*, 30 (2): 203–212.

Elander, G. and Hermérén, G. (1995) Placebo effect and randomized clinical trials. *Theoretical Medicine*, 16: 171–182.

Eldridge, S.M., Ashby, D., Feder, G.S., Rudnicka, A.R. and Ukoumunne, O.C. (2004) Lessons for cluster randomized trials in the twenty-first century: A systematic review of trials in primary care. *Clinical Trials*, 1: 80–90.

Eldridge, S., Spencer, A., Cryer, C., Parsons, S., Underwood, M. and Feder, G. (2005) Why modelling a complex intervention is an important precursor to trial design: Lessons from studying an intervention to reduce falls-related injuries in older people. *Journal of Health Services Research and Policy*, 10 (3): 133–142.

Elkin, I., Falconnier, L., Martinovich, Z. and Mahoney, C. (2006) Therapist effects in the National Institute of Mental Health Treatment of Depression Collaborative Research Program. *Psychotherapy Research*, 16 (2): 144–160.

Ellis, P.M. (2000) Attitudes towards and participation in randomized clinical trials in oncology: A review of the literature. *Annals of Oncology*, 11: 939–945.

Embi, P.J., Jain, A., Clark, J., Bizjack, S., Hornung, R. and Harris, M. (2005) Effect of a clinical trial alert system on physician participation in trial recruitment. *JAMA Internal Medicine*, 165: 2272–2277.

Epstein, R.M. and Peters, E. (2009) Beyond information: Exploring patients' preferences. *Journal of the American Medical Association*, 302 (2): 195–197.

Epstein, R.S. (2000) Responsiveness in quality-of-life assessment: Nomenclature, determinants, and clinical applications. *Medical Care*, 38 (9, Suppl II): 91–94.

Eremenco, S., Cella, D. and Arnold, B. (2005) A comprehensive method for the translation and cross-cultural validation of health status questionnaires. *Evaluation and the Health Professions*, 28 (2): 212–232.

Ferriter, M. and Huband, N. (2005) Does the non-randomized controlled study have a place in the systematic review? A pilot study. *Criminal Behaviour and Mental Health*, 15 (2): 111–120.

Finnis, D.G., Kaptchuk, T.J., Miller, F. and Benedetti, F. (2010) Biological, clinical, and ethical advances of placebo effects. *The Lancet*, 375: 686–695.

Fischer, D., Stewart, A.L., Boch, D.A. et al. (1999) Capturing the patients' view of change as a clinical outcome measure. *Journal of the American Medical Association*, 282: 1157–1162.

Fitzpatrick, R., Ziebland, S., Jenkinson, C., Mowat, A. and Mowat, A. (1993) Transition questions to assess outcomes in rheumatoid arthritis. *British Journal of Rheumatology*, 32: 807–811.

Fixsen, D.L., Naoom, S.F., Blase, K.A., Friedman, R.M. and Wallace, F. (2005) *Implementation Research: A Synthesis of the Literature*. Tampa: University of South Florida.

Fleiss, J.L. (1986) Analysis of data from multiclinic trials. *Controlled Clinical Trials*, 7 (4): 267–275.

Floyd, A.H.L. and Moyer, A. (2010) Effects of participant preferences in unblinded randomized controlled trials. *Journal of Empirical Research on Human Research Ethics*, 5: 81–93.

Forbes, A. (2009) Clinical intervention research in nursing. *International Journal of Nursing Studies*, 46: 557–568.

Forgatch, M.S., Patterson, G.R. and DeGarmo, D.S. (2005) Evaluating fidelity: Predictive validity for a measure of competent adherence to the Oregon model of parent management training. *Behaviour Therapy*, 36 (1): 3–13.

Fraenkel, L., Rabidou, N., Wittink, D. and Fried, T. (2007) Improving informed decision-making for patients with knee pain. *The Journal of Rheumatology*, 34 (9): 1894–1898.

Freedman, D.H. (2010) Lies, damned lies, and medical science. *The Atlantic*, November.

Fuertes, J.N., Mislowack, A., Bennett, J., Paul, L., Gilbert, T.C., Fontan, G. and Boylan, L.S. (2007) The physician–patient working alliance. *Patient Education and Counseling*, 66: 29–36.

Ganguli, M., Lytle, M.E., Reynolds, M.D. and Dodge, H.H. (1998) Random versus volunteer selection for a community-based study. *The Journals of Gerontology Series A: Biological Sciences and Medical Sciences*, 53 (1): M39–M46.

Gearing, R.E., El-Bassel, N., Ghesquiere, A., Baldwin, S., Gillies, J. and Ngeow, E. (2011) Major ingredients of fidelity: A review and scientific guide to improving quality of intervention research implementation. *Clinical Psychology Review*, 31: 79–88.

Gilbert, J.P., McPeek, B. and Mosteller, F. (1978) Statistics and ethics in surgery and anesthesia. *Science*, 78: 684–689.

Givens, J.L, Houston, T.K., Van Voorhees, B.W., Ford, D.E. and Cooper, L.A. (2007) Ethnicity and preferences for depression treatment. *General Hospital Psychiatry*, 29: 182–191.

Glasgow, R.E., Magid, D.J., Beck, A., Ritzwoller, D. and Estabrooks, P.A. (2005) Practical clinical trials for translating research to practice: Design and measurement recommendations. *Medical Care*, 43 (6): 551–559.

Glasziou, P., Chalmers, I., Rowlins, M. and McCulloch, P. (2007) When are randomized trials unnecessary? Picking signal from noise. *British Medical Journal*, 334: 349–351.

Glazerman, S., Levy, D.M. and Myers, D. (2003) Nonexperimental versus experimental estimates of earning impacts. *The Annals of the American Academy*, 589: 63–93.

Goldfried, M.R. and Eubanks-Carter, C. (2004) On the need for a new psychotherapy research paradigm: Comment on Westen, Novotny, and Thompson-Brenner (2004). *Psychological Bulletin*, 130 (4): 669–673.

Graham, J.W. and Donaldson, S.I. (1993) Evaluating interventions with differential attrition: The importance of nonresponse mechanisms and use of follow up data. *Journal of Applied Psychology*, 78 (1): 119–128.

Grapow, M.T.R., von Wattenwyl, R., Guller, U., Beyersdorf, F. and Zerkowski, H.R. (2006) Randomized controlled trials do not reflect reality: Real world analyses are critical for treatment guidelines. *The Journal of Thoracic and Cardio Surgery*, 132 (1): 5–7.

Green, J. (2000) The role of theory in evidence-based health promotion practice. *Health Education Research*, 15: 125–129.

Grimshaw, J., Campbell, M., Eccles, M. and Steen, N. (2000) Experimental and quasi-experimental designs for evaluating guideline implementation strategies. *Family Practice*, 17 (1): S11–S16.

Guentner, K., Hoffman, L.A., Happ, M.B., Kim, Y., DeVito Dabbs, A., Mendelson, A.B. and Chelluri, L. (2006) Preferences for mechanical ventilation among survivors of prolonged mechanical ventilation and tracheostomy. *American Journal of Critical Care*, 15: 65–77.

Gum, A.M., Arean, P.A., Hunkeler, E., Tang, L., Katon, W., Hitchcock, P., Steffens, D.C., Dickens, J. and Unützer, J. (2006) Depression treatment preferences in older primary care patients. *The Gerontologist*, 4: 14–22.

Guyatt, G.H., Haynes, B., Jaeschke, R., Cook, D., Greenhalgh, T., Meade, M, Green, L., Naylor, C.D., Wilson, M., McAlister, F. and Richardson, W.S. (2002) Introduction: The philosophy of evidence-based medicine. In G. Guyatt and D. Rennie (eds), *Users' Guides to the Medical Literature: A Manual for Evidence-based Clinical Practice*. Chicago: AMA Press, pp. 3–12.

Gwadry-Sridher, F., Guyatt, G.H., Arnold, M.O., Massel, D., Brown, J., Nadeau, L. and Lawrance, S. (2003) Instruments to measure acceptability of information and acquisition of knowledge in patients with heart failure. *The European Journal of Heart Failure*, 5: 783–791.

Haaga, D.A.F. (2004) A healthy dose of criticism for randomized trials: Comment on Western Novotny, and Thompson-Brenner. *Psychological Bulletin*, 130 (4): 674–676.

Haidich, A-B. and Ioannidis, J.P.A. (2001) Patterns of patient enrollment in randomized controlled trials. *Journal of Clinical Epidemiology*, 54: 877–883.

Hamunen, K. and Kalso, E. (2005) A systematic review of trial methodology, using the placebo groups of randomized controlled trials in pediatric postoperative pain. *International Association for the Study of Pain*, 116: 146–158.

Hardeman, W., Sutton, S., Griffin, S., Johnston, M., White, A., Wareham, N.J. and Kinmonth, A.L. (2005) A causal modelling approach to the development of theory-based behaviour change for programmes for trial evaluation. *Health Education Research*, 20 (6): 676–687.

Hark, T.T. and Stump, D.A. (2008) Statistical significance versus clinical significance. *Seminars in Cardiothoracic and Vascular Anesthesia*, 12 (1): 5–6.

Harris, K.M., Florey, F., Tabor, J., Bearman, P.S., Jones, J. and Udry, J.R. (2003) The national longitudinal study of adolescent health: Research design. Carolina Population Center, University of North Carolina at Chapel Hill. Retrieved from: www.cpc.unc.edu/projects/addhealth/faqs/aboutdata/weight1.pdf (accessed 3 September 2008).

Harris, P.M. (1998) Attrition model. *American Journal of Evaluation*, 19 (3): 293–305.

Harris, R. and Dyson, E. (2001) Recruitment of frail older people to research: Lessons learnt through experience. *Journal of Advanced Nursing*, 36 (5): 643–651.

Hart, E. (2009) Treatment definition in complex rehabilitation interventions. *Neuropsychological Rehabilitation*, 19 (6): 824–840.

Hasson, H. (2010) Systematic evaluation of information fidelity of complex intervention in health and social care. *Implementation Science*, 5: 67–75.

Hawe, P., Schiell, A. and Riley, T. (2004) Complex interventions: How 'out of control' can a randomized controlled trial be? *British Medical Journal*, 328: 1561–1563.

Hazlett-Stevens, H., Craske, M.G., Roy-Byrne, P.P., Sherbourne, C.D., Stein, M.B. and Bystritsky, A. (2002) Predictors of willingness to consider medication and psychosocial treatment for panic disorder in primary care patients. *General Hospital Psychiatry*, 24: 316–321.

Heaman, M. (2001) Conducting health research with vulnerable women: Issues and strategies. *Canadian Journal of Nursing Research*, 33 (3): 81–86.

Heinsman, D.T. and Shadish, W.R. (1996) Assignment methods in experimentation: When do nonrandomized experiments approximate answers from randomized experiments? *Psychological Methods*, 1 (2): 154–169.

Heit, M., Rosenquist, C., Culligan, P., Graham, C., Murphy, M. and Shott, S. (2003) Predicting treatment choice for patients with pelvic organ prolapse. *The American College of Obstetrics and Gynecology*, 101: 1279.

Hertzog, M.A. (2008) Considerations in determining sample size for pilot studies. *Research in Nursing and Health*, 31: 180–191.

Hicks, C. (1998) The randomized controlled trial: A critique. *Nurse Researcher*, 6 (1): 19–32.

Hitchcock Noël, P., Marsh, G., Larme, A.C., Correa, A., Meyer, J. and Pugh, J.A. (1998) Patient choice in diabetes education curriculum. *Diabetes Care*, 21: 896–901.

Hofmann, S.G., Barlow, D.H., Papp, L.A., Detweiler, M.F., Ray, S.E., Shear, M.K. et al. (1998) Pretreatment attrition in a comparative treatment outcome study on panic disorder. *American Journal of Psychiatry*, 155: 43–47.

Hollis, S. and Campbell, F. (1999) What is meant by intention to treat analysis? Survey of published randomised controlled trials. *British Medical Journal*, 319 (7211): 670–674.

Holtz, A. (2007) Comparative effectiveness of health interventions: Strategies to change policy and practice. Report from ECRI Institute's 15th Annual Conference, pp. 1–8.

Homer, C.S. (2002) Using the Zelen design in randomized controlled trials: Debates and controversies. *Journal of Advanced Nursing*, 38 (2): 200–207.

Horn, S.D., DeJong, G., Ryser, D.K., Veazie, P.J. and Teraoka, J. (2005) Another look at observational studies in rehabilitation research: Going beyond the holy grail of the randomized controlled trial. *Archives of Physical Medicine and Rehabilitation*, 86 (2): S8–S15.

Horwitz, R.I. (1987) Complexity and contradiction in clinical trial research. *The American Journal of Medicine*, 82: 498–510.

Howard, L. and Thornicroft, G. (2006) Patient preference and randomized controlled trials in mental health research. *British Journal of Psychiatry*, 188: 303–304.

Huibers, M.J.H., Bleijenberg, G., Beurskens, A.J.H.M., Kant, I., Knottnerus, J.A., Van der Windt, S.A.W.M. et al. (2004) An alternative trial design to overcome validity and recruitment problems in primary care research. *Family Practice*, 21 (2): 213–218.

Huppert, J.D., Bufka, L.F., Barlow, D.H., German, J.M., Shear, M.K. and Woods, S.W. (2001) Therapists, therapist variables, and cognitive-behavioral therapy outcome in a multicenter trial for panic disorder. *Journal of Consulting and Clinical Psychology*, 69: 747–755.

Hussey, M.A. and Hughes, J.P. (2007) Design and analysis of stepped wedge cluster randomized trials. *Contemporary Clinical Trials*, 28: 182–191.

Hyde, P. (2004) Fool's gold: Examining the use of gold standards in the production of research evidence. *British Journal of Occupational Therapy*, 67 (2): 89–94.

Ibrahim, S. and Sidani, S. (2013) Strategies to recruit minority persons: A systematic review. *Journal of Immigrant and Minority Health*, 5 (11): 1784–1790.

Ilnyckyj, A., Shanahan, F., Anton, P.A., Cheang, M. and Bernstein, C.N. (1997) Quantification of the placebo response in ulcerative colitis. *Gastroenterology*, 112: 1854–1858.

Imbens, G.W. and Lemieux, T. (2008) Regression discontinuity designs: A guide to practice. *Journal of Econometrics*, 142 (2): 615–635.

Institute of Medicine (2001) *Crossing the Quality Chasm: A New Health System for the 21st Century*. Washington, DC: National Academy Press.

Ioannidis, J.P.A. (2005) Why most published research findings are false. *PLoS Medicine*, 2 (8): 696–701.

Ioannidis, J.P.A., Haidich, A.B., Pappa, M., Pantazis, N., Kokori, S.I., Tektonidou, M.G. et al. (2001) Comparison of evidence of treatment effects in randomized and nonrandomized studies. *Journal of the American Medical Association*, 286 (7): 821–830.

Jacobs, G.D., Pace-Schott, E.F., Stickgold, R. and Otto, M.W. (2004) Cognitive behavior therapy and pharmacotherapy for insomnia: A randomized controlled trial and direct comparison. *Archives of Internal Medicine*, 164: 1888–1986.

Janevic, M.R., Janz, M.K., Dodge, J.A., Lin, X., Pan, W., Sinco, B.R. and Clark, N.M. (2003) The role of choice in health education intervention trials: A review and case study. *Social Science and Medicine*, 56: 1581–1594.

Jenkins, V. and Fallowfield, L. (2000) Reasons for accepting or declining to participate in randomized clinical trials for cancer therapy. *British Journal of Cancer*, 82 (11): 1783–1788.

Jepsen, P., Johnsen, S.P., Gillman, M.W. and Sorensen, H.T. (2004) Interpretation of observational studies. *Heart*, 90: 956–960.

Jo, B. (2002) Statistical power in randomized intervention studies with noncompliance. *Psychological Methods*, 7 (2): 178–193.

Jo, B., Muthen, B.O., Asparouhov, T., Ialongo, N.S. and Hendricks-Brown, C. (2008) Cluster randomized trials with treatment noncompliance. *Psychological Methods*, 13 (1): 1–18.

Jobe, J.B. (2003) Cognitive psychology and self-reports: Models and methods. *Quality of Life Research*, 12: 219–227.

Jolly, K., Lip, G.Y., Taylor, R.S., Mant, J.W., Lane, D.A., Lee, K.W. and the BRUM Steering Committee (2005) Recruitment of ethnic minority patients to a cardiac rehabilitation trial: The Birmingham Rehabilitation Uptake Maximisation (BRUM) study. *BMC Medical Research Methodology*, 5 :18.

Joyce, A.S., Ogradniczuk, J.S., Piper, W.E. and McCallum, M. (2003) The alliance as mediator of expectancy effects in short-term individual therapy. *Journal of Clinical and Consulting Psychology*, 71 (4): 672–679.

Jüni, P., Witschi, A., Bloch, R. and Egger, M. (1999) The hazards of scoring the quality of clinical trials for meta-analysis. *Journal of the American Medical Association*, 282: 1054–1060.

Kang, J., Robertson, R.J., Hagberg, J.M., Kelley, D.E., Goss, F.L., Dasilva, S.G., Suminski, R.R. and Utter, A.C. (1996) Effect of exercise intensity on glucose and insulin metabolism in obese individuals and obese NIDDM patients. *Diabetes Care*, 19 (4): 341–349.

Kaptchuk, T.J. (2001) The double-blind, randomized, placebo-controlled trial: Gold standard or golden calf? *Journal of Clinical Epidemiology*, 54: 541–549.

Kaptchuk, T.J., Friedlander, E., Kelley, J.M., Sanchez, M.N., Kokkotou, E., Singer, J. P. et al. (2010). Placebos without deception: A randomized controlled trial in irritable bowel syndrome. *Public Library of Science One*, 5 (12): 1–7.

Karanicolas, P.J., Montori, V.M., Devereaux, P.J., Schünemann, H. and Guyatt, D.H. (2009) A new 'mechanistic-practical' framework for designing and interpreting randomized trials. *Journal of Clinical Epidemiology*, 62: 479–484.

Kaufman, J.S., Kaufman, S. and Poole, C. (2003) Causal inference from randomized trials in social epidemiology. *Social Science and Medicine*, 57: 2397–2409.

Kaul, S. and Diamond, G.A. (2010) Trial and error: How to avoid commonly encountered limitations of published clinical trials. *Journal of the American College of Cardiology*, 55: 415–427.

Kazdin, A.E. (1980) Acceptability of alternative treatments for deviant child behavior. *Journal of Applied Behavior Analysis*, 13: 259–273.

Kazdin, A.E. (2003) *Research Design in Psychology*. Boston: Allyn and Bacon.

Keith, R.E., Hopp, F.P., Subramanian, U., Witala, W. and Lowery, J.C. (2010) Fidelity of implementation: Development and testing of a measure. *Implementation Science*, 5: 99–109.

Keller, C.S., Gonzales, A. and Fleuriet, K. J. (2005) Retention of minority participants in clinical research studies. *Western Journal of Nursing Research*, 27 (3): 292–306.

Keller, C., Fleury, J., Sidani, S. and Ainsworth, B. (2009) Fidelity to theory in physical activity intervention research. *Western Journal of Nursing Research*, 31 (3): 289–311.

Kemmer, L. and Júlia Paes da Silva, M. (2007) How can one choose what is unknown? A study on the image of nurses by high school students. *Acta Paulista de Enfermagem*, 20 (2): 125–130.

Kerlikowske, K. (2012) Screening mammography in women less than age 50 years. *Current Opinion in Obstetrics and Gynecology*, 24 (1): 38–43.

Kernan, W.N., Viscoli, C.M., Makuch, R.W., Brass, L.M. and Horwitz, R.I. (1999) Stratified randomization for clinical trials. *Journal of Clinical Epidemiology*, 52 (1): 19–26.

Kiesler, D.J. and Auerbach, S.M. (2006) Optimal matches of patient preferences for information, decision-making and interpersonal behavior: Evidence, models, and interventions. *Patient Education and Counseling*, 61: 319–341.

Kim, D-M., Wampold, B.E. and Bolt, D.M. (2006) Therapist effects in psychotherapy: A random-effects modeling of the National Institute of Mental Health Treatment of Depression Collaborative Research Program data. *Psychotherapy Research*, 16 (2): 161–172.

King, M., Nazareth, I., Lampe, F., Bower, P., Chandler, M., Morou, M., Sibbald, B. and Lai, R. (2005) Impact of participant and physician intervention preferences on randomized trials: A systematic review. *Journal of the American Medical Association*, 293: 1089–1099.

Kjaergaard, J., Clemmensen, I.H. and Storm, H.H. (2001) Validity and completeness of registration of surgically treated malignant gynaecological diseases in the Danish National Hospital Registry. *Journal of Epidemiology and Biostatistics*, 6 (5): 387–392.

Klaber-Moffett, J.K., Torgerson, D., Bell-Syer, S., Jackson, D., Llewlyn-Phillips, H., Farrin, A. and Barber, J. (1999) Randomised controlled trial of exercise for low back pain: Clinical outcomes, costs, and preferences. *British Medical Journal*, 319 (7205): 279–283.

Kleinman, P.H., Woody, G.E., Todd, T.C., Millman, R.B., Kang, S-Y., Kemp, J. and Lipton, D.S. (1990) Crack and cocaine abusers in outpatient psychotherapy. In L.S. Onken and J.D. Blaine (eds), *Psychotherapy and Counseling in the Treatment of Drug Abuse*. National Institute on Drug Abuse (NIDA) Research Monograph Series 104. Washington, DC: US Department of Health and Human Services, pp. 24–35.

Koedoot, C.G., de Haan, R.J., Stiggelbout, A.M., Stalmeier, P.F.M., de Graeff, A., Bakker, P.J.M. et al. (2003) Palliative chemotherapy or best supportive care? A prospective study explaining patients' treatment preference and choice. *British Journal of Cancer*, 89: 2219–2226.

Kok, G., Schaalma, H., Ruiter, R.A.C., Van Empelen, P. and Brug, J. (2004) Intervention mapping: A protocol for applying health psychology theory to prevention programmes. *Journal of Health Psychology*, 9 (1): 85–98.

Kovach, C.R. (2009) Some thoughts on the hazards of sloppy science when designing and testing multicomponent interventions, including the Kitchen Skin phenomenon. *Research in Nursing and Health*, 32: 1–3.

Kownacki, R.J. (1997) *A meta-analysis of the alcoholism treatment outcome literature: Selection with randomized and quasi-experiments* (Doctoral dissertation, University of Memphis).

Kraemer, H.C. and Fendt, K.H. (1990) Random assignment in clinical trials: Issues in planning (infant health and development program). *Journal of Clinical Epidemiology*, 43 (11): 1157–1167.

Kraemer, M.S., Martin, R.M., Sterne, J.A.C., Shapiro, S., Dahhou, M. and Platt, R.W. (2009) The double jeopardy of clustered measurement and cluster randomization. *British Medical Journal*, 339: 503–505.

Kunz, R. and Oxman, A.D. (1998) The unpredictability paradox: Review of empirical comparisons of randomised and non-randomised clinical trials. *British Medical Journal*, 317: 1185–1190.

Kwan, B.M., Dimidjian, S. and Rizvi, S.L. (2010) Treatment preferences, engagement, and clinical improvement in pharmacotherapy versus psychotherapy for depression. *Behavior Research and Therapy*, 48: 799–804.

LaLonde, R. (1986) Evaluating the econometric evaluations of training programs. *American Economic Review*, 76: 604–620.

Lambert, N., Rowe, G., Bowling, A., Ebrahim, S., Laurence, M. et al. (2004) Reasons underpinning patients' preferences for various angina treatments. *Health Expectations*, 6: 246–256.

Lancaster, G.A., Dodd, S. and Williamson, P.R. (2004) Design and analysis of pilot studies: Recommendations for good practice. *Journal of Evaluation in Clinical Practice*, 10 (2): 307–312.

Larzelere, R.E., Kuhn, B.R. and Johnson, B. (2004) The intervention selection bias: An under recognized confound in intervention research. *Psychological Bulletin*, 130 (2): 289–303.

Lawlor, D.A., Smith, G.D., Bruckdorfer, K.R., Kundu, D. and Ebrahim, S. (2004) Those confounded vitamins: What can we learn from the differences between observational versus randomized trial evidence? *The Lancet*, 363: 1924–1927.

Leach, M.J. (2003) Barriers to conducting randomized controlled trials: Lessons learnt from the Horsechestnut and Venous Leg Ulcer Trial (HAVLUT). *Contemporary Nurse*, 15: 37–47.

Lee, E., McNally, D.L. and Zuckerman, I.H. (2004) Evaluation of a physician-focused educational intervention on Medicaid children with asthma. *The Annals of Pharmacotherapy*, 38 (6): 961–966.

Leeman, R., Quiles, Z., Molinelli, L., Terwal, D., Nordstrom, B., Garvey, A. and Kinnunen, T. (2006) Attrition in a multi-component smoking cessation study for females. *Tobacco Induced Disease*, 3 (2): 59–71.

Lehman, A.F. and Steinwachs, D.M. (2003) Evidence-based psychosocial treatment practices in schizophrenia: Lessons from the Patient Outcomes Research Team (PORT) Project. *Journal of the American Academy of Psychoanalysis and Dynamic Psychiatry*, 31 (1): 141–154.

Leigh, J.P., Ward, M.M. and Fries, J.F. (1993) Reducing attrition bias with an instrumental variable in a regression model: Results from a panel of rheumatoid arthritis patients. *Statistics in Medicine*, 12 (11): 1005–1018.

Leon, A.C., Davis, L.L. and Kraemer, H. C. (2011) The role and interpretation of pilot studies in clinical research. *Journal of Psychiatric Research*, 45 (5): 626–629.

Leventhal, H. and Friedman, M.A. (2004) Does establishing fidelity of treatment help in understanding treatment efficacy? Comment on Bellg et al. (2004). *Health Psychology*, 23 (5): 452–456.

Lewis, B.A., Napolitano, M.A., Whiteley, J.A. and Marcus, B.H. (2006) The effect of preferences for print versus telephone interventions on compliance and attrition in a randomized controlled physical activity trial. *Psychology of Sport and Exercise*, 7: 453–462.

Leykin, Y., DeRubeis, R.J., Gallop, R., Amsterdam, J.D., Shelton, R.C. and Hollon, S.D. (2007) The relation of patients' treatment preferences to outcome in a randomized clinical trial. *Behavior Therapy*, 38: 209–217.

Liang, M.H. (2000) Longitudinal construct validity: Establishment of clinical meaning in patient evaluative instruments. *Medical Care*, 38 (9, Suppl II): 84–90.

Linde, K., Scholz, M., Ramirez, G., Clausius, N., Melchart, D. and Jonas, W.B. (1999) Impact of study quality on outcome in placebo-controlled trials of homeopathy. *Journal of Clinical Epidemiology*, 52 (7): 631–636.

Lindsay, B. (2004) Randomized controlled trials of socially complex nursing interventions: Creating bias and unreliability? *Journal of Advanced Nursing*, 45 (1): 84–94.

Lindsay Davis, L., Broome, M.E. and Cox, R.P. (2002) Maximizing retention in community-based clinical trials. *Journal of Nursing Scholarship*, 34: 47–53.

Lippke, S. and Ziegelman, J.P. (2008) Theory-based health behavior change: Developing, testing, and applying theories for evidence-based interventions. *Applied Psychology: An International Review*, 57 (4): 698–716.

Lipsey, M.W. (1990) *Design Sensitivity: Statistical Power for Experimental Research*. Thousand Oaks, CA: Sage.

Lipsey, M.W. and Wilson, D.B. (1993) The efficacy of psychological, educational, and behavioral treatment: Confirmation from meta-analysis. *American Psychologist*, 48: 1181–1209.

Little, R.J.A. and Rubin, D.B. (2002) *Statistical Analysis with Missing Data* (2nd ed.). Hoboken, NJ: John Wiley and Sons.

Lowenstein, P.R. and Castro, M.G. (2009) Uncertainty in the translation of preclinical experiments to clinical trials: Why do most Phase III clinical trials fail? *Current Gene Therapy*, 9 (5): 368–374.

Luborsky, L., McLellan, A.T., Diguer, L., Woody, G. and Selignman, D.A. (1997) The psychotherapist matters: Comparison of outcomes across twenty two therapists and seven patient samples. *Clinical Psychology: Science and Practice*, 4: 53–65.

Lugtenberg, M., Burgers, J.S. and Westert, G.P. (2009) Effects of evidence-based clinical practice guidelines on quality of care: A systematic review. *Quality and Safety in Health Care*, 18: 385–392.

Lutz, W., Leon, S.C., Martinovich, Z., Lyons, J.S. and Stiles, W.B. (2007) Therapist effects in outpatient psychotherapy: A three-level growth curve approach. *Journal of Counseling Psychology*, 54 (1): 32–39.

Lyons, K.S., Carter, J.H., Carter, E.H., Rush, K.N., Stewart, B.J. and Archbold, P.G. (2004) Locating and retaining research participants for follow-up studies. *Research in Nursing and Health*, 27: 63–68.

Macias, C., Barreira, P., Hargreaves, W., Bickman, L., Fisher, W. and Aronson, E. (2005) Impact of referral source and study applicants' preference for randomly assigned service on research enrollment, service engagement, and evaluative outcomes. *American Journal of Psychiatry*, 162: 781–787.

MacKinnon, D.P. and Fairchild, A.J. (2009) Current directions in mediation analysis. *Current Directions in Psychological Science*, 18 (1): 16–20.

MacLehose, R.R., Reeves, B.C., Harvey, I.M., Sheldon, T.A., Russell, I.T. and Black, A.M.S. (2000) A systematic review of comparisons of effect sizes derived from randomized and non-randomised studies. *Health Technology Assessment*, 4 (34): 1–154.

Maclure, M. (2009) Explaining pragmatic trials to pragmatic policymakers. *Journal of Clinical Epidemiology*, 62: 476–478.

Man-Son-Hing, M., Hart, R.G., Berquist, R., O'Connor, A.M. and Laupacis, A. (2001) Differences in treatment preferences between persons who enroll and do not enroll in clinical trials. *Annals of the Royal College of Physicians and Surgeons*, 34 (5): 292–296.

Marcellus, L. (2004) Are we missing anything? Pursuing research on attrition. *Canadian Journal of Nursing Research*, 36 (3): 82–98.

Margo, C.E. (1999) The placebo effect. *Survey of Ophthalmology*, 44 (1): 31–44.

Martin, K.A., Bowen, D.J., Dunbar-Jacob, J. and Perri, M.G. (2000) Who will adhere? Key issues in the study and prediction of adherence in randomized controlled trials. *Controlled Clinical Trials*, 21: 195S–199S.

McCarney, R., Warner, J., Iliffe, S., Van Haselen, R., Griffin, M. and Fisher, P. (2007) The Hawthorne Effect: A randomized controlled trial. *BMC Medical Research Methodology*, 7: 30.

McLean, S. (1997) No consent means not treating the patient with respect. *British Medical Journal*, 314:1076.

McClelland, G.H. (1997) Optimal design in psychological research. *Psychological Methods*, 2 (1): 3–19.

McDonald, A.M., Knight, R.M., Campbell, M.K., Entwhistle, V.A., Grant, A.M., Cook, J.A. et al. (2006) What influences recruitment to randomized controlled trials? A review of trials funded by two UK funding agencies. *Trials*, 7: 9.

McEwen, A. and West, R. (2009) Do implementation issues influence the effectiveness of medications? The case of nicotine replacement therapy and bupropion in UK Stop Smoking Services. *BMC Public Health*, 9: 28–36.

McKay, J.R., Alterman, A.I., McLellan, T., Boardman, C.R., Mulvaney, F.D. and O'Brien, C.P. (1998) *Journal of Consulting and Clinical Psychology*, 66 (4): 697–701.

McKee, M., Britton, A., Black, N., McPherson, K., Sanderson, C. and Bain, C. (1999) Interpreting the evidence: Choosing between randomised and non-randomised studies. *British Medical Journal*, 19: 312–315.

McKnight, P.E., McKnight, K.M., Sidani, S. and Figueredo, A.J. (2007) *Missing Data: A Gentle Introduction*. New York: Guilford Publications.

McRae, A.D., Weijer, C., Binik, A, Grimshaw, J.M., Baruch, R., Brehaut, J.C., Donner, A., Eccles, M.P., Saginur, R., White, A. and Taljaard, M. (2011a) When is informed consent required in cluster randomized trials in health research? *Trials*, 12: 202.

McRae, A.D., Weijer, C., Binik, A., White, A., Grimshaw, J.M., Baruch, R., Brehaut, J.C., Donner, A., Eccles, M., Saginur, R., Zwarenstein, M. and Taljaard, M. (2011b) Who is the research subject in cluster randomized trials in health research? *Trials*, 12: 183.

Melde, C., Esbensen, F.A. and Tusinski, K. (2006) Addressing program fidelity using onsite observations and program provider descriptions of program delivery. *Evaluation Review*, 30 (6): 714–740.

Messer, S.B. and Wampold, B.E. (2002) Let's face facts: Common factors are more potent than specific therapy ingredients. *Clinical Psychology and Scientific Practice*, 9: 21–25.

Messick, S. (1995) Validity of psychological assessment. *American Psychologist*, 50 (9): 741–749.

Methodology Committee of the Patient-Centered Outcomes Research Institute (PCORI) (2012) Methodological standards and patient-centeredness in comparative effectiveness research. The PCORI perspective. *Journal of the American Medical Association*, 307 (15): 1636–1640.

Miao, L.L. (1977) Gastric freezing: An example of the evaluation of medical therapy by randomized clinical trials. In J.P. Bunker, B.A. Barnes and F. Mosteller (eds), *Costs, Risks, and Benefits of Surgery*. New York: Oxford University Press, pp. 198–211.

Mihalic, S. (2002) The importance of implementation fidelity. 442 UCB. Retrieved from: http://incrediblyears.comwww.incredibleyears.com/Library/items/fidelity-importance.pdf

Millat, B., Borie, F. and Fingerhut, A. (2005) Patients' preference and randomization: New paradigm of evidence-based clinical research. *World Journal of Surgery*, 29: 596–600.

Miller, J.N., Colditz, G.A. and Mosteller, F. (1989) How study design affects outcomes in comparisons of therapy. II: Surgical. *Statistics in Medicine*, 8: 455–466.

Mills, N., Donovan, J.L., Wade, J., Hamdy, F.C., Neal, D.E. and Lane, J.A. (2011) Exploring treatment preferences facilitated recruitment to randomized controlled trials. *Journal of Clinical Epidemiology*, 64: 1127–1136.

Miranda, J. (2004) An exploration of participants' treatment preferences in a partial RCT. *Canadian Journal of Nursing Research*, 36 (3): 100–114.

Moffett, J.A., Jackson, D.A., Richmond, S., Hahn, S., Coulton, S., Farrin, A., Mance, A. and Torgerson, D.J. (2005) Randomised trial of a brief physiotherapy intervention compared with usual physiotherapy for neck pain patients: Outcomes and patients' preferences. *British Medical Journal*, 330: 75–80.

Montoro-Rodriguez, J. and Smith, G.C. (2010) When cost meets efficiency: rethinking ways to sample a rare population (pp. 136–146). In D.L. Streiner and S. Sidani (eds), *When Research goes off the* Rails. New York: Guilford Press.

Moser, D.K., Dracup, K. and Doering, L.V. (2000) Factors differentiating dropouts from completers in a longitudinal, multicenter clinical trial. *Nursing Research*, 49 (2): 109–116.

Mowbray, C.T., Holter, M.C., Teague, G.B. and Bybee, D. (2003) Fidelity criteria: Development, measurement, and validation. *American Journal of Evaluation*, 24 (3): 315–340.

Murray, D.M., Varnell, S.P. and Blitstein, J.L. (2004) Design and analysis of group randomized trials: A review of recent methodological developments. *American Journal of Public Health*, 94 (3): 423–432.

Najavits, L.M. and Weiss, R.D. (1994) Variations in therapist effectiveness in the treatment of patients with substance use disorders: An empirical review. *Addiction*, 89: 679–688.

Nallamothu, B.K., Hayward, R.A. and Bates, E.R. (2008) Beyond the randomized clinical trial: The role of effectiveness studies in evaluating cardiovascular therapies. *Circulation*, 118: 1294–1303.

Nápoles-Springer, A.M., Santayo-Olsson, J., O'Brien, H. and Stewart, A.L. (2006) Using cognitive interviews to develop surveys in diverse populations. *Medical Care*, 44: S21–S30.

National Institute of Neurological Disorders and Stroke [NINDS] (1995) Tissue plasminogen activator for acute ischemic stroke. *The New England Journal of Medicine*, 333: 1581–1587.

National Institutes of Health, National Cancer Institute (2005) *Theory at a Glance: A Guide for Health Promotion Practice* (2nd ed.). Retrieved from: http://www.cancer.gov/cancertopics/cancerlibrary/theory.pdf

Noar, S.M. and Mehrotra, P. (2011) Toward a new methodological paradigm for testing theories of health behavior and health behavior change. *Patient Education and Counseling*, 82 (3): 468–474.

Nock, M.K. (2007) Conceptual and design essentials for evaluating mechanisms of change: Alcoholism. *Clinical and Experimental Research*, 31 (S3): 4S–12S.

Norman, G.R. and Streiner, D.L. (2008) *Biostatistics: The Bare Essentials* (3rd ed.). Shelton, CT: PMPH US.

Norris, S.L. and Atkins, D. (2005) Challenges in using randomized studies in systematic reviews of treatment interventions. *Annals of Internal Medicine*, 142 (12): 1112–1119.

North West Uro-Oncology Group (2002) A preliminary report on patient-preference study to compare treatment options in early prostate cancer. *British Journal of Urology International*, 90: 253–256.

Nunnally, J.C. and Bernstein, I.H. (1994) *Psychometric Theory* (3rd ed.). New York: McGraw-Hill.

Nystuen, P. and Hagen, K.B. (2004) Telephone reminders are effective in recruiting nonresponding patients to randomized controlled trials. *Journal of Clinical Epidemiology*, 57: 773–776.

O'Reilly, P. Martin, L. and Collins, G. (1999) Few patients with prostate cancer are willing to be randomized to treatment. *British Medical Journal*, 318 (197): 1556.

Oakley, A., Strange, V., Torogan, T., Wiggins, M., Roberts, I. and Stephenson, J. (2003) Using random allocation to evaluate social interventions: The recent U.K. examples. *The Annals of American Academy of Political and Social Science*, 589: 170–189.

Okiishi, J., Lambert, M.J., Nielson, S.L. and Ogles, B.M. (2003) Waiting for supershrink: An empirical analysis of therapist effects. *Clinical Psychology and Psychotherapy*, 10: 361–373.

Ong, J.C., Kuo, T.F. and Manber, R. (2008) Who is at risk for dropout from group cognitive-behavior therapy for insomnia? *Journal of Psychosomatic Research*, 64: 419–425.

Ong-Dean, C., Hofsletter, C.H. and Strick, B.R. (2011) Challenges and dilemmas in implementing random assignment in educational research. *American Journal of Evaluation*, 32 (1): 29–49.

Oremus, M., Cosby, J.L. and Wolfson, C. (2005) A hybrid qualitative method for pre-testing questionnaires: The example of a questionnaire to caregivers of Alzheimer's disease patients. *Research in Nursing and Health*, 28: 419–430.

Osoba, D., Hsu, M.A., Copley-Merriman, C., Coombs, J., Johnson, F.R., Hauber, B., Manjunath, R. and Pyles, A. (2006) Stated preferences of patients with cancer for health-related quality-of-life (HRQOL) domains during treatment. *Quality of Life Research*, 15: 273–283.

Ottenbacher, K. (1992) Impact of random assignment on study outcome: An empirical examination. *Controlled Clinical Trials*, 13: 50–61.

Oxman, A.D., Lombard, C., Treweek, S., Gagnier, J.J., Maclure, M. and Zwarenstein, M. (2009) Why we will remain pragmatists: Four problems with the impractical mechanistic framework and a better solution. *Journal of Clinical Epidemiology*, 62: 485–488.

Oxman, T.E., Schulberg, H.C., Greenberg, R.L., Dietrich, A.J., Williams, J.W., Nutting, P.A. and Bruce, M.L. (2006) A fidelity measure for integrated management of depression in primary care. *Medical Care*, 44 (11): 1030–1037.

Padhye, N.S., Cron, S.G., Gusick, G.M., Hamlin, S.K. and Hanneman, S.K. (2009) Randomization for clinical research: An easy-to-use spreadsheet method. *Research in Nursing and Health*, 32: 561–566.

Painter, J.E., Borba, C.P.C., Hynes, M., Mays, D. and Glanz, K. (2008) The use of theory in health behavior research from 2000–2005: A systematic review. *Annals of Behavioral Medicine*, 35: 358–362.

Pallesen, S., Mitsem, M., Kvale, G., Johnsen, B.H. and Molde, H. (2005) Outcome of psychological treatments of pathological gambling: A review and analysis. *Addiction*, 100 (10): 1412–1422.

Pawson, R. and Tilley, N. (1997) *Realistic Evaluation*. London: Sage.

Peabody, J.W., Luck, J., Jain, S., Bertenthal, D. and Glassman, P. (2004) Assessing the accuracy of administrative data in health information systems. *Medical Care*, 42 (11): 1066–1072.

Pearson, M.L., Wu, S., Schaefer, J., Bonomi, A.E., Shortell, S.M., Mendel, P.J. et al. (2005) Assessing the implementation of the chronic care model in quality improvement collaboratives. *Health Services Research*, 40 (4): 978–996.

Peduzzi, P., Henderson, W., Hartigan, P. and Lavori, P. (2002) Analysis of randomized controlled trials. *Epidemiologic Reviews*, 24 (1): 26–38.

Pincus, T. (2002) Limitations of randomized clinical trials in chronic diseases: Explanations and recommendations. *Advances*, 18 (2): 14–21.

Podsakoff, P.M., MacKenzie, S.B., Lu, J-Y. and Podsakoff, N.P. (2003) Common method biases in behavioral research: A critical review of the literature and recommended remedies. *Journal of Applied Psychology*, 88 (5): 879–903.

Polit, D.F., Beck, C.T. and Owen, S.V. (2007) Is the CVI an acceptable indicator of content validity? Appraisal and recommendations. *Research in Nursing and Health*, 30 (4): 459–467.

Porter, R., Frampton, C., Joyce, P.R. and Mulder, R.T. (2003) Randomized controlled trials in psychiatry. Part 1: Methodology and critical evaluation. *Australian and New Zealand Journal of Psychiatry*, 37: 257–264.

Preference Collaborative Review Group (2009) Patients' preferences within randomized trials: Systematic review and patient level meta-analysis. *British Medical Journal Online.* Retrieved 3 February 2009.

Proctor, R.W. and Capaldi, E.J. (2001) Empirical evaluation and justification of methodologies in psychological science. *Psychological Bulletin,* 127 (6): 759–772.

Project MATCH Research Group (1998) Therapist effects in three treatments for alcohol problems. *Psychotherapy Research,* 8: 455–474.

Pruitt, R.H. and Privette, A.B. (2001) Planning strategies for the avoidance of pitfalls in intervention research. *Journal of Advanced Nursing,* 35 (4): 514–520.

Quitkin, F.M. (1999) Placebos, drug effects, and study design: A clinician's guide. *American Journal of Psychiatry,* 156 (6): 829–836.

Raudenbush, S.W. and Bryk, A.S. (2002) *Hierarchical Linear Models: Applications and Data Analysis Methods* (2nd ed.). Thousand Oaks, CA: Sage.

Raue, P.J., Schulberg, H.C., Heo, M., Klimstra, S. and Bruce, M.L. (2009) Patients' depression treatment preferences and initiation, adherence, and outcome: A randomized primary care study. *Psychiatric Services,* 60: 337–343.

Relton, C., Torgerson, D., O'Cathain, A. and Nicholl, J. (2010) Rethinking pragmatic randomized controlled trials: Introducing the 'cohort multiple randomized controlled trial' design. *British Medical Journal,* 340: 963–967.

Resio, M.A., Baltch, A. and Smith, R.P. (2004) Mass mailing and telephone contact were effective in recruiting veterans into an antibiotic treatment randomized clinical trial. *Journal of Clinical Epidemiology,* 57: 1063–1070.

Ribisl, K.M., Walton, M.A., Mowbray, C.T., Luke, D.A., Davidson, W.S. and Bootsmiller, B.J. (1996) Minimizing participant attrition in panel studies through the use of effective retention and tracking strategies: Review and recommendations. *Evaluation and Program Planning,* 19(1): 1–25.

Robey, R.R. (2004) A five phase model for clinical-outcome research. *Journal of Communication Disorder,* 37: 401–411.

Robinson, E.J., Kerr, C.E.P., Stevens, A.J., Lilford, R.J., Brauholtz, D.A., Edwards, S.J., Beck, S.R. and Rowley, M.G. (2005) Lay public's understanding of equipoise and randomisation in randomised controlled trials. *Health Technology Assessment,* 9 (8).

Rohrer, J.E. (2000) Rigor at the expense of relevance equals rigidity: Where to next in the study of medical care utilization? *Health Services Research,* 34 (6): 1307–1314.

Rosenberger, W.F. (1999) Randomized play-the-winner clinical trials: Review and recommendations. *Controlled Clinical Trials,* 20: 328–342.

Ross, S., Grant, A., Counsell, C., Gillespie, W., Russell, I. and Prescott, R. (1999) Barriers to participation in randomized controlled trials: A systematic review. *Journal of Clinical Epidemiology,* 52 (12): 1143–1156.

Rossi, P.H., Freeman, H.E. and Lipsey, M.W. (2004) *Evaluation: A Systematic Approach* (7th ed.). Thousand Oaks, CA: Sage.

Rothwell, P.M. (2005) External validity of randomized controlled trials: 'To whom do the results of this study apply?' *The Lancet*, 365: 82–93.

Rücker, G. (1989) A two-stage trial design for testing treatment, self selection and treatment preference effects. *Statistics in Medicine*, 8(4): 477–485.

Russell, K. and Walsh, D. (2009) Can the use of behavioural intervention studies support change in professional practice behaviours? A literature review. *Evidence Based Midwifery*, 7 (2): 54–59.

Sackett, D.L. (2007) Commentary: Measuring the success of blinding in RCTs: Don't, must, can't or needn't? *International Journal of Epidemiology*, 36: 664–665.

Sacks, H., Chalmers, T.C. and Smith, H. (1982) Randomized versus historical controls for clinical trials. *The American Journal of Medicine*, 72: 233–240.

Sacks, H.S., Chalmers, T.C. and Smith, H. (1983) Sensitivity and specificity of clinical trials: Randomized v. historical controls. *Archives of Internal Medicine*, 143: 753–755.

Salyer, J., Geddes, N., Smith, C.S. and Mark, B.A. (1998) Commitment and communication: Keys to minimizing attrition in multisite longitudinal organizational studies. *Nursing Research*, 47 (2): 123–125.

Saunders, R.P., Evans, M.H. and Joshi, P. (2005) Developing a process-evaluation plan for assessing health promotion program implementation: A how to guide. *Health Promotion Practice*, 6 (2): 134–147.

Savard, J., Simard, S., Hervouet, S., Ivers, H., Lacombe, L. and Fradet, Y. (2005) Insomnia in men treated with radical prostatectomy for prostate cancer. *Psycho-Oncology*, 14: 147–156.

Say, R.E. and Thomson, R. (2003) The importance of patient preferences in treatment decisions: Challenges for doctors. *British Medical Journal*, 327: 542–545.

Schafer, J.L. and Kang, J. (2008) Average causal effects from nonrandomized studies: A practical guide and simulation example. *Psychological Methods*, 13 (4): 279–313.

Schellings, R., Kessels, A.G., ter Riet, B., Knottnerus, J.A. and Stumans, F. (2006) Randomized consent designs in randomized controlled trials: systematic literature search, *Contemporary Clinical* Trials, 27 (4): 320–332.

Schmidt, F. (2010) Detecting and connecting the lies that data tell. *Perspectives on Psychological Science*, 5 (3): 233–242.

Schochet, P.Z. (2008) Statistical power for random assignment evaluations of education programs. *Journal of Educational and Behavioral* Statistics, 33(1); 62–87.

Schulz, K.F. and Grimes, D.A. (2002a) Generation of allocation sequences in randomised trials: Chance, not choice. *The Lancet*, 359: 515–519.

Schulz, K.F. and Grimes, D.A. (2002b) Allocation concealment in randomised trials: Defending against deciphering. *The Lancet*, 359: 614–618.

Schulz, K.F., Chalmers, I., Hayes, R.J. and Altman, D.G. (1995) Empirical evidence of bias: Dimensions of methodological quality associated with estimates of treatment effects in controlled trials. *Journal of the American Medical Association*, 273(5): 408–412.

Schwartz, C.E. and Fox, B.H. (1995) Who says yes? Identifying selection biases in a psychosocial intervention study of multiple sclerosis. *Social Science and Medicine*, 40 (3): 359–370.

Schwartz, C.E., Chesney, M.A., Irvine, J. and Keefe, F.J. (1997) The control group dilemma in clinical research: Applications for psychosocial and behavioural medicine trials. *Psychosomatic Medicine*, 59: 362–371.

Schwartz, C.E., Merriman, M.P., Reed, G.W. and Hammes, B.J. (2004) Measuring patient treatment preferences in end-of-life care research: Applications for advance care planning interventions and response shift research. *Journal of Palliative Medicine*, 7: 233–245.

Sellors, J., Cosby, R., Trim, K., Kaczorowski, J., Howard, M., Hardcastle, L. et al. for the Seniors Medication Assessment Research Trial (SMART) Group (2002) Recruiting family physicians and patients for a clinical trial: Lessons learned. *Family Practice*, 19 (1): 99–104.

Sepucha, K. and Ozanne, E.M. (2010) How to define and measure concordance between patients' preferences and medical treatments: A systematic review of approaches and recommendations for standardization. *Patient Education and Counseling*, 78: 12–23.

Shadish, W.R. (2010) Campbell and Rubin: A primer and comparison of their approaches to causal inference in field settings. *Psychological Methods*, 15 (1): 3–17.

Shadish, W.R. and Ragsdale, K. (1996) Random versus nonrandom assignment in controlled experiments: Do you get the same answer? *Journal of Consulting and Clinical Psychology*, 64 (6): 1290–1305.

Shadish, W.R., Hu, H., Glaser, R.R., Kownacki, R. and Wong, S. (1998) A method for exploring the effects of attrition in randomized experiments with dichotomous outcomes. *Psychological Methods*, 3 (1): 3–22.

Shadish, W.R., Matt, G.E., Navarro, A.M. and Phillips, G. (2000) The effects of psychological therapies under clinically representative conditions: A meta-analysis. *Psychological Bulletin*, 126 (4): 512–529.

Shadish, W.R., Cook, T.D. and Campbell, D.T. (2002) *Experimental and Quasi-experimental Design for Generalized Causal Inference*. Boston: Houghton-Mifflin.

Shadish, W.R., Galino, R., Wong, V.C., Steiner, P.M. and Cook, T.D. (2011) A randomized experiment comparing random and cutoff-based assignment. *Psychological Methods*, 16: 179–191.

Shapiro, D.A. and Shapiro, D. (1982) Meta-analysis of comparative therapy outcome studies: A replication and refinement. *Psychological Bulletin*, 92: 581–604.

Shapiro, S.L., Figueredo, A.J., Caspi, O., Schwartz, G.E., Bootzin, R.R., Lopez, A.M. and Lake, D. (2002) Going quasi: The premature disclosure effect in a randomized clinical trial. *Journal of Behavioural Medicine*, 25 (6): 605–621.

Shetty, N., Friedman, J.F., Kieburtz, K., Marshall, F.J., Oakes, D. and the Parkinson Study Group. (1999) The placebo response in Parkinson's disease. *Clinical Neuropharmacology*, 22 (4): 207–212.

Shumaker, S.A., Dugan, E. and Bowen, D.J. (2000) Enhancing adherence in randomized controlled clinical trials. *Controlled Clinical Trials*, 21: S226–S232.

Sidani, S. (2006) Random assignment: A systematic review. In R.R. Bootzin and P.E. McKnight (eds), *Strengthening Research Methodology: Psychological Measurement and Evaluation*. Washington, DC: American Psychological Association Books, pp. 125–141.

Sidani, S. and Braden, C.J. (1998) *Evaluating Nursing Interventions: A Theory-driven Approach*. Thousand Oaks, CA: Sage.

Sidani, S. and Braden, C.J. (2011) *Design, Evaluation, and Translation of Nursing Interventions*. Ames, IA: Wiley-Blackwell.

Sidani, S., Epstein, D.R., Bootzin, R.R., Moritz, P. and Sechrest, L. (2007) *Alternative Methods for Clinical Research* (NP 05075). Final report submitted to the National Institute of Nursing Research.

Sidani, S., Epstein, D.R. and Miranda, J. (2006) Eliciting patient treatment preferences: a strategy to integrate evidence-based and patient-centred care, *Worldviews on Evidence-Based Nursing*, 3(3): 116–123.

Sidani, S., Miranda, J., Epstein, D. and Fox, M. (2009a) Influence of treatment preferences on validity: A review. *Canadian Journal of Nursing Research*, 41 (4): 52–67.

Sidani, S., Epstein, D.R., Bootzin, R.R., Moritz, P. and Miranda, J. (2009b) Assessment of preferences for treatment: Validation of a measure. *Research in Nursing and Health*, 32: 419–431.

Sidani, S., Guruge, S., Miranda, J., Ford-Gilboe, M. and Varcoe, C. (2010) Cultural adaptation and translation of measures: An integrated method. *Research in Nursing and Health*, 33: 133–143.

Silverman, E. and skinner, J. (2004) Medicare upcoding and hospital ownership, *Journal of Health Economics*, 23: 369–389.

Simmons, J.P., Nelson, L.D. and Somonsohn, U. (2011) False-positive psychology: Undisclosed flexibility in data collection and analysis allows presenting anything as significant. *Psychological Science*, 22 (11): 1359–1366..

Sinnot, P.L., Joyce, V.R. and Barnett, P. (2007) *Preference Measurement in Economic Analysis. Guidebook*. Menlo Park, CA: VA Palo Alto, Health Economic Resource Center.

Slater, M.D. (2006) Specification and misspecification of theoretical foundations and logic models for health communication campaigns. *Health Communication*, 20 (2): 149–157.

Smith, M.L., Glass, G.V. and Miller, T.I. (1980) *The Benefits of Psychotherapy*. Baltimore, MD: Johns Hopkins University Press.

Sørensen, H.T., Lash, T.I. and Rothman, K.J. (2006) Beyond randomized controlled trials: A critical comparison of trials with non-randomized studies. *Hepatology*, 44: 1075–1082.

Sox, H.C., Helfand, M., Grimshaw, J., Dickerson, K., The PLoS Medicine, Torvey, D. et al. (2010) Comparative effectiveness research: Challenges for medical journals. *Trials*, 7 (4): e1000269.

Spencer, S.M. and Patrick, J.H. (2010) Revisiting traditional survey methodology to recruit and surevy lesbian, gay and bisexual older adults(pp.211–218). In D.L. Streiner and S. Sidani (eds), *When Research goes off the* Rails. New York: Guilford Press.

Spillane, V., Byrne, M.C., Byrne, M., Leathem, C.S., O'Malley, M. and Cupples, M.E. (2007) Monitoring treatment fidelity in a randomized controlled trial of a complex intervention. *Journal of Advanced Nursing*, 60 (3): 343–352.

Spiro, S.G., Gower, N.H., Evans, M.T., Facchini, F.M. and Rudd, R.M., on behalf of the Big Lung Trial Steering Committee (2005) Recruitment of patients with lung cancer into a randomised clinical trial: Experience at two centres. *Thorax*, 55: 463–465.

Staines, G.L., Cleland, C.M. and Blankertz, L. (2006) Counselor confounds in evaluations of vocational rehabilitation methods in substance dependency treatment. *Evaluation Review*, 30 (2): 139–170.

Stalmeier, P.F.M., Van Tol-Geerdink, J.J., Van Lin, E.N.J.T., Schimmel, E., Huizenga, H., Van Daal, W.A.J. et al. (2007) Doctors' and patients' preferences for participation and treatment in curative prostate cancer radiotherapy. *Journal of Clinical Oncology*, 25 (21): 3096–3100.

Stanford Encyclopedia of Philosophy (2008) Counterfactual theories of causation.

Stein, K.F., Sargeant, J.T. and Rafaels, N. (2007) Establishing fidelity of the independent variable in nursing clinical trials. *Nursing Research*, 56 (1): 54–62.

Steinke, E.E. (2004) Research ethics, informed consent, and participant recruitment. *Clinical Nurse Specialist*, 18 (2): 88–97.

Stevens, T. and Ahmedzai, S.H. (2004) Why do breast cancer patients decline entry into randomized trials and how do they feel about their decision later: A prospective, longitudinal, in-depth interview study. *Patient Education and Counseling*, 52: 341–348.

Stewart-Williams, S. and Podd, J. (2004) The placebo effect: Dissolving the expectancy versus conditioning debate. *Psychological Bulletin*, 130 (2): 324–340.

Stirman, S.W., DeRubeis, R.J., Brody, P.E. and Crits-Christoph, P. (2003) Are samples in randomized clinical trials of psychotherapy representative of community outpatients? A new methodology and initial findings. *Journal of Consulting and Clinical Psychology*, 71 (6): 963–972.

Stirman, S.W., DeRubeis, R.J., Crits-Christoph, P. and Rothman, A. (2005) Can the randomized controlled trial literature generalize to nonrandomized patients? *Journal of Consulting and Clinical Psychology*, 73 (1): 127–135.

Stone, G.W. and Pocock. S.J. (2010) Randomized trials, statistics, and clinical inference. *Journal of the American College of Cardiology*, 55 (5): 428–431.

Streiner, D.L. (2002) The 2 'Es' of research: Efficacy and effectiveness trials. *Canadian Journal of Psychiatry*, 47 (6): 552–556.

Streiner, D.L. and Norman, G.R. (2008) *Health Measurement Scales: A Practical Guide to Their Development and Use* (4th ed.). Oxford: Oxford University Press.

Streiner, D.L. and Sidani, S. (eds) (2010) *When Research Goes Off the Rails: Why it Happens and What You Can Do About it*. New York: The Guilford Press.

Swift, J.K., Callahan, J.L. and Vollmer, B.M. (2011) Preferences. *Journal of Clinical Psychology: In Session*, 67 (2): 155–165.

Tacher, J.A., Morey, E. and Craighead, W.E. (2005) Using patient characteristics and attitudinal data to identify depression treatment preference groups: A latent-class model. *Depression and Anxiety*, 21: 47–54.

Tarlov, A.R., Ware, J.E., Greenfield, S., Nelson, E.C., Perrin, E. and Zubkoff, M. (1989) The medical outcomes study: An application of methods for monitoring the results of medical care. *Journal of the American Medical Association*, 262 (7): 925–930.

Tarrier, N., Liversidge, T. and Gregg, L. (2006) The acceptability and preference for the psychological treatment of PTSD. *Behaviour Research and Therapy*, 44: 1643–1656.

TenHave, T.R., Coyne, J., Salzer, M. and Katz, I. (2003) Research to improve the simple randomized clinical trial. *General Hospital Psychiatry*, 25: 115–123.

Thomas, E., Croft, P.R., Paterson, S.M., Dziedzic, K. and Hay, E.M. (2004) What influences participants' treatment preference and can it influence outcome? Results from a primary care-based randomized trial for shoulder pain. *British Journal of General Practice*, 54: 93–96.

Thomas Becker, P. (2008) Publishing pilot intervention studies. *Research in Nursing and Health*, 31(1): 1–3.

Thoolen, B., de Ridder, D., Bensing, J., Gorter, K. and Rutten, G. (2007) Who participates in diabetes self-management interventions? Issues of recruitment and retainment. *The Diabetes Educator*, 33 (3): 465–474.

Thorpe, K.E., Zwarenstein, M., Oxman, A.D., Treweek, S., Furberg, C.D., Altman, D.G., Tunis, S., Bergel, E., Harvey, I., Magid, D.J. and Chalkidou, K. (2009) A pragmatic – explanatory continuum indicator summary (PRECIS): A tool to help trial designers. *Journal of Clinical Epidemiology*, 62: 464–475.

Tilley, N. (2000) Realistic evaluation: An overview. Paper presented at the Founding Conference of the Danish Evaluation Society.

Torgerson, C.J. and Torgerson, D.J. (2004) The need for pragmatic experimentation in educational research. *Economics of Innovation and New Technology*, 16 (5): 323–330.

Torgerson, D.J., Klaber-Moffatt, J. and Russell, I.T. (1996) Patient preference in randomized trials: Threat or opportunity? *Journal of Health Science Research and Policy*, 1 (4): 194–197.

Towne, L. and Hilton, M. (2004) Implementing randomized field trials in education: Report of a workshop. Committee on Research in Education, National Research Council. Washington, DC. National Academy Press.

Travaodo, L., Grassi, L., Gil, F., Ventura, C., Martins, C. and the Southern European Psycho-Oncology Study (SEPOS) Group (2005) Physician–patient communication among southern European cancer physicians: The influence of psychosocial orientation and burnout. *Psycho-Oncology*, 14: 661–670.

Tunis, S.R., Stryer, D.B. and Clancy, C.M. (2003) Practical clinical trials: Increasing the value of clinical research for decision making in clinical and health policy. *Journal of the American Medical Association*, 290 (12): 1624–1632.

US Government Accountability Office (2009) Program evaluation: A variety of rigorous methods can help identify effective interventions. Retrieved from: http://www.gao.gov/products/GAO-10-30

Valentine, J.C. and McHugh, C.M. (2007) The effects of attrition on baseline comparability in randomized experiments in education: A meta analysis. *Psychological Methods*, 12 (3): 268–282.

Vallance, J.K., Courneya, K.S., Taylor, L.M., Plotnikoff, R.C. and Mackey, J.R. (2008) Development and evaluation of a theory-based physical activity guidebook for breast cancer survivors. *Health Education and Behavior*, 35 (2): 174–189.

Vandelanotte, C., Bourdeaudhuij, I. and Brug, J. (2004) Acceptability and feasibility of an interactive computer-tailored fat intake intervention in Belgium. *Health Promotion International*, 19 (4): 463–470.

Van der Berg, M., Timmermans, D.R.M., Knol, D.L., Van Eijk, J.M., de Smit, D., Van Vugt, J.M.G. and Van der Wal, G. (2008) Understanding pregnant women's decision making concerning prenatal screening. *Health Psychology*, 27 (4): 430–437.

Van der Wejden, T., Légaré, F., Boivin, A., Burgers, J.S., Van Veenendaal, H., Stiggelbout, A.M., Faber, M. and Elwyn, G. (2010) How to integrate individual patient values and preferences in clinical practice guidelines? A research protocol. *Implementation Science*, 5: 10–18.

Van Die, D.M., Bone, K.M., Burger, H.G. and Teede, H.J. (2009) Are we drawing the right conclusions from randomized placebo-controlled trials? A post-hoc analysis of data from a randomized controlled trial. *BioMed Central Medical Research Methodology*, 9: 41–47.

Veitch, C., Hollins, J., Worley, P. and Mitchell, G. (2001) General practice research: Problems and solutions in participant recruitment retention. *Australian Family Physician*, 30 (4): 399–406.

Victora, C.G., Habicht, J.-P. and Bryce, J. (2004) Evidence based public health: Moving beyond randomized trials. *American Journal of Public Health*, 94 (3): 400–406.

Vist, G.E., Hagen, K.B., Devereaux, P.J., Bryant, D., Kristofferson, D.T. and Oxman, A.D. (2005) Systematic review to determine whether participation in a trial influences outcome. *British Medical Journal*, 330: 1175–1181.

Vuorma, S., Teperi, J., Hurskainen, R., Aalto, A., Rissanen, P. and Kujansuu, E. (2003) Correlates of women's preferences for treatment of heavy menstrual bleeding. *Patient Education Counseling*, 49: 125–132.

Waller, G. (2009) Evidence-based treatment and therapist drift, *Behavioural Research and Therapy*, 47: 119–127.

Waltz, J., Addis, M.E., Koerner, K. and Jacobson, N.S. (1993) Testing the integrity of a psychotherapy protocol: Assessment of adherence and competence. *Journal of Consulting and Clinical Psychology*, 61 (4): 620–630.

Wampold, B.E. and Brown, G.S. (2005) Estimating variability in outcomes attributable to therapists: A naturalistic study of outcomes in managed care. *Journal of Consulting and Clinical Psychology*, 73 (5): 914–923.

Watson, B., Procter, S. and Cochrane, W. (2004) Using randomized controlled trials (RCTS) to test service interventions: Issues of standardisation, selection and generalisability. *Nurse Researcher*, 11 (3): 28–42.

Weijer, C., Grimshaw, J.M., Taljaard, M., Binik, A., Boruch, R., Brehaut, J.C., Donner, A., Eccles, M.P., Gallo, A., McRae, A.D., Saginur, R. and Zwarenstein, M. (2011) Ethical issues posed by cluster randomized trials in health research. *Trials*, 12: 100.

Weinberger, M., Oddone, E.Z., Henderson, W.G., Smith, D.M., Huey, J., Giobbie-Hurder, A. and Feussner, J.R. (2001) Multisite randomized controlled trials in health services research: Scientific challenges and operational issues. *Medical Care*, 39 (6): 627–634.

Weinberger, M., Oddone, E.Z., Henderson, W.G., Smith, D.M., Huey, J., Giobbie-Hurder, A. and Feussner, J.R. (2002a) Multisite randomized controlled trials in health services research: Scientific challenges and operational issues. *Medical Care*, 39: 627–634.

Weinberger, M., Murray, M.D., Marrero, D.G., Brewer, N., Lykens, M., Harris, L.E. et al. (2002b) Issues in conducting randomized controlled trials of health services research interventions in nonacademic practice settings: The case of retail pharmacies. *Health Services Research*, 37(4): 1067–1077.

Welleck, S. and Blettner, M. (2012) On the proper use of the crossover design in clinical trials: part 18 of a series on evaluation of scientific publications. *Deutsches Arzteblatt* International, 109(15): 276–281.

Wertz, R.T. (1995) Intention to treat: Once randomized, always analyzed. *Clinical Aphasiology*, 23: 57–64.

West, S.G. and Thoemmes, F. (2010) Campbell's and Rubin's perspectives on causal inference. *Psychological Methods*, 15 (1): 18–37.

Westen, D., Novotny, C.M. and Thompson-Brenner, H. (2004) The empirical status of empirically supported psychotherapies: Assumptions, findings, and reporting in controlled clinical trials. *Psychological Bulletin*, 130 (4): 631–663.

Westerberg, V.S., Miller, W.R. and Tonigan, J.S. (2000) Comparison of outcomes for clients in randomized versus open trials of treatment for alcohol use disorders. *Journal of Studies on Alcohol*, 6(5): 720–732.

Wierzbicki, M. and Pekarik, G. (1993) A meta-analysis of psychotherapy dropout. *Professional Psychology: Research and Practice*, 24 (2): 190–195.

Wilder, E.T. and Hollister, R. (2002) *How Close is Close Enough? Testing Non-experimental Estimates of Impact against Experimental Estimates of Impact with Education Test Scores as Outcomes*. Madison, WI: Institute for Research on Poverty.

Williams, A.C., Nicholas, M.K., Richardson, P.H., Pither, C.E. and Fernandes, J. (1999) Generalizing from a controlled trial: The effects of patient preference versus randomization on the outcome of impatient versus outpatient chronic pain management. *Pain*, 83: 57–65.

Wilson, D.B. and Lipsey, M.W. (2001) The role of method in treatment effectiveness research: Evidence from meta-analysis. *Psychological Methods*, 6 (4): 413–429.

Wiltsey-Stirman, S., DeRubeis, R.J., Crits-Christoph, P. and Brody, P.E. (2003) Are samples in randomized controlled trials of psychotherapy representative of community outpatients? A new methodology and initial findings. *Journal of Consulting and Clinical Psychology*, 71 (6): 963–972.

Wingerson, D., Sullivan, M., Dager, S., Flick, S., Dunner, D. and Roy-Byrne, P. (1993) Personality traits and early discontinuation from clinical trials in anxious patients. *Journal of Clinical Psychopharmacology*, 13 (3): 194–197.

Wood, L., Egger, M., Gluud, L.L., Schulz, K.F., Jüni, P., Altman, D.G., Gluud, C., Martin, R.M., Wood, A.J. and Sterne, J.A. (2008) Empirical evidence of bias in treatment effect sizes in controlled trials with different interventions and outcomes: Meta-epidemiological study. *British Medical Journal*, 336: 601.

Woods, M., Harris, K., Mayo, M., Catley, D., Scheibmeir, M. and Ahluwalia, J. (2002) Participation of African Americans in a smoking cessation trial: A quantitative and qualitative study. *Journal of the National Medical Association*, 94 (7): 609–618.

Worrall, J. (2002) What evidence in evidence-based medicine? *Philosophy of Science*, 69 (S3): S316–S330.

Yong, E. (2012) Bad copy. *Nature*, 485: 298–300.

Young, B., Beidel, D., Turner, S., Ammerman, R., McGraw, K. and Coaston, S. (2006) Pretreatment attrition and childhood social phobia. *Anxiety Disorders*, 20: 1133–1147.

Zatzick, D.F., Kang, S.-M., Hinton, L. et al. (2001) Posttraumatic concerns: A patient-centered approach to outcome assessment after traumatic physical injury. *Medical Care*, 39 (4): 327–339.

Zelen, M. (1979) A new design for randomized clinical trials. *The New England Journal of Medicine*, 300: 1242–1245.

Zoeller, L.A., Feeny, N.C., Cochran, B. and Pruitt, L. (2003) Treatment choice for PTSD. *Behaviour Research and Therapy*, 41: 879–886.

Zwarenstein, M. and Treweek, S. (2009) What kind of randomized trials do we need? *Canadian Medical Association Journal*, 180 (10): 998–1000.

INDEX